D0069573

Carrying Jackie's Torch

The Players Who Integrated
Baseball—and America

Steve Jacobson

Lawrence Hill Books

Library of Congress Cataloging–in–Publication Data

Jacobson, Steve.
     Carrying Jackie's torch : the players who integrated baseball . . . and America
/ Steve Jacobson.
        p.   cm.
     Includes bibliographical references and index.
     ISBN–13: 978–1–55652–639–8
     ISBN–10: 1–55652–639–3
     1. African American baseball players—Biography.   2. Baseball players
—United States—Biography.   3. Discrimination in sports—United
States.   4. Baseball—United States—History.   I. Title.

GV865.A1J34 2007
796.3570922—dc22
[B]2006014278

Cover design: Todd Petersen
Interior design: Pamela Juàrez
Interior photo credits: Page xxiv, Jackie Robinson of the Brooklyn Dodgers; page 2, Jackie
Robinson in 1946; page 14, Monte Irvin; page 28, Larry Doby; page 40, Ed Charles;
page 54, Mudcat Grant; page 66, Ernie Banks; page 76, Elston Howard completing a
World Series home run; page 86, Alvin Jackson; page 96, Charlie Murray; page 106,
Chuck Harmon; page 116, Maury Wills; page 128, Emmett Ashford; page 138, Frank
Robinson; page 152, Tommy Davis; page 164, Bob Gibson; page 178, Curt Flood; page
192, Henry Aaron; page 208, Dusty Baker; page 220, Lou Brock breaking records for
stolen bases; page 230, Bob Watson; page 240, Jackie Robinson and Branch Rickey.
All photos courtesy of The Baseball Hall of Fame.

© 2007 by Steve Jacobson
All rights reserved
First edition
Published by Lawrence Hill Books
An Imprint of Chicago Review Press, Incorporated
814 North Franklin Street
Chicago, Illinois 60610
ISBN–13: 978–1–55652–639–8
ISBN–10: 1–55652–639–3
Printed in the United States of America
5 4 3 2 1

To my parents, Roselyn and Harold Jacobson, who taught me honesty and the deception of the curveball.

To my wife, Anita, who was her father's first son at Ebbets Field and who encouraged me to expand the stories I brought home from the ballpark.

To my grown children, Mathew and Neila, who smile because I am their father, and laugh because there is nothing I can do about it. And to Susan, Mathew's wife, who hardly knew what she was getting into.

Contents

Acknowledgments

SPECIAL THANKS TO Tommy Carney, who heard my thoughts over the bar and demanded that I write them, and Bob Sales, my favorite newspaper copyeditor, who made sense out of my original text. Thanks to agents Jane Dystel and Miriam Goderich, who found an unafraid publisher, and to Cynthia Sherry and Lisa Rosenthal, who helped me convert decades of sports page idiom for people who might not be able to recite the infield fly rule.

Introduction

I WASN'T NEARLY as worldly and sophisticated as I thought, growing up in New York in the 1940s and 1950s. We had good schools in suburban Long Island. There weren't a lot of black people in the community but the schools were integrated and so were the sports teams and the recreation leagues.

Of course the schools in New York taught about Abraham Lincoln and the Emancipation Proclamation. We knew about segregation laws in the South, but that was a distant land to us. What we knew was that after the pain and tension of World War II, Americans craved peace and good new days. We weren't yet aware of the great ferment to change.

I grew up rooting for the Brooklyn Dodgers, who played in Ebbets Field, an hour away at the other end of the Long Island Railroad. The Dodgers planted milestones in my life. Year after year they were almost as good as the damn Yankees, who were so smug and elite in their corporate pinstripes, which they wore like royal robes. Not only were the Dodgers good on the field, we felt they were right-thinking in the front office, too. They opened their dugout and the ball field—the major-league ball field, that is—to Jackie Robinson.

Jackie Robinson's body of work that earned him his place in the Baseball Hall of Fame was from 1947 to 1956, when he retired at age 38 rather than accept a trade to the hated New York Giants. It wasn't long before it became obvious that this 28–year–old rookie, Robinson, was the most exciting player in the National League. He would toy with fielders on a rundown play so deftly it would make you laugh. He would cross first base with an ostentatious limp and on the next pitch, steal second. He stole home 28 times in his career. Whoever heard of such a thing?

Social scientists tell us we cling to images we form when we're 17. I had just turned 17 and was learning to do my own laundry as a brand–new 1951 freshman at Indiana University with the radio broadcaster telling me what to see in the Dodgers' crucial last game of the season. The floor of the laundry room was deep in soapsuds because a freshman football player, who would from this day forward be known as Bubbles, had put too much soap in the machine. I remember the bubbles and I remember wishing I could watch the baseball action unfold and yet still feel the tension as if I was there. So maybe I hadn't separated the colors properly and my T–shirts would come out pink as my mother warned. My mind was on the game in Philadelphia.

The Dodgers were such sweet agony, always. Now the chill of having the hated Giants come from so far behind clutched me. My Dodgers had been 13½ games in front in August and now the Giants were ahead and it was the last day of the season. Now it was the Dodgers who had to come from behind. They were losing in Philadelphia—this was the win–or–die game.

The Dodgers and Phillies were tied, and in the last of the 12th, the game fell to Robinson. Games come to great players. With the bases full and two outs, Eddie Waitkus lined one up the middle for the Phillies: it was going to win the game. The Dodgers were finished. Robinson at second base flung himself to his right, glove outstretched. As he struck the ground and crumpled motionless, the ball was lost to view. His teammates rolled him onto his back, revealing the ball clutched in his glove. Did Robinson trap the ball and deliberately deceive the umpires? He would never tell. We know he made it happen. And in the 14th inning he won the game with a home run. He got the Dodgers into that infernal Bobby Thomson play–off game with the Giants. He showed that a black man could stand up to the pressure. What he showed every day of his career told all but the most blindly racist owners that talented black players could make their teams better.

How could it have been that no black man was permitted to play in Major League Baseball until Jackie Robinson came along? To many people in the North the only baseball we knew was the major leagues and so we'd never seen black ballplayers in action. Now the door was open.

My friends and I had some awareness that water fountains and restrooms in the South were separate. The extent of this separate–and–

unequal was beyond us: that buses and restaurants and housing were segregated in other parts of the country, and that shops in the South and even in California didn't permit black people to try on clothes or hats. In our suburban cocoon, integrated on the surface, we didn't know that in most places in America white people sat down front at the movies while blacks sat in the balcony—if they were allowed in the theater at all. So much of the life that I lived was closed to black people elsewhere. Years later, when I was covering the Yankees for *Newsday*, I learned that outfielder Bill Robinson's father in Pittsburgh in the 1950s was the first black crane operator at United States Steel. But life in the North wasn't as blatantly oppressive for Negroes and the subtlety of racism escaped our awareness.

❖

Harry Truman ordered the army to integrate in 1948. I didn't expect life in the army to be anything other than integrated when I was inducted in 1956. On that day I was at 33 Whitehall Street in New York taking my pre–induction physical and, being judged of sound mind and body by U.S. Army standards, headed for two years of active duty. It was October 10, 1956.

Two days before my induction, Don Larsen pitched his perfect game against my Dodgers, which I choose not to include among my memorable dates. The next day the Dodgers beat the Yankees, 1–0, on Jackie Robinson's 10th–inning hit, which tied the Series at three games each and led me to the moment of my pre–induction physical. As I recall, every time a doctor asked me to cough, Yogi Berra hit one of his two two–run homers off Don Newcombe. And the Yankees got nothing off Johnny Kucks. The Dodgers failed and I passed. And with this sad knowledge I went on to Fort Dix for basic training.

Movies on post were thoroughly integrated. So were the places where you could buy a hamburger, if you had any money or free time. Whites and blacks lived together, slept in the same barracks, and ate the same bad food in the same mess hall. We took orders from white and black drill instructors and saluted white and black officers. After basic I was assigned to the Psychological Warfare Center at Fort Bragg, North Carolina. My unit was heavily white and college educated, but we had several black officers and sergeants. There were two golf courses on post, and they were segregated by officers and enlisted men, not by race. Off post I saw the old slave market in Fayetteville and stored it in my mind. I read about frequent racial issues with the Lumbee Indians nearby. On post, blacks and whites mixed freely. Fort Bragg was the largest military installation in the world at the time, but it was an island to itself in the midst of North Carolina with its history of the Old South.

In the spring of 1957 I watched the telecast as the University of North Carolina won the NCAA basketball championship beating Wilt Chamberlain and Kansas in the final, and immediately North Carolina license plates were boasting the state's victory. Wise Sergeant Eberhardt, whose wife was Korean, asked if the proud Carolinians really were aware that the best player, Lenny Rosenbluth, was a Jew.

I was playing on a battalion baseball team at Fort Bragg in 1957, 10 years after Jackie came to Brooklyn. When we went to play off post, I was forced to face the piney woods of the reality of North Carolina. All of us got off the bus for lunch in uniform. Then Davey Williams, head down, came back out of the roadside restaurant and dragged himself back onto the bus. This crummy restaurant refused to serve him because he was black.

I had never heard of such a thing or even imagined it happening as it did in the army. Even though he had grown up in Buffalo, Davey surely must have known the way of the South. Yet while he was serving in the U.S. Army, he was refused lunch in his own country. Davey was our second baseman and our guy. I could only imagine his pain as he stared out the window of that bus. Larry Van Gelder, another New Yorker, and I got back on the bus with Davey. Somebody must have brought out sandwiches for us. I've forgotten that, but I haven't forgotten feeling sick to my stomach at the outrage. "It was horrible," my friend Van Gelder recalls nearly 50 years later. When we got back on the bus with Davey, we didn't think of it in terms of defiance or solidarity or anything especially altruistic, but we could try to be company for him and maybe help ease his pain. Without putting it into words, we knew what he was going through was wrong.

Lieutenant Harold Luck, the coach and a decent man, later apologized. He was from Greensboro, North Carolina, and he seemed genuinely embarrassed by the incident. He said, "That's the way it is." And so it was, not to be changed by us. I don't think the other players gave it that much thought. They had their lunch and the thought that a teammate couldn't eat with them—if they gave the matter any thought at all—apparently was "the way it is." That's how unthinking or unfeeling America still was.

One day in September 1957, I returned to the barracks from baseball practice, opened my copy of the *New York Times*, and read that the Dodgers had played their last game in Brooklyn. They were reassigned to Los Angeles. I sat on the khaki blanket of my neatly made bunk and thought: "Damn! I'm never going to watch the Brooklyn Dodgers again." And so it was.

The Dodgers had left their indelible mark on asphalt schoolyards in New York and on suburban sandlots. From the early moments of Robinson's time with the Dodgers, when he first danced on the base paths and threatened to steal home, boys in sneakers danced on the bases and said, "I'm Jackie Robinson." For the first time, white children at play emulated a black athlete. The impact was profound. Stars are important. America was being transformed. Give the Brooklyn Dodgers credit for making history turn.

Several years ago a gray–whiskered black taxi driver in St. Louis—he must have been nearing 80 years old—told me he had always rooted for the Cardinals because they were the team in town, but when Robinson came to the Dodgers, he became a Dodgers fan. "Jackie told me we could make it in the big leagues," the driver said. "He told us we could be something."

⋆⋮⋆

I developed a love of baseball and learned about black baseball from my father, who once mentioned that he had pitched for the volunteer firemen and beat the cops. At the dinner table when the potatoes were passed from my father to me to my mother, she would say, "Tinker to Evers to Chance." At the time I was growing up, black baseball wasn't extensively covered by the general newspapers. My father grew up in the Bronx, not far from the Polo Grounds. He lived in the same building as Hank Mathewson, a pitcher for the Giants and brother of the great pitcher Christy Mathewson. My father was a fan of the Giants and told me how Hank would play ball in the street with the kids on his day off. Dad said he went to a lot of games when the gates were opened to non–ticket holders in the seventh inning, something no team does anymore. During the World Series when he was a kid he would stand outside a newspaper office and watch as the play–by–play was posted on a big board.

When my father was older, occasionally he went to Negro League games when they were played in New York, and he told me about some of their legendary players. He spoke of the wonders of Satchel Paige—"he would call in his outfielders and infielders and strike out the side"—and Josh Gibson—"he could hit a ball farther than Babe Ruth"—and Cool Papa Bell—"they said he could shut the light and be in bed before the room got dark." But they played in a league apart. On occasion they played against barnstorming white players and more than held their own, but that was "after the season" and therefore didn't count.

Nobody really knew how good the black players were. Could it be they were as good as the whites? In more recent times, a theater production of Lee Blessing's *Cobb* dealt with the paradox of Ty Cobb, one of the greatest white players and a profound bigot. They called him the Georgia Peach. The play depicted Cobb in three stages of his life. Interrupting Cobb's monologue was the figure of Oscar Charleston, pushing a broom, haunting him. Oscar Charleston was known as the black Ty Cobb. Would he have been as good as Cobb if he played against the same competition? Cobb would never know. Neither will we.

When I grew up to cover baseball and the damn Yankees for *Newsday*, some of the veterans of the Brooklyn era would tell me that I should have been around to cover the Dodgers. I missed something.

And nobody was up to PeeWee Reese, the captain and shortstop of the Dodgers who was called "Cap'n" by his teammates even years after he was through playing. He was that wonderful Kentuckian who defied the jeering Cincinnati crowd to put his arm around Jackie in support. That moment when Reese displayed his courage and sense of decency is now memorialized by a bronze statue in Brooklyn. (Once at a dinner in Cooperstown, PeeWee sat next to my wife, Anita, who often accompanied her father to Dodgers games, and our daughter, Neila, who had heard me talk of PeeWee. He kissed Anita's cheek and that spot remains a family landmark.)

Brooklyn, where the Dodgers played, was a distinctive place in 1947, probably the single best illustration of the melting pot of America. Until then the most popular player in Brooklyn history was right fielder Dixie Walker, from the heart of Dixie. But Walker was a leading voice in the petition to keep Jackie Robinson from playing with the Dodgers. So when the Dodgers set foot in Ebbets Field after spring training, Brooklyn fans booed Walker and cheered Robinson, who had never played a game for them. That's in public memory. Reese was always popular, partly for his consistently high performance on the field, partly for his unfailing class, and very much for his open support of Robinson.

How slowly and painfully widespread acceptance of black players in baseball came, however, we hardly knew. It was only 50 years or so ago and what the black players who came after Robinson endured for the next 20 years is hardly appreciated—even by black players who reap the rewards of those who came before. The experience of the early blacks playing in the minor leagues presents a good picture of life in our country, an aspect that went unseen by many Americans.

Mario Cuomo, former governor of New York, was a minor–league baseball player during that time. Cuomo's first profound experience with the hatefulness of segregation came as a ballplayer and prompted him into a career as a liberal politician and brought him close to running for president of the United States. In 1951 he went from St. John's

University in New York to play center field in Brunswick, Georgia, in the Georgia–Florida League for the Pittsburgh Pirates' farm system.

He grew up in South Jamaica in the borough of Queens, the son of an Italian immigrant greengrocer. "We weren't the most civilized or sophisticated or educated community, but we were varied with Jews and blacks and Catholics and people who had just come to America and didn't speak English," Cuomo recalled in a recent interview. "That was the world I lived in. I took it all for granted that's what the world was. We didn't know what a luxury that growing–up was."

In 1951, four years after Robinson's entrance into Brooklyn, the Georgia–Florida League had not yet had its first black player. Brunswick was a town of about 15,000 with a fine ballpark, and going to watch the Pirates was a popular evening out. "We had seats at home for 3,000," Cuomo recalled. "There was a separate bleacher entrance in right field with wooden benches and that's where blacks were permitted to sit. They let in about 100 and that was it.

"It was just incredible to me," he reflected, "that at that advanced stage in this society's history you could tell these human beings, you have to sit out there; you can't sit with us. We weren't allowed to say hello to them."

The display of bigotry wasn't limited to blacks. Cuomo was a rare Italian. In one game he stepped up to bat and the catcher, a man named Red Skeleton, snarled that Cuomo was "a Dago." Cuomo took a punch at him and was thrown out of the game. Worse, Skeleton was wearing his catcher's mask when Cuomo hit him, and he just laughed at the punch. Cuomo's hand swelled as he walked back to his dugout. "That," said manager Mickey O'Neill, "was the dumbest thing I've ever seen."

"I don't know if it was the dumbest thing I ever did," Cuomo said, "but it was the dumbest thing I ever did in baseball."

Bigotry is woven into the fabric of America. The house I live in today is on real estate that excluded Jews in the 1930s. In 1960 when the Yankees made their annual spring training trip from St. Petersburg, Florida, to Miami, they stayed at the Kenilworth Hotel, owned by popular entertainer Arthur Godfrey. The Jewish newsmen covering the Yankees became the first Jews ever accepted at this hotel. And one of these reporters, Len Shecter, the acid–witted man from the *New York Post*, repeatedly had a bellman walk the lobby intoning, "Paging Stanley Isaacs. Paging Stanley Isaacs."

Perhaps the people who best understood the pain of bigotry aimed at others were people who had been victims themselves. In 1939 young Billie Holliday sang "Strange Fruit," a brilliantly bold protest song written by Abe Meeropol, a Jewish schoolteacher from the Bronx, the uncle who adopted the sons of executed Julius and Ethel Rosenberg. Billie Holiday sang:

> Southern trees bear strange fruit,
> Blood on the leaves and blood at the root,
> Black bodies swinging in the southern breeze,
> Strange fruit hanging from the poplar trees.

This song shouted and mourned the lynchings that were too common in America. The year Jackie broke baseball's color barrier in Brooklyn, four black World War II veterans were lynched in the South. And it wasn't until 2005 that the United States Senate made a formal apology and passed a law making lynching a federal crime. And yet 15 Republican senators declined to cosponsor the bill. Laws are passed one by one intended to end the legal brutality of segregation, but the customs of bigotry and repression are slow to die.

Life for a black person was, in the words of Hall of Fame baseball player Lou Brock, under the cloud of "the ever–present danger."

Do we know that in 1954, when Willie Mays won his first Most Valuable Player Award, 14–year–old Emmett Till from Chicago, vacationing with relatives in Mississippi, was dragged from bed, brutally beaten, and murdered, accused of whistling at a white woman? And further, that the courts wouldn't convict anyone in the group of killers? Two men later confessed, for a price, to *Look* magazine. In 1964, the year Bob Gibson was named Most Valuable Player in the World Series, three civil rights workers pushing for the right of black citizens to vote—James Chaney, Michael Schwerner, and Andrew Goodman—were murdered for trying to overturn the dismal traditions of the South. It was that ever–present danger. It wasn't until 2005 that a Mississippi court convicted the instigator, a preacher and Ku Klux Klan member, by then 80 years old.

When Mudcat Grant, one of the leading pitchers of the 1960s, tells his grandchildren his often harrowing story of growing up in America, and they say, "No, Grandpa, it wasn't like that." He tells them that indeed, it was. Grant and Gibson in 1965 became the first black pitchers to win 20 games.

Do people know that the season before Robinson's debut in Brooklyn, when he was playing with the Montreal Royals, a player named Red Treadway left the Royals and his hope of a baseball career, because he would not play with Robinson? Do we know that permitting blacks to play on the same field as whites in the American South was seen by many as the first step toward destruction of the Southern way of life?

Do we know that Jim and Leander Tugerson, black brothers who were barred from the Cotton States League, wrote, "Are we fit to work in your homes, your fields only? We can talk for you and help elect you when it's time for voting. When you were young, was it fair for a Negro maid to raise you? . . . We don't want to, as Negroes, stay with you or eat with you. All we want to do is play baseball for a living." These are barely known tales.

A dozen years ago in New York, the Mets had a black player named Vince Coleman. He'd been in the major leagues a few years. He'd even spent time in college, maybe even sat in a history class. "I don't know no Jackie Robinson," Coleman said, "and don't care to." He had no concept of his debt to Jackie and those who followed him.

"Some of the young players don't have a clue," said Hank Aaron, in a roundtable discussion with *Newsweek* in 1997. Aaron, then and still senior vice president of the Braves, made it his obligation, once he was an established star, to guide the progress of young black players. He taught them. He comforted them. He continues to do so.

"It's not just athletes," says sports historian Jeffrey Sammons of New York University. "Jackie Robinson means very little to black students today."

When baseball was celebrating the 50th anniversary of Jackie breaking the color barrier with the Brooklyn Dodgers in 1947, I spoke to a group of students at a Long Island high school. I asked who could identify Jackie Robinson. Of the 40 students in the group, six hands were raised. One young man whose hand was not raised was a black student. His father taught history, of all subjects, at that very school. He couldn't have imagined what Davey Williams felt. Clearly there was a significant chapter in American history that had not been taught in this school or in his home.

Jackie Robinson quickly became a dominant player, demonstrating for all to see that a black man really could compete as an equal with whites. In its way, it was a peacetime parallel to the lesson of the Tuskegee Airmen who proved that black men were brave enough, disciplined enough, and intelligent enough to fly America's fighter planes with the best in the world. But these stories are being lost.

The trials of Robinson and the black players who followed illustrate the history of black and white America of their time. First, the laws that had stood for a century were against them. Then, even as the oppressive laws were forced to change, the attitudes of many Americans hardly softened at all. And still remnants of segregation and discrimination linger today in the North as well as the South.

"How do you know yourself if you don't know your history and the history of the game you love?" asks Willie Randolph, manager of the Mets and the first black man to manage a New York team.

The society that forgot Emmett Till for a half century can't imagine that conditions were so oppressive for black ballplayers destined for the Hall of Fame, men who would never quit on the ball field, were treated so poorly both on and off the field that they considered quitting and going home. Some did quit and we, and they, will never know what they might have accomplished. But they felt it was better to quit than to submit to the abuse.

Bob Gibson, a member of the Baseball Hall of Fame and an outstanding college basketball player, and Oscar Robertson, a member of the Basketball Hall of Fame, were being recruited to play basketball at my school, Indiana University. That is, until each received a letter stating: "Our quota of Negroes has been filled." Today the president of Indiana University, Dr. Adam Herbert, is a black man. Until I told him this story, no one had informed Dr. Herbert of this piece of embarrassing history.

The prevailing attitudes of the 1950s, even in a great educational institution, resisted the laws promoting integration and prejudices were stronger than the pressures to win on the athletic field. Great athletes were rejected because of race. Those bigoted attitudes and the decisions they prompted were hidden and unresolved for decades.

So much of the dark side of our history has been obscured or lost in some kind of emotional denial. On the day I returned from the 50th reunion of my graduating class at Indiana University, I saw in the *New York Times* a photo of the lynching of two black men with white spectators carrying on as if it were a carnival. The event took place in Marion, Indiana in 1930. The ever–present danger.

⋯⋰⋰⋯

Our mainstream newspapers, especially in New York, should have pressed regularly for the acceptance of blacks in baseball. They didn't. Lester Rodney campaigned nobly for this for 11 years in the Communist *Daily Worker*. He was largely dismissed as "that commie." For years the torch was carried almost exclusively by the black press, most influentially by Wendell Smith in the *Pittsburgh Courier*. His work was dismissed because it was in the "Negro press."

I'm disappointed in myself for not dealing more with the issue in my first years of covering spring training for *Newsday* in St. Petersburg, Florida, in the early 1960s, when the few black players with the Yankees had to find private homes because they were not accepted at the team's hotel. For years a Dr. Ralph Wimbish found housing for the few black players with the Yankees, sometimes in his own home. Dr. Wimbish also was an activist and a constant irritant to whites for his efforts to break down segregation rules in the community. His son, Ralph Jr., says whites often called his father "The Devil," because he made hell for people. Dr. Wimbish got his share of "Dear nigger" letters and cross burnings on his lawn. A few years later arsonists burned his home.

I didn't deal enough with the fact that the St. Petersburg Chamber of Commerce had an annual breakfast at the yacht club for the Yankees and Cardinals. It was understood: don't bring your black players, please. But I was young and not confident enough to make an issue—and there was that insidious sense of that's how it is. The Yankees certainly weren't going to make an issue about getting that changed.

"We hated the Yankees for their reluctance to sign black players," Percy Sutton, borough president of Manhattan and a Harlem resident, said.

Bob Gibson, in his way, says the struggle of the black players is repetition. "It was the same for all of us," he said.

Not so, says Bob Watson, the black general manager of the Yankees in 1996 and 1997 when they reestablished their dynasty. "Each of us," he said, "is one of the tiles in a mosaic that makes the big picture."

Mudcat Grant urged me to tell the story of those black pioneers who followed Jackie "before we're all gone." Frank Robinson encouraged me. He said, "If a black man wrote it, it would sound like whining." I committed to recording the details of these players' lives, victories, and defeats because these are stories that need to be told.

I've listened to the stories of these players during 40 years of covering baseball, and came to understand the personal strength that persistence and survival demanded. Over the past two years of working on this book, I've conducted additional interviews, and players said they'd never told these things before. It's a dark shadow on journalism that nobody ever asked them to tell these stories.

The details of their stories remembered across the years may not be exactly accurate. Some names and dates are clouded. The truth is not. My hope is that *Carrying Jackie's Torch* will help others learn of the struggle of early black baseball players, those who followed Jackie Robinson, so we can understand our debt to these pioneers.

1

Equal but Separate

Before Jackie Changed Everything

BY THE FIRST LIGHT of day, they'd stop the bus on the all–night roll from one game in one town to one more game in another town. They'd pick up the newspapers and open directly to the box scores. How did Jackie do? He was one of theirs the way a man's heart is a part of him.

In their hearts, Jackie Robinson was playing for them and they were playing every game with him. "He was the idol," Lester Lockett recalled, still in awe of Robinson's success more than a generation later. "It told them maybe they had a chance." By the time Robinson pushed open the door the first crack with the Brooklyn Dodgers, Lockett was 35 years old and reconciled to the fact that his time had come and gone playing infield in the Negro League.

It was 1947, the summer after the great Josh Gibson had died with the big leagues still closed to him, and nobody would ever know how good he might have been. But Jackie was in the big leagues now and maybe the young ones could go through that door after him. It was that first summer of Jackie that Lockett and the Baltimore Elite Giants were in Covington, Kentucky, across the river from Cincinnati, where the Dodgers were in town to play the Reds.

"The bridge from Covington was loaded," Lockett recalled. "People on crutches were going to see him. Boy, I'm telling you, all those people!" Awe and joy mixed in Lockett's voice, and there was probably a well–hidden tear as well. It must have been a wondrous scene.

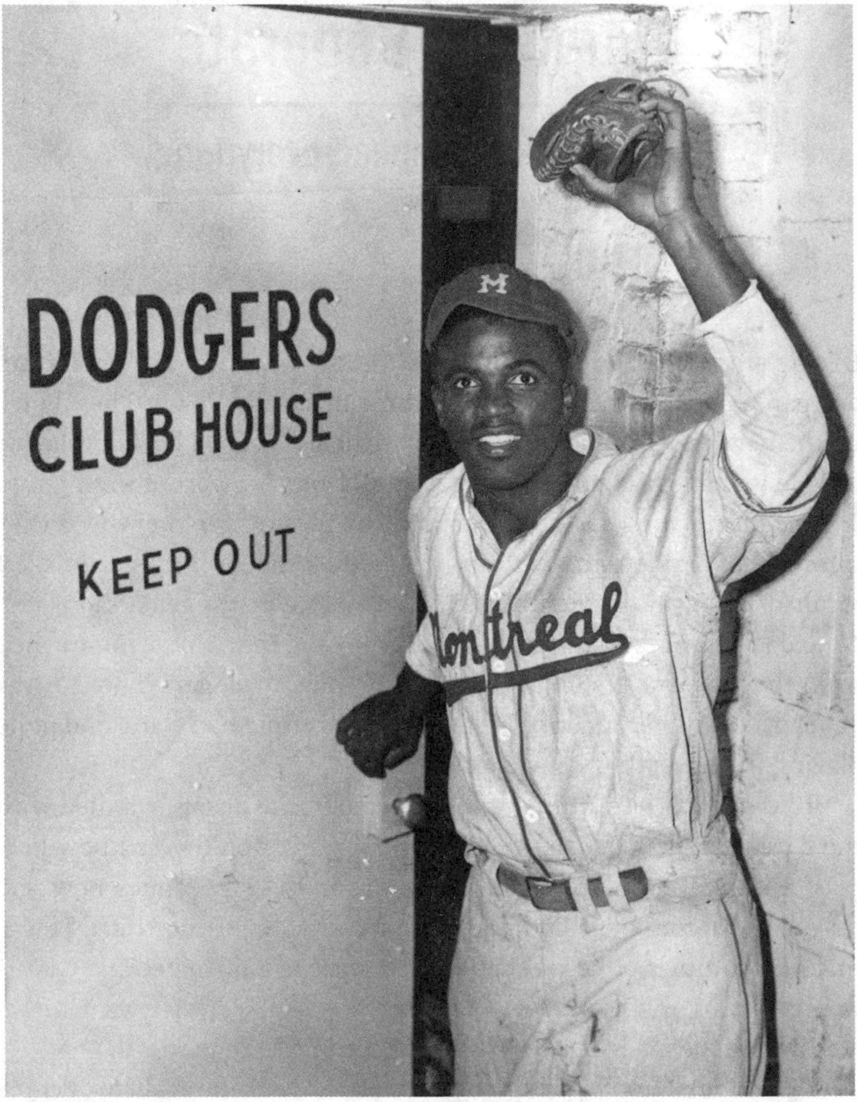
DODGERS
CLUB HOUSE
KEEP OUT
Montreal

Black players—politely called Negroes when they weren't called nig
gers—had played in what was the beginning of Major League Baseball in the 19th century. Then with Cap Anson, now a member of the
National Baseball Hall of Fame, leading the way, blacks were systemati-
cally excluded. "Get that nigger off the field" was how Anson put it. But
Negroes continued to play baseball and form teams and loose leagues
of their own.

From the 1920s to the late 1950s, the Negro Leagues played in
loosely defined competition, ultimately with contracts and schedules
similar to the major leagues. In many cases they played in the same
ballparks when the home teams were out of town. They played other
games where they could find a crowd. And when the major–league
seasons were over—which was in early October, when the weather was
still mild and there was still money to be made—many major–league
players barnstormed mostly through the South competing against players from the Negro Leagues.

More than a few of the white stars, including Joe DiMaggio, said
Satchel Paige, the legendary pitcher of the Negro Leagues—as wondrous as he was flamboyant—was the best pitcher they'd ever seen.
Josh Gibson would have been a star catcher in any league without question. But the major leagues wouldn't let Paige or Gibson in, and for the
players in the Negro Leagues, that's how it was. Competing in those
postseason barnstorming tours against major–league players or in their
own leagues was as good as it got. The big–time baseball remained for
whites only.

So they lived the life they loved and loved the life they lived. They
were playing baseball during the Depression, and the money was pretty
good for black men. These black players, some of them wonderfully
talented, were relegated and resigned to hotels oftentimes without hot
water, rickety buses, meals cobbled together on those buses. "We'd call
it Dutch lunch—baloney and cheese and stuff—and we'd buy it before

the games so we'd have something to eat after; a lot of places wouldn't serve us," Josh Gibson Jr., the great catcher's son, an infielder in the Negro Leagues, said.

At a time when so many of the current stars of the big leagues are black men who would have been fated to ride those buses, too, these recollections come without bitterness. During those barnstorming tours they got the notion that many of them were as good as the white big leaguers, but they would never know.

Their schedules were mixed with exhibition games to make a much–needed buck. They played on teams that used different names from town to town because there was only so much revenue they could draw from any one place. There was no videotape then. Film from that era is scarce and statistics are unreliable. "You just have to go by what we tell you," said Monte Irvin, who made his big–league debut in 1949, at age 30, after 11 years in the Negro Leagues. "We didn't know how good we were, either."

For teams with the stability to play in one hometown and still pay their bills, the living was pretty good. The Kansas City Monarchs was one of them. "We didn't eat on the bus," Buck O'Neill, the historian and patriarch, said. "We stayed at some of the best hotels and restaurants in the country, but they were black. It wasn't like a lot of people thought; we were in our big leagues." (Orchestra leader Duke Ellington explained that he adapted by eating steak every morning at a good hotel because "I never knew when the next meal was coming.")

O'Neill played and managed in the Negro Leagues from 1937 to 1955, played with Jackie Robinson and Ernie Banks, then scouted and coached for the Cubs. The day Banks signed his first contract with the Cubs, Buck O'Neill signed to scout for them.

"The black guys in the white minor leagues in the South had it tough," he said. "I knew where to go in Greenville, Mississippi, but I didn't know where to go in Newark, New Jersey. When I scouted for the Cubs, I would drive all the way from Tucson to Mesa and when I get there they see that I'm black and they say that they have no reservation, and a white person come up right behind me and gets the room." Perhaps the name O'Neill fooled them.

Maybe we don't really understand the racism of that period in America. It was much more blatant then than now, but we're still passing through it. Buck O'Neill was in the segregated navy in World War II. He was on the train transferring German prisoners of war from Virginia to Fort Leavenworth in Kansas, and the prisoners rode in the front of the train. The American Negro sailors had to ride in the back. Even though the German soldiers were prisoners, they sat ahead of the men guarding them. "Pitiful," O'Neill says. "The American uniform didn't make any difference."

The players on the Monarchs who had played a few seasons in the league knew how to make those oppressive rules work as best they could. And young black players who grew up in Harlem or inner Chicago knew about the rules. "If we got a kid from Albany or something, it was tough on them," O'Neill said. "I knew where to take them. We had a book of places to go and stay all over the country. In Chicago we'd ask the guys on the Chicago American Giants, in Kansas City we'd tell them about the Blue Room, the jazz club in the Streets Hotel."

Management at the Streets Hotel kept the Monarchs' schedule always in mind. Duke Ellington and Count Basie would be booked for the Blue Room for weekends when the Monarchs were playing at home so the upper–class Negroes from Wichita and St. Joe could make a weekend out of the trip. (Years later when the author was a young reporter covering the Yankees, the Blue Room was a prize destination after a night game.) O'Neill's book on places to go and things to do is now on display in the Museum of the Negro Leagues in Kansas City.

Branch Rickey signed Jackie for the Dodgers organization late in 1945 and assigned him to their Montreal Royals farm team. But the wheels had been turning with agonizing frustration for some time.

Some recall the bittersweet memory of those players who experienced the Negro Leagues in the later years when they knew Robinson's success as a rookie in 1947 would break open the big leagues and mean the end of their league. If Major League Baseball was open to the best of the Negro Leagues, then the life of the baseball they loved, however restricted, was being closed down. They were pleased that at long last one of their own was getting a chance at the major leagues. The sadness for almost all of them was that they would never have that chance for themselves. Their time as baseball players was past for all but a few of the youngest and most talented players.

"Oh man," O'Neill said. "Jackie signing actually was the death knell of Negro League baseball. The guys I used to sign for the Monarchs out of high school or college, now they're signing with organized baseball. It really hurt us, but even with that we were so happy that it had finally happened. This is why they were forced to organize the Negro Leagues in the first place."

❖

The first major–league tryout of black players was hidden in secrecy in April 1945, two years before Jackie's debut. Columnist Wendell Smith, who had campaigned relentlessly in the black *Pittsburgh Courier* for the gates to open, was bolstered by Boston city councilman Isadore Muchnik, who threatened to revoke the Red Sox's permit to play Sunday games at Fenway Park unless the Red Sox granted a tryout to three black players.

Smith selected shortstop Marvin Williams, outfielder Sam Jethroe, and former UCLA running back Jackie Robinson, who was about to begin his first season with the Monarchs. Robinson, a great college athlete in football, baseball, track, and basketball, was fresh out of the army and had not played any baseball for six years. The workout was supposed to be supervised by four Red Sox Hall of Famers: Joe Cronin, the manager; 78–year–old Hugh Duffy, a coach; owner Tom Yawkey, a South Carolina lumberman; and Eddie Collins, the general manager. The workout was, of course, a sham.

Cronin refused to give an evaluation of the players he'd seen. Duffy said one workout wasn't enough. Yawkey said any judgment had to come from his baseball people. And Collins said he couldn't be there because of a previous engagement. Don't call us, we'll call you—and the Red Sox never did call.

Smith recommended Robinson to Rickey, and in 1947 Robinson was Rookie of the Year. Jethroe was the Rookie of the Year in 1950 for the Boston Braves. The Red Sox had a farm team in Birmingham, Alabama, in the late 1940s and early 1950s, and teenager Willie Mays was blossoming with the Negro League team in town, but the Red Sox declined to sign him. A few years later Red Sox manager Pinky Higgins, a favorite of owner Yawkey, gave a simple explanation: "There'll be no niggers on this ball club as long as I have anything to say about it."

In the 13 seasons after Robinson and before the Red Sox in 1959 became the last team to field a black player, eight black players were Rookie of the Year in the National League and nine were MVP. No black player won either award in the American League in that same time. Scouts say that when National League teams were trying to sign black players, they emphasized that they would be more comfortable in the National League, while American League teams told white prospects they wouldn't have to deal with black players.

Red Sox management wasn't the only team to let bigotry handicap them on the field. The dynasty Yankees, who had dominated the standings for four decades with brilliant scouting and money, lost some of their advantage by not elevating black players. Their only exception was Elston Howard in 1954. The Yankees were content with their success in signing the best white players in the South and advised scout Tom Greenwade, who had found Mickey Mantle, "not to go down dark alleys." Once the flow of black players to the majors became a steady stream, the Yankees went from 1965 until 1976 without winning a pennant. The Red Sox, who won the American League pennant in 1946, the last year of the all–white major leagues, did not win another pennant until 1967. The effect was clear.

❖

When Robinson got his chance, the ripple effect was profound in the mind of black athletes who had never before felt they had a chance. For those in the Negro Leagues, it was a flash of brilliant light. Maybe they did have a chance before it was too late. Larry Doby got his chance 11 weeks after Robinson in 1947. Monte Irvin got his chance in 1949 and Ernie Banks in 1953. Henry Aaron was the last big leaguer to come out of the Negro Leagues in 1953. It was too late for Buck Leonard and Cool Papa Bell and who knows how many more. Ray Dandridge, one of the greats, got a taste of the minor leagues, but by the time baseball was open to him, his time had passed.

Who knows how good they really were? That evaluation exists only in legend and in the few old gray heads that were there. "You just have to take our word for it," said Monte Irvin, a member of the group who selects long–overlooked players to the Hall of Fame. Irvin was elected to the Hall of Fame in 1973, partly because of his play over eight seasons in the major leagues but more in recognition of his greater accomplishments in the Negro Leagues.

"Oscar Charleston was the Willie Mays of his day," Irvin said. "Nobody ever played center field better than Willie Mays. Suppose they had never given Willie a chance, and we said that, would anybody believe there was a kid in Alabama who was that good? Or there was a black guy in Atlanta who might break Babe Ruth's home run record? No.

"Charleston," Irvin said. "Of all of the players in our league, he was the best. Rifle for an arm, strong as two men, had no weaknesses. I played six years with Willie; Oscar would be comparable to him. Some players say Oscar was better.

"You should have seen Willie Wells play shortstop: as good as Ozzie Smith and a better hitter. How I wish people could have seen Ray Dandridge play third base, as good as Brooks Robinson and Craig Nettles and all of those. He was bowlegged; a train might go through there but not a baseball."

Who knows if Satchel Paige was even greater than my father told me? At a Biblical age of at least 42, Paige got to the Cleveland Indians in 1948 in time to help them to the American League pennant. He compiled a 6–1 record and a 2.48 earned–run average, so he must have been some pitcher when he was younger. He lasted until 1953 with the St. Louis Browns. In a token appearance in 1965 for the Kansas City Athletics, he pitched three scoreless innings at the age of something like 59. If that was a token of what he was when he was young, who knows what he was in his prime.

The evidence of how great these players really were must be in their success once they got the chance. Clearly the myth that they weren't good enough to play with white players was exposed.

Josh Gibson may have been the best of them in the Negro Leagues, maybe the best of any of them anywhere. He was a catcher with a strong arm, speed, and extraordinary power who played from 1930 to 1946, when he died of high blood pressure and a brain hemorrhage at 35. Legend says he might have followed Robinson to the majors in 1947.

"That's what's so ironic," said Josh Gibson Jr., himself a Negro Leagues infielder for two seasons. "My father was never bitter. The everyday Negro might have felt bitter, but not the players. My father didn't die of a broken heart. Put that in there."

❖

So the players in the Negro Leagues got on the bus from one town with some sort of stadium to another, to play three games in one day on occasion, perhaps a doubleheader in the morning in Brooklyn and a night game in New Jersey a couple of hours away. Maybe it would be a game against one of the Negro League teams or maybe it would be against a team of local hotshots. Sometimes they'd stay at private homes or at a hotel that had one shower, and they'd wait their turn until there was only cold water. Meal money at the time the Negro Leagues were winding down had reached a high of $2 a day. Sometimes payday depended on a bet between owners.

"You had to laugh a lot; you did, you did," Lester Lockett, a longtime veteran of the leagues, said at the age of 80. Good times, they were not forgotten.

"It was like riding the wagon," Ted (Double Duty) Radcliffe said. "Ride all night, play all day, sing all night."

Radcliffe died in 2005 at the age of 103. He loved participating in a benefit for the Negro League Baseball Players Association at Shea

Stadium in New York in 1992 and was full of memories and smiles on that occasion. This was a good and worthwhile event because Major League Baseball and its players' association were very late in finding a place to honor what those players contributed. For that benefit event they wore replicas of their old uniforms and wreaths of nostalgia. In recent years historians like Monte Irvin have selected a number of Negro League players for inclusion in a special category at the Baseball Hall of Fame.

However painful it was to accept that there was no way to the top for all those years, what those outcasts remembered was the joy. Radcliffe, at age 90, was full of smiles at the recollections. He put out his hand. "*See* that," he said. The five fingers of his right hand pointed in five directions. He was a catcher, also a pitcher, which accounts for the nickname an appreciative Damon Runyon hung on him. One time Radcliffe caught Satchel Paige in the first game of a doubleheader and hit a grand slam. "And I was sitting on the bus hustling girls for the night," Radcliffe said. "Every town we went to was like being on vacation. And I loved the girls.

"The owner comes out and says he needs me to pitch the second game. I said, 'Sweeten the ante,' and he did. I pitched a one–hitter."

Radcliffe played for 36 years. At the same time he was pitcher, catcher, general manager, and club secretary for $650 a week. Gibson was their Babe Ruth of the payrolls. Gibson's son recalled his father, the great man of the Negro Leagues, was paid $1,000 or $1,200 a month at the time. That was pretty good money when $80 a week was a reasonable living for most Americans. Ruth, of course, was being paid $80,000 a year then, more than even President Hoover.

❖

Robinson changed everything. He changed things even before he got to Brooklyn. Sure the Monarchs could have Dutch lunch while they rolled, but a restroom–equipped bus was not part of the equipment.

"We could buy gas because they wanted the money, but we couldn't go to the restroom," O'Neill said.

"When Jackie came with us, we'd been going to a town in Okla-homa for 20 years; we'd been going to that same gas station. But the sign on the restroom door said 'White Men Only.' Jackie came with us and we'd go to this town and fill up the ballpark. Next morning we'd be fixing to leave and go to the filling station.

"The man comes out, puts the hose in the tank. He says, 'You guys played baseball last night, filled up the ballpark, and put on a great show.' Jackie gets off the bus and starts to the restroom. 'Where you goin,' boy?' the man says.

"'I'm goin' to the restroom.'

"'Boy, you know you can't go to that restroom.'

"Jackie said, 'Take the hose out of the tank.'"

"Man thought awhile now because we got a 50-gallon tank on this side and we got a 50-gallon tank on that side. He's not going to sell that much gas at one time any day soon. You know what he said: 'You boys can go to the restroom but don't stay long.'

"From that day on, we never went to a gas station where we couldn't use the restroom. We never played in a town where we didn't have a place to sleep or a place where we could eat. Jackie said we're making money for these people; I think we've been putting up with a lot of stuff we don't have to."

Surely Branch Rickey's dossier before he signed Robinson must have included information like that. Robinson changed everything. Maybe there was a better player in the Negro Leagues; his peers thought he was the superior man. "Like a lot of things, we had to be better," Lester Lockett said.

O'Neill, elegant and eloquent at 94, was the lead speaker at Hall of Fame induction ceremonies in 2006 when a five-year study presented 17 Negro Leagues players and executives for inclusion. He pointed out that in the great years of the Negro Leagues 8 percent of major-league players had been to college. Since the Negro Leagues usually had spring training on the campus of a black college, 40 percent of the black play-ers had been to college. "We helped build a bridge across the chasm of prejudice," he said.

At that time Negro Leagues baseball was the third–largest black industry, behind black insurance and cosmetics. The departure of their Robinson was the arrival of Robinson on the bigger stage. It meant the opening of doors and it meant the best talent was going to the big leagues. It meant the end of the Negro Leagues. And that's a little bad. But also a whole lot good.

2

He Made His Own History

Monte Irvin Might Have Been First

(Born Columbia, Alabama, February 25, 1919-)

As Monte Irvin remembers the details, he might have become the first black man in Major–League Baseball. There was a meeting of NAACP officials and the executives of the Negro Leagues. It was shortly after the 1941 baseball season, and the NAACP was planning to pressure the Fair Employment Commission to urge baseball to drop its barrier to Negro players.

"My name was brought up as the one to break the barrier," Irvin recalled in a swirl of recollections from his more than 60 years as a baseball man and 80 years as a black man.

Josh Gibson, Ray Dandridge, Satchel Paige, and Buck Leonard were already stars in their league, but Irvin was young, had two years of college, and was coming off three great years in the Negro Leagues. "I was second to none in the five things a great player should have," he said a career later. "I could run, throw, field, hit, and hit for power. I had solid fundamentals and I was easy to get along with."

He was 22 years old. Jackie Robinson, a multisport star at UCLA, hadn't yet decided he was a baseball player. But America was expending all its physical and emotional energy fighting World War II to save the world from the foreign evil. The plight of the Negro wasn't a priority. The time wasn't right to change America at home. The time was never right until the time somebody made it right.

Irvin is one of the very rare characters in the integration of baseball. Not only was he a significant player, fortunate to have a substantial career in the newly integrated major leagues, abbreviated as it was, beginning as a rookie at the age of 31, but he had a significant career in the Negro Leagues among those fabled names whose talent is attested to only by memory. There are so few of them left, and there are no comparison statistics that hold Oscar Charleston up against Ty Cobb.

Nobody knows how good those players were. Monte Irvin doesn't know how good he might have been if his time had come when he was 22 like so many of the names in the official record book. He was one of the lucky ones who still had time left to play eight seasons in the big leagues; still he missed 7 or 8 or 10 of his prime years.

While he was playing with the Newark Eagles of the Negro National League, he and some of the guys would go to Yankee Stadium and compare. "I'd watch DiMaggio," he said. "I didn't think he could do more than I did, and I had a better arm. I did learn to pull the ball by watching him."

False modesty is not part of his memory bank. In high school in Orange, New Jersey, he was one of four boys ever named all-state in four sports. The most recent was Larry Doby. Irvin turned down a scholarship to the University of Michigan because the brutal wisdom of the day said he'd be torturing himself because stardom there would only be a dead end. If he went to Lincoln University in Pennsylvania he could make Negro business contacts that would serve him all his life.

He played for the Eagles under the created name of Jimmy Nelson so he could stay eligible to play college ball at Lincoln—until he got tired of being broke and went full-time to the Eagles—and winter ball in Puerto Rico and Cuba. Statistics are sketchy but they say Irvin at 20 batted .403. In 1941, at 22, he led his league with .395.

The Eagles were paying him $150 a month. Jorge Pasquel, the wealthy promoter and major owner of the Mexican League, invited him to play in Mexico for $750 a month. He asked Eagles owner Effa Manley, the mother of the league, for $175. "I wanted to stay," Irvin said. "She said she couldn't afford the other $25 so I went."

He married Dorinda, known as Dee, went to Mexico City, hit .370 on his honeymoon, and experienced life without segregation. "It was the first time I ever felt free," he said.

We should think what free means today and what it meant then. Compare that kind of money and freedom against the obstacles in the life of a black man in America, even in New Jersey, and the very mixed joys and rewards of playing in the Negro Leagues.

Buck O'Neill, the patriarch of black baseball, noted that young men coming out of Harlem adjusted to the restrictions placed on their lives, but a man growing up integrated into suburban Orange, New Jersey, as Irvin did, might find his awakening very demanding.

.·:⋄:·.

Irvin is an aware man with the philosophy that he could accomplish more by being diplomatic than by expressing anger. He was born in Alabama and his parents took their understanding of Alabama life with them to New Jersey. Monte Irvin learned the value of being compliant. Veteran players told the new ones where to go, what to wear, and how to get along. "It's not comfortable, but you get used to it. And you want to do something to, you know, get ahead, to make some decent money," he said. "So you accepted the rules, but you tried to change them."

In the big leagues, black players would complain about those harsh rules to owners or the general manager or the traveling secretary, all of whom who would say the segregation rules weren't the club's rules, and the black players just had to go along with them. And the executives usually added that they hoped the rules wouldn't last much longer. They had been in place so long already.

In the Negro Leagues there was another kind of reality. "It beat pushing a broom or running an elevator," Irvin said. "You knew you had to play well or go home and follow the mule." Meal money was $1 a day so they ate a lot of cold cuts and cheese and crackers and drank soda on the bus. Journeymen in the major leagues were being paid $600 a month while Irvin was making his $175 as a star, but black people outside of baseball were making $15 a week operating elevators, he said.

So they might play two games—one against the Bushwicks and one against the Springfield Grays—in the morning in Newark and travel 60 miles to play at night in Trenton. The bus was uncomfortable, but when they won the 1946 championship, the Eagles got a new $15,000 air-conditioned bus.

It was good considering the boundaries. "We were living high on the hog," Irvin said. They played in Yankee Stadium and the Polo Grounds. Ella Fitzgerald or Sugar Ray Robinson would throw out the first ball. "When they played in the Bushwicks in Brooklyn it was a big event. "You made sure your uniform was clean and your shoes shined," he said. "When we played at the Bushwicks, the fans almost all wore ties."

Reality was that it was as good as it got for them. "We couldn't aspire to the major leagues; we knew that was closed," Irvin said. "We aspired to our All-Star Game and the three-day weekend in Chicago" where the annual East-West game was played, beginning in 1933. Black newspapers conducted polls to select the teams. Urban blacks couldn't sustain the cost of a lengthy parallel to the World Series so the East-West game was the highlight of the season and regularly drew 50,000 fans, white and black, to Comiskey Park.

There was no misconception that the level of play in the Negro Leagues—top to bottom—was as good as the major leagues. The realistic issue always was the comparison of the best of the black players with the best of the white. There never was genuine and direct competition so there could be no definitive answer. There was always the tantalizing prism of barnstorming. Through the early 1960s the major-league season ended in the first week of October, when the weather was still warm enough for baseball, especially in the South. There were still the original 16 major-league teams, none farther south than Washington or St. Louis, and television essentially had not brought images of the stars of baseball around the country. So after the World Series a major white star like Bob Feller of the Cleveland Indians would assemble a team of players, some-

times filling in with high–level minor leaguers, and travel through the
South playing against another troupe of major leaguers in Montgomery,
Alabama, or New Orleans or Birmingham or smaller cities that had
little exposure to what America regarded as the best.

The best of the Negro League teams played in the North where
the economics were better, but the large majority of black people lived
in the South. Often the white all–stars would tour side–by–side with
a group of black all–stars, so it would be Bob Feller's All–Stars playing against Satchel Paige's All–Stars. They could play in arenas that
wouldn't permit whites and blacks on the same teams.

Sometimes they'd fly—separate planes, of course. More often they'd
go by bus, whites in white hotels and blacks in black facilities, and
they'd meet at the ballpark. Holding down costs was especially significant so the black teams would travel with a core of stars and pick up the
best of the local crop at each stop along the way. Players could double
their salaries, especially players from the Negro Leagues who weren't
making as much as the white big leaguers.

While the black teams often played the big leaguers even and sometimes outplayed them, the public and the black players realized that the
white players already had played their season and were playing these
exhibition games for the money. The Negro League players, however,
were driven to prove themselves to the whites and to themselves.

They were haunted by what Irvin called athlete's pride. Those black
stars never knew how good they were. Could they play a whole season
in the major leagues?

Black players would talk to friendly whites—Stan Musial was one of
the best—who could see how good the black players were and ask them
to talk up an end to big–league barriers. "They'd say it won't do any
good; they don't think you can play up here with us," Irvin said. "It was
the same ball and same bat and if we could play with them barnstorming, why couldn't we play with them in the big leagues?"

Hadn't he fought on the same side in the Battle of the Bulge in
1944, when General Patton called for help from black soldiers who
hadn't been issued weapons before? And the black troops responded
that they were already on the way. Equality to fight and die came

instantly. "Then the weather cleared, the Germans were stopped, and we went back to segregation. No change," Irvin said.

The irony of having fought in the segregated army against the very thing they were subject to was not lost. "When you wanted to cry, you had to laugh; you had to be courteous when you wanted to be otherwise," Irvin said. "When you'd go in to buy something, they wouldn't take money out of your hand, had to put it on the counter. Had to always say 'Miss' this and 'Miss' that. Don't linger too long. Then when we got on a public facility, the sign said Negroes load from back. If there were no seats for whites, you had to get up and stand."

Irvin pointed out that in the town of Rosewood, Florida, a few miles from his present home in Homosassa, in 1923 virtually a whole town of colored people was wiped out. The residents were murdered or driven into the swamps to escape raging whites. The court dismissed charges for "insufficient evidence."

Southern black players told Northern teammates that being called "alligator bait" was no joke because there were people who disappeared and were just never found. So when the white cops stopped the bus that was going 60 miles per hour and said they were speeding at 70, they were going 70. When the bus broke down carrying Negro League players, sometimes they had to pay a ransom to have it fixed in time to get to the next game. Sometimes they couldn't get it fixed at any price. Then they had to scramble to get to the game or just couldn't show up.

"Don't overdramatize," Irvin's wife Dee cautioned while we were talking over glasses of Irish Cream in his living room. "We know the tone of society then," she said. Do we really? Do we know that an early issue of *Time* carried a letter objecting to Negroes being referred to as "Mr." in print? Dee Irvin remembered; she lived it.

"You got along as a matter of survival: if you're in jail, how smart are you? If you're dead, what good are you?" Irvin said. They played by the same rules that made Marion Anderson, a star with the Metropolitan Opera, return to a store in Dallas after hours in order to buy a gown for her performance because the store wouldn't serve her when whites were around.

"When we were young we weren't thinking about civil rights," he said. "You wanted to play to please the owners, to please the fans, but mostly to please yourself. All we wanted to do was, where can we find a good–looking broad, and play ball. You knew things were almost hopeless because nobody was making any progress. So we would try to be good enough to stay there, make some money, hope that things would change and eventually they'd get the message that a human being is a human being."

Irvin came back from the war, changed uniforms, and went to play in Puerto Rico to get into shape.

Then Branch Rickey signed Jackie Robinson and assigned him to Montreal for the 1946 season. And wherever players in the Negro Leagues might find a newspaper with AAA International League box scores they'd look to see how Jackie did. As important, they'd look all the way down to the last line that gave the attendance. Were people staying away because there was a black player on the Royals, or were they coming out because that black player made the team better? Attendance for the Royals and the whole International League was up considerably, but that's difficult to interpret because crowds at sports events were greater all over with the end of World War II. We do know that Robinson's presence certainly didn't make fans stay away.

The insightful ones might have thought Rickey signed a black player not out of Christian altruism, but because Robinson would eventually make the Brooklyn Dodgers better and bring in more money. Rickey had the courage not to care that Robinson was black. That was the highest principle and the most pragmatic.

"Then we knew we had a chance; we said we wished it had come 10 years before," Irvin said. "Then they would have had the cream of our crop." Some of the black players didn't think Robinson was the right man because he had played only a few months in their league while Roy Campanella had played 10 years and Irvin four. There was jealousy, but there was hope. Irvin went back to the Eagles, played shortstop with Larry Doby at second base, and hit .404, and so on. Rickey made another pitch.

Mrs. Manley railed that Rickey had taken black pitcher Don New-combe from her to the Dodgers for nothing. She demanded $5,000 for Irvin and hired lawyers. Rickey backed away. Bill Veeck declined to take Irvin with Doby. A young executive with the Giants, Chub Feeney, who had gone to high school in Orange, New Jersey, with Irvin, recommended him. New York Giants owner Horace Stoneham had seen the success of Robinson with the hated Dodgers, gave the lady $5,000, and grabbed Irvin.

"I figured I deserved a split from Mrs. Manley," Irvin said. "She said no, she'd keep it all, pay the lawyers and 'I'll buy myself a fur stole.'

"I said, 'Don't you feel funny giving me nothing? Maybe I won't report. She said, 'You'll report.' I did."

Years later, in 1975, Mrs. Manley and Irvin, then a member of the Baseball Hall of Fame and assistant to the commissioner of baseball, were honored at the Ashland, Kentucky, Negro League Museum. "She wore that stole," Irvin said. "I asked, 'Mrs. Manley, is that it?' She said, 'It looks good and it keeps me nice and warm.'"

In 2006 Mrs. Manley was inducted into the Hall of Fame.

✦

In 1949, as an outfielder, Irvin hit .373 in the AAA International League and played a month with the Giants. In 1950 he was hitting .510 when he was called up to be a 31-year-old rookie with the Giants. In his first full season, the year of the Giants' 1951 miracle comeback, Irvin hit .312 and led the league with 121 RBI.

Larry Doby and Jackie Robinson had talked often in their first year in the majors. So it was Doby, once a young protégé of Irvin's in New Jersey, who spoke often with Irvin in his first year. They informed each other of who the good guys were and who the bad guys were, where they could go and where they couldn't, and what the pitfalls of the road were. Irvin was the wise old head who tutored 19-year-old Willie Mays of Fairfield, Alabama, on the ways of the world in the big leagues and the big city.

"He was brought up to take what they had to throw at you, then fight back like crazy," Irvin said. "When he came to our club and played so well, we thought, here we got a diamond in the rough, a superstar, and he was so good it became a pleasure coming to the ballpark."

When the few black players in the National League came to New York, Irvin would show them Count Basie's or Ray Robinson's place in Harlem or Killer Johnson's restaurant on 63rd Street. After a game at the Polo Grounds they'd say, "*See* you at the Red Rooster." When the Boston Celtics came to New York, black Bill Russell would take white Bob Cousy and Bill Sharman to the Rooster.

But when Irvin went to Sanford, Florida, for his first spring training in the Giants' organization, he couldn't stay at the team's hotel. Horace Stoneham, who owned the Giants, also owned the hotel, but the law said no Negro could stay there. So when the team traveled, Irvin would sleep on the train whenever possible.

Give Leo Durocher, the often acid manager of the Giants, credit. He wanted to win and didn't care who helped him win. When Irvin and Henry Thompson, another star from the Negro Leagues, joined the team, Durocher called a clubhouse meeting to introduce the two new men. As Irvin recalled it, Durocher said, "This is what I'm gonna say about race and color: I don't care what color you are, but if you can help this team, help us win, help us earn more money, you can play on this team. Now get to know each other. Work together and let's have a successful season."

But in Arizona, the Adams Hotel had a separate dining room for the players in order to protect the proper guests. When *Sports Illustrated* had a cover photo of Durocher and his blonde actress wife Laraine Day with their arms around this black kid Mays, the uproar was great, and not exclusively from the South. Irvin stood firm, like the black players who had the strength to bear the abuses, who told themselves they were going to succeed, who were going to show everyone they could play.

There was the time in 1951 when the Giants and the Indians were playing each other on the way north from training in Arizona. Big Luke Easter of the Indians missed a throw at first base and one loud voice to be heard all over the stadium yelled to Cleveland manager Al

Lopez, as Irvin remembered, "Get some of those [Irvin paraphrased with 'N–people'] out of there and maybe you could win something."

At that time, if there was a black player on the team, he was playing. A clearly outstanding black player, such as Willie Mays, would rise through the system. Even the most racist of organizations wanted talent. If the player had the major–league talent, there was little room for him on the bench as a utility player. That job was for a white player. And there was a quota, no matter how many good black players there were.

In 1948 Phillies manager Ben Chapman, who had bitterly opposed Robinson's acceptance with the Dodgers, said to Jackie, "You're a hell of a ballplayer. You're still a nigger." In 1967, Phillies manager Harry Walker, once one of those who objected to Robinson in 1947, wrote out a lineup with eight black players and a white pitcher, whose turn it was to pitch. One day in 1971 the Pittsburgh Pirates put nine black players on the field, and manager Danny Murtaugh was asked about that. He said he hadn't noticed, and those were his best players. Some of the rigid mentality was changing.

Irvin recalled that with substitutions in a game in St. Louis in the 1950s, the only white on the field for the Giants was shortstop Alvin Dark, from Louisiana. "And," Irvin said, "another guy with a shrill voice yells, 'Hey, Alvin, now I know why they call you Dark.' Alvin laughed and said, 'What am I doing out here?'" Alvin Dark's nickname was Blackie. The man from Louisiana was growing, although years later as manager of the San Francisco Giants, Dark still expressed his conviction that black players could not be fully alert on the field—not even Willie Mays or Elston Howard. Centuries of prejudice didn't wipe clear so quickly.

Philadelphia, home of the Liberty Bell, was one of the northern cities where hotels didn't accept black ballplayers. Frank Sinatra had to threaten to break his contract until the Las Vegas hotel where he and the Rat Pack were appearing, accepted Sammy Davis Jr.

In Orange, New Jersey, Irvin was refused when he tried to buy property to build a home. So he hired a lawyer and told him to buy the land and Irvin would buy it from him. "He said, 'No, I'm afraid of that and I'm president of the Republican Club'," Irvin said. "What I did was change to a lawyer who happened to be a Democrat."

⁜

In 1951 Irvin was at the core of the Giants' stunning comeback from 13½ games behind the hated Dodgers in August. When the Giants began to sense they had a chance, almost every night they were on the road many of them would congregate in the hotel room of one of the veteran leaders. Often it would be in Irvin's room; he was leading the league in runs batted in, and he had poise and bearing they all recognized. They would order sandwiches and talk about what they had to do to keep winning and to catch the Dodgers.

The Dodgers hated the Giants and the Giants hated them right back. Irvin recalled that on August 9 the Dodgers had beaten them in Brooklyn for the 12th time in 15 games and taunted them. Jackie Robinson, who could win a game as well as any man who ever played, sat beating a din into the Giants' ears with a baseball bat against the wall between the two clubhouses.

Eddie Stanky, a son of Alabama, responded with a racial slur. "That goes for me, too," added Monte Irvin." He had not forgotten that, like Robinson, he was a veteran of the Negro Leagues, but he had become a member of the Giants. For that moment Irvin's color was black and orange as his Giants cap.

It is a footnote to history that before Bobby Thomson hit his dramatic ninth–inning playoff home run to win the pennant for the Giants, Irvin made the only out. Waiting to hit behind Thomson for the unneeded moment was Irvin's protégé, rookie Willie Mays.

In 1952, the spring after being part of the thunder and lightning in the Giants' comeback, Irvin was expecting more from himself. On April 2, in an exhibition game, he broke his ankle. He came back in 1953 to hit .329 with 97 RBI, but the speed that enabled him to steal home against the Yankees in the 1951 World Series was blunted.

His career was winding down. He was 34 years old. In five full major–league seasons he batted .300 three times. He was a respected professional. What might he have done if he had been Rickey's original selection? "I know he could have handled it," Dee said with a wife's certainty. "Failing was the furthest thing from my mind."

Looking back, Irvin wonders if he made a mistake in not making himself a candidate for Rickey instead of thinking he needed time to make himself ready. "I would be proud to have been the first," he said. He doesn't complain. He admires Robinson's greatness at rising to the occasion and above it time and again.

"Jackie said, 'Let them keep throwing at me; I'll take it out on the ball,'" Irvin said. "Guys thought, 'I would have done it if I had the chance.' They didn't give Jackie the credit he deserved. He got the chance and made it. He knew how to get things done. He stood for education as well as athletics. He made it better not only for baseball, but all the other sports—for black people. He made it better for America. It isn't as good as it should be, but it's better."

When the 1974 season opened with Henry Aaron one home run short of equaling Babe Ruth's career home run record, the Braves wanted to hold Aaron out of the first series in Cincinnati so he could do it on the first homestand. Commissioner Bowie Kuhn said no. Aaron had to play in Cincinnati and on his first at bat homered to tie Ruth. When the Braves came home, instead of Kuhn making himself present for Aaron's passing of the most cherished milestone in baseball, Kuhn blundered by sticking to a commitment to a booster club event in Cleveland. In some quarters ignoring the new home run king was seen as racist. Irvin, a member of the commissioner's office, was sent to Atlanta as official representative of baseball in place of the commissioner. He stood and took the booing that was really due Kuhn, and Irvin stood up gracefully.

Recently, at home in his Homosassa neighborhood, Monte Irvin looked around and reflected on the change in times since the Rosewood massacre. He and Dee, married since 1943, live in a handsome home in a nice neighborhood of whites and blacks. "We get along," he said. The house on the corner has a trout stream running through the living room. Irvin laughed. He never could have dreamed the neighborhood would have accepted them.

"I feel awful bad for the guys who never got to play," he said. "At least I got a piece of the pie.

"I think we were doing a job, not realizing how important it was. We wanted, you know, to pioneer in our own way, pioneer by playing well. Make it better for those who came after us. And apparently we succeeded. I think so."

3

Second, and Second to None

Larry Doby Bears the Burden with Grace

*(Born Camden, South Carolina, December 13, 1923.
Died Montclair, New Jersey, June 18, 2003.)*

IN THE DEEPEST SPOT in his memory bank, where the years of indignity and insult might endure, Larry Doby kept one image of the joy of what life ought to be. It was in his mind even more prominently than it was on display in his home in Montclair, New Jersey.

It's a moment preserved from the 1948 World Series when Larry Doby was 23 years old and barely a year removed from resigning himself to a career in the Negro Leagues. He and pitcher Steve Gromek, a white teammate, embrace in the Cleveland Indians' clubhouse after Doby's home run won the crucial fourth game of the World Series, giving Cleveland a lead of three games to one over the Boston Braves. "That's what America is all about, or what it's supposed to be all about," Doby said two generations later. "We could have rehearsed all day and never got that joy on our faces. It was genuine. I hit a home run to win the game for him.

"And don't you think he didn't get heat for that when he got back home to Hamtramck [Michigan]. Steve said, 'Larry won a game for me. He's my teammate.'

"I think I feel good about that photograph more than anything."

It's an illustration of the fairy tale of what equality is all about, which too often does not exist in reality. Doby was a teammate. How

tragically simple that was and sometimes still is. It was the best of what Doby held in his mind. "Fifty–one years ago there were two black folks playing Major League Baseball," he reflected one afternoon years later. There was Jackie Robinson and there was Larry Doby. "There are more than two now," he said.

On the occasion of Doby's funeral in 2003, in the community that he graced with his grace, a bit of pointed philosophy by master sports author Red Smith from an earlier time suited the moment: "Dying is easy; the least of us can do that. Living is the trick."

Larry Doby died at 79. He didn't get all the credit he deserved for living so gracefully in center field and everyplace else. We all should know that Jackie Robinson was first. Doby referred to him in admiration as "Mr. Robinson" for being the first of their race in the major leagues. Doby rarely let on how difficult it had been to be second. He rarely revealed his disappointment at being overlooked, which is how it goes to be second in history. Who was second to fly? Who was second on the moon?

Larry Doby was the second black manager, too.

All of that is relevant today, when black athletes are commonplace across the spectrum of sports. They are more frequent, too, among Americans who wear neckties and carry briefcases to work every day than in the days when Doby was a trailblazer in his profession. Prejudice is less virulent than it was 30 or 40 or 50 years ago. But the path is still especially demanding and lonely even if the resentment is muted.

"Things are better for all of America; I'd have to say baseball is ahead," Doby said. "We did this without someone writing a bill; this was before civil rights legislation, before Dr. King, before [Brown v.] Board of Education."

Doby is remembered, but "unforgotten" might be a more appropriate word. Until the celebration of the 50 years since Jackie Robinson first set pigeon toe in the National League in Brooklyn, April 15, 1947, Doby's role was overshadowed and overlooked. "I understood what

Jackie went through. Do you think it was any easier 11 weeks later?" he asked, not exactly expecting an answer.

He endured his trial over 13 seasons in the big leagues, six in a row as an all–star—whether or not anybody appreciated how difficult it was for him. Whether the slights were intended or not, whether they were only in his mind, they were there. Bill Veeck, the wonderful renegade owner who gave Doby his chance with the Cleveland Indians, thought the man's sensitivity hurt his performance and made his time more difficult.

Veeck, who died in 1986, recalled in his *Veeck as in Wreck* how often a plate umpire would call a strike and Doby would back out of the batters box and point to the color of the skin on his hand. The implication was clear. Whether Doby's perception of persecution interfered with his concentration on the rest of his time at bat and the times that followed is forever immeasurable.

❖

Doby's father's father was a slave. Can any young person today appreciate what that felt like to a young boy growing up?

Larry was born in Camden, South Carolina, and lived in the section known as the "black bottom" until he was 14 when his family moved to Paterson, New Jersey, and he was introduced to integrated schools and an integrated neighborhood. The residue of South Carolina was still strong in his home. Wealthy whites used to ride through black bottom with horse and buggy. As he recalled it, the buggies had gold wheels. The white swells would toss nickels and dimes out to the colored kids and when they picked up the coins, the swells would rub the little kids' heads. That was supposed to be good luck, of course

And Larry's grandma would admonish him: "Don't you ever, don't you ever do that." She didn't explain until he was 10 or 12 years old. Sure there was a chance for "kids who never had a nickel or a dime to buy some kind of treat, but grandma saw there was no dignity in picking up those coins," he said. There was dignity in her grandson turning his back.

In Paterson he'd go to the movies with high school teammates and white friends. They'd sit downstairs and he'd go upstairs where theater owners felt he belonged. Some people called that "nigger heaven." That's how it was. But when the movie was over, they'd get together for sodas. When their football team won the state championship, they were invited to play a game in Florida—but the hosts insisted that Doby could not be included with his teammates. The team stood with Doby and voted not to go.

He was the only black on his high school football team, one of two on the basketball team, and the only one on the baseball team. He was a solid basketball player at Long Island University, when LIU was a major college basketball power. He played a season of semipro basketball before going into the navy. He went and did things with white teammates and white schoolmates. He surely knew about Jim Crow and bigotry, but he'd never lived with it. In the big leagues he was alone. It was shocking to him.

Eleven weeks after Jackie broke the color barrier, Larry played a Fourth of July doubleheader for the Newark Eagles of the Negro National League, hit a home run on his last at bat, and caught a train to Chicago where the Cleveland Indians were playing. He walked into the visitors' clubhouse to be greeted by silence. He met with player–manager Lou Boudreau and introduced himself to his new teammates. Four of them, Doby recalled, refused to shake his hand. He refused to name them.

"That never happened," Hall of Fame pitcher Bob Feller insisted years later. (Author's note: From what I've been told, I accept Doby's version. In a biography of Jackie Robinson, *Great Time Coming*, author David Falkner wrote that Feller at first asked not to share the same platform with Robinson during their inauguration into the Baseball Hall of Fame in 1962.)

On Doby's first day, he put on his gray road uniform and went out for warm–ups, but there was nobody to throw the ball around with. If the Gromek photo marks Doby's sweet moment, then this was the bitter. For some aching minutes Doby stood alone and rejected until second baseman Joe Gordon waved his glove to throw him the ball.

Gordon, catcher Jim Hegan, and coach Bill McKechnie risked being what Doby called "N–word–lovers" to more than accept him. For the rest of the year Doby warmed up with Gordon. For the rest of his life he gave credit to Gordon.

In the smothering pressure of the first weeks, when Doby struck out, he'd go to the end of the dugout and sit alone. Once, after a week or so of that, Gordon struck out and went to sit next to Doby on the bench. Gordon had been a solid pro for a long time and knew how to absorb striking out. In his way he was telling Doby not to beat himself up. Gordon was one of the good guys.

In later years Doby saw a few of the guys he felt "weren't real friendly" and they said, "Let's have a drink."

Doby replied, "Um, I've got to go someplace."

The hard times, he told his son, Larry Junior, were of the past and to read about in the history books. The father didn't need to dwell on them. Years later Larry Junior heard from Bob Lemon, who was a star pitcher, how he liked having Doby playing behind him in center field. When father and son would watch baseball on television and Jim Hegan would appear on screen, coaching for the Yankees, the father would say, "Good man."

Ultimately, Doby had to deal alone with the hardest times. There was the time Boudreau told Doby to find a first baseman's mitt because that's where he was playing in order to give Eddie Robinson a rest. Robinson refused to let Doby use his mitt. Feller says that was only natural because players don't like anybody using their glove. Doby eventually borrowed one from the White Sox. Another time Boudreau sent Doby up to pinch–hit for popular Dale Mitchell, an accomplished contact–hitter, with two strikes against a tough pitcher. It was a clear invitation to embarrassment.

Doby never would identify publicly the bad guys. Often in that first year Doby and Jackie Robinson would speak on the phone and tell one another who were the good and bad guys, and which were the good places and bad places, and how each understood what it was to be alone. "People don't understand what that is," Doby said. "Who tells you about the balls you hit hard that weren't hits? Who tells you he should have had the ball you were charged with an error on? What do you do when everybody goes out of the ballpark after a game and you go alone?

"It's a loneliness where you're glad when the next day comes, because you know you're back in the ballpark. The best time was the time on the field."

And, as Doby said, don't think Gromek didn't get heat when he went home to Hamtramck. Gromek recalled overhearing something at a bar. "A friend of mine, a priest," Gromek said, "was sitting at a table and he said to another guy, 'Can you imagine him kissing Doby?' I mean, Larry won me my ball game. What more could I ask for?" In several cities Doby could not even take a taxi to or from the ballpark with teammates or eat with them after a game. "It was awful for him," Gromek said.

Over the years when Doby was insulted, rejected from hotels, and subjected to the continuing indignity, he would try to think of that moment—less the home run off Johnny Sain than the picture with Gromek.

⋄

Doby's dignity was in how he conducted his life, married to his high school sweetheart Helyn for 55 years until she died, in how he raised his five children, and how he worked as administrator with Major League Properties. There was his personal dignity in his willingness to thank Joe Gordon and Indians owner Bill Veeck, white people on his side.

One might understand if Doby resented that he was overlooked. Not resentful of "Mr. Robinson," but of the whole mechanism that makes one man stand in the light of history and cast a shadow on the other. How could Larry Doby not have been remembered?

While Robinson was starring in Brooklyn, Doby helped the Indians get to the World Series twice and the White Sox once—the only years the Yankees didn't win the American League pennant between 1946 and 1964. That first half season he was a second baseman as he had been with the Eagles, but he was overwhelmed by the jump to the major leagues and the burden of being for the first time in his life a black man in a white man's world. Ted Williams and Dominic DiMaggio congratulated him and wished him luck when they played the Red Sox, then the most racist of organizations, but there wasn't enough of that to cut the gloom. Doby struck out in his first at bat and compiled a dismal .156.

The next spring he was converted to a center fielder and immediately emerged as a fine player. He was the first black on a World Series–winning team. He batted in 100 runs five times and hit 20 home runs eight times in the era when both numbers were significant milestones. He scored 90 runs six times and once went 166 games in center field without an error. He was the first black to lead either major league in home runs. In 1954, when the Indians won 112 games, then the American League record, he led the league in home runs and RBI.

In the 1948 World Series, Doby batted .318. Feller, it may be noted, was the Cleveland losing pitcher in the two games the Braves won.

Lou Brissie, a white pitcher from South Carolina who came home from the war with a reconstructed leg, and who was a teammate of Doby's, recalled that there was no ballplayer he "admired more as an athlete and a man" than Doby.

In 1948, in his first spring training, Doby was shut out of the hotel of his white teammates in Tucson, Arizona. Like so many of the other black players in the minors and majors, he had to find a place to stay with a black family. In Texarkana, Arkansas, he was escorted in full uniform to the back of the ballpark because he couldn't go in the front entrance.

In Houston in 1948 he couldn't get a cab driver to take him to the ballpark. When he went to the plate for the first time he was roundly booed. He then hit what Veeck recalled as the longest home run Houston had ever seen. He hit another homer, two doubles, and a triple and made two remarkable catches at his new position. That was the day Doby made the team.

It was not the day the pain went away. Veeck described Doby as too sensitive to shake off the slights. He knew that many of the pitches that knocked him down were based on the pitchers' notion that if they knocked down a black player, he didn't want to dig in anymore. Veeck recalled that when Luke Easter got up and hit a home run, he'd laugh; when Doby would get up and hit a home run, he didn't laugh.

There were emotional blows from so many directions. In Columbus, Georgia, Dr. Thomas Brewer, a black dentist, opened his home to the traveling ballplayer. "Without those people you could have never made it through those towns," Doby said.

In the heat of the civil rights demonstrations in 1956, Dr. Brewer was shot and killed by a white merchant when he refused to leave a segregated lunch counter. He was shot seven times and the merchant was acquitted on grounds of self-defense.

"It's hard to believe you can get shot for sitting at a counter and all you're doing is representing what is right," Doby said. "Today more than ever we have to stick together as people. We have to get it right."

In 1998, the year after the Robinson commemoration, Doby was selected for the Baseball Hall of Fame and named honorary captain of the American League All-Star team. He wore the Hall of Fame ring the rest of his life. At least some of the slight was washed away. "Now that it's happened, I feel great," he said. "I didn't think I'd feel this good. I know my numbers are not as good as some, and better than some. For us to do what we did in the circumstance we played in, and not have hate, I think we accomplished something."

And he was almost the first black manager. He went back to Cleveland as a coach, hoping to learn enough about the players and teams in the American League after several seasons with Montreal so he could be next in line with the Indians. However, the Indians chose Frank Robinson; again Doby was second to a Robinson.

In 1978, Veeck, that wonderful maverick, bought the White Sox, and when Bob Lemon left, Doby became manager for half a season. Veeck gave the man his chance. Again. That was the kind of man Veeck was. Doby's experience would not have emerged if not for Veeck.

In 1942, when World War II had skimmed the cream off the big leagues, Veeck tried to buy the bankrupt Philadelphia Phillies. He intended to bolster the seventh–place roster with players of color, wherever he could find them. He thought he could steal the pennant. After he told Commissioner Kennesaw M. Landis of his plan, Veeck found a surprise buyer for the Phillies had emerged.

Realistically, Veeck couldn't have been the man to break the color barrier. For one thing, he was in Cleveland, not Brooklyn, and he wasn't nearly as powerful as Branch Rickey was in Brooklyn, nor was his public image so profoundly and righteously Christian. Veeck did have his own sense of what was right. "He never wanted to make a lot of money, which is very unusual," Doby said.

The two had a special relationship. "He had a deep feeling, a deep feeling," Doby said, stammering. "Not based on, on color or nationality, based on human being."

Veeck had owned the minor–league Milwaukee Brewers, who trained in Ocala, Florida. One time he emerged from the clubhouse in left field and sat down nearby among the worst seats in the house, which of course were in the Jim Crow section. When the sheriff and the mayor threatened to throw Veeck out, Veeck threatened to move his team out of Ocala. Other owners preferred not to contest local segregation laws.

When Veeck took the Indians to train in Tucson, the stands weren't segregated, but the team's hotel was. Veeck got a promise that Doby would be accepted for 1949. Veeck lamented that Doby would have to swallow the indignity until the next year. Everywhere the team moved through the exhibition schedule in the South, Veeck had alternative sites to get around Texas laws against mixed races on the field.

As Rickey did with Jackie Robinson, Veeck set out guidelines for Doby to get through those early years: Don't fight back. Don't argue with umpires. Close your ears to the fans. "They kept emphasizing," Doby recalled, "if you did anything out of character, you're out and the next person ain't going to get the opportunity."

It was a great responsibility to carry, to represent a whole race under unfair scrutiny. Unfair or not, it was there.

Many years later when some recognition came, Doby welcomed it earnestly. "You've been a part of something that a lot of people would have loved to have been a part of," he said. He ticked off the names of Satchel Paige, Josh Gibson, Cool Papa Bell, and Double Duty Radcliff. If the game had opened up for them in the 1930s, "you'd have seen some great players."

The time came for Larry Doby in 1947. Maybe America wasn't ready for it, but then maybe America never would have been ready without a push. To the end Doby wondered how he got through it.

Years later Veeck wondered in print what Doby might have become if he had come to baseball when black players were more common and hostility was less common, if he had come along when he had a black confidant on the team instead of spending so much of his early time alone. Veeck wondered what Doby might have become if he didn't feel he had to bear the burden of being a trailblazer.

"If Larry had come up just a little later, when things were just a little better," Veeck wrote, "he might very well have become one of the greatest players of all time."

4

A Closed World Opens Up

Ed Charles Finds There Is a Chance

(Born Daytona Beach, Florida, April 29, 1933-)

JACKIE IS COMING. Jackie is coming! Jackie Robinson is coming to my town! The Brooklyn Dodgers are playing an exhibition game in St. Petersburg and Jackie is coming to town. We can see Jackie Robinson!

Ed Charles was 13 years old in St. Petersburg, Florida, in the spring of 1947 and thought of himself as a baseball player. But until then there were no black players in the major leagues. They were not allowed, so he was not allowed. Life told Charles every moment of the day he was an inferior being. Life told him black people weren't good enough to play baseball with white players. His parents had taught him those were the facts of life all the years of their lives.

The afternoon the Dodgers were coming to town Ed Charles was going to cut school and try to get a glimpse of Jackie Robinson—always both names said in awe—through the fence at Al Lang Field, where major-league teams played springtime exhibition games. He bubbled with excitement. As they peered through openings in the fence, Ed and his friends found out the Dodgers were going to leave town on the train. After the game they dashed to the depot and there was the train, but the players had already boarded.

"So now we're walking down the platform, looking in the windows trying to see where Jackie was seated," Charles recalled, the feeling strong in his mind despite the gap of decades separating that memory

and now. "Finally we come to the right coach and there is Jackie, playing cards. We waved and, you know, he waved back to us.

"Then the train starts pulling out and we start slowly walking
with it, just waving to Jackie. The train picked up speed and we picked
up speed. We kept running and waving till the train got out of sight.
Things liked that, you know, I can recall so vividly because they were
very special moments in my life and in the life of the country. It was
like the Messiah had come."

In October of 1945, Branch Rickey, the boss of the Dodgers,
announced signing Robinson to a minor-league contract as the first
black to play in what was known as Organized Baseball. They sent
him to 1946 spring training with their highest minor-league team, the
Montreal Royals, in Daytona Beach, Florida.

Ed Charles lived in Daytona Beach then. There his parents taught
him about being black in America. They taught him what to expect and
how to behave so as not to be punished for being black. And he heard
all those words from white people saying he and all the other black
people were inferior.

"You want to have the same opportunities to everything in society
like everyone else," Charles said. "But it was denied to you. So it was
like being on pins and needles all the time. You're afraid that you're
going to cross the line."

At home, being caught crossing the line meant he'd be severely reprimanded, or maybe it meant there'd be a strap across his backside. Just
how strong that line was is almost impossible to comprehend across
the generations—unless you lived it. Charles's parents were punishing
him in order to protect him. The severity of punishment for breaking
the rules was at the whim of someone who saw him as less than a full
human being.

"Well, you ran the risk of being put in jail or beaten up if you took
the liberty to drink out of a water fountain that was designated whites
only," Charles said. "Anything that was designated for whites only, you
did not cross that line. You stayed within 'black only.'"

He was speaking 30 years after the end of his big-league time.
What began for him as a 29-year-old rookie, he managed to extend to

an eight–season career of some accomplishment. He was speaking also after retiring from 13 years in the juvenile justice system of the City of New York as liaison with the board of education. He worked with kids in detention, kids who never in their lives had anyone tell them they were worth "more than diddley squat."

When those detained kids learned that Charles had played with the Miracle Mets of 1969, the team that rose from years of ridicule to win the World Series, they asked what he was doing there. He answered, "I'm here because you're here."

Those kids had no idea who Jackie Robinson was, much less Michael Schwerner, James Chaney, and Andrew Goodman, the three young civil rights workers who were murdered in Mississippi in 1964 because they were working to gain voting rights for black people. The kids Charles was trying to help had been drawn to the culture of the street.

Avoiding the street and its pitfalls was drummed into Charles's mind every day at home. If he absorbed the lesson, maybe it would save him from the terrible fate of Emmett Till, a Chicago boy of 14 who didn't know the rules when he went to spend a summer with his grandparents in Mississippi in 1954. A white woman claimed that he dared to whistle at her, and his brutal lynching is legend.

Ed was 9 or 10 when he and his three brothers were visiting their grandfather's farm in rural central Florida, in a tiny community of one store and maybe a dozen families. The train ran through town. The Charles brothers and their friends used to play with some discarded wagon rims and put them away each time they were finished. One Sunday they hurried to get home from church before Granddaddy got home. Granddaddy was a Baptist minister and he believed Sunday was the Lord's day and not for child's play.

"We got to the house—and no rims," Charles said. "Who got the rims? We heard noise from white kids playing across the tracks. They were having a ball with our rims. We go over to retrieve our rims and a brawl breaks out. When we got back to the house, those kids' father came over to talk with Granddaddy. We knew we were in trouble.

"So after the man had left, Granddaddy got his little razor strap, called us out one by one and as he was lashing our behind parts with that strap he kept saying, 'Don't you know, Mr. So–and–so could have lynched all of us.'"

As trivial as their childhood dispute was, Ed and his brothers could have been hanged from a tree. It had happened before. Every day it was beaten into their lives that they were accountable to the whites they saw every day. It was a matter of course for them to accept that they were inferior. Society was telling them that. Courts in their part of the world had confirmed as much for a century.

"From the day I was born, the word was there," Charles said. "All the signs saying, 'blacks here, whites there.' It's working on your psyche— the laws denying you opportunities and access to public accommodations and everything else. They're saying you're not good enough. We grew up under this banner.

"But in my school, this all–black school we had some strong, focused teachers. And they kept drumming it into my head that you got to study; you got to be twice as good as whites. That's all I heard: You don't have time to fool around. You got to prove to the world. They didn't let us forget that the weight is on me: I got to prove myself. After that the doors would open, but I got to be able to prove myself. I could not say honestly at that time that I thought, 'Oh—now I'm good enough.'"

Charles dreamed of baseball for himself, but those who dreamed as he did dared to dream only to themselves. "You knew you couldn't dream of being elevated to the major leagues," Charles said. "You knew where there were barriers. So we'd play our little stickball games and listen to Dodgers baseball games on radio. They had this nickname Bums and, you know, that's sort of like how I was feeling about blacks in this country. We were both low on the totem pole."

Word that a black player had signed with the Dodgers organization came from elders by way of the grapevine, then from the black publications like the *Pittsburgh Courier*. "It was a big deal," Charles said. "We wanted to have opportunities, to aspire to greatness just like anyone else. If Jackie were successful, it was going to open doors. We were portrayed as unproductive, that we couldn't do this or that. Jackie could soften that. Everyone in our community knew the significance, where it might lead. This was monumental in the South. He became my hero, my idol."

Jackie Robinson was sent for his first spring training to Daytona with the Dodgers' Montreal farm team, which presented a problem. "I was very excited and apprehensive, too," Charles said, "because that was against the law. Blacks were not allowed to play games or have any action or intercourse with whites. Period. Will they set upon him? Will they lock him up in jail? Will they try to prevent him from playing with the whites? I recall saying a lot of prayers."

The Montreal team trained at the big recreation center across the street from the Charles house, and Ed, not yet 13, would go to the field to watch practice. White people would watch, too. Florida law forbade blacks from playing in the stadiums in Florida, so what was to be seen was the Montreal Royals training among themselves. "I'm praying that Jackie Robinson never makes an error, that every time he comes to bat he gets a base hit," Charles said. "You just want him to succeed, to show the white community that, given the opportunity, blacks could fit in and could excel.

"I never had the nerve to go up to him with the other kids and get his autograph. I'd be standing back so where I was just looking at him as if he was God, you know."

⁘

Charles's parents separated and he went with his mother to St. Petersburg when he was 14. He had little interest in school and saw no future in continuing so he dropped out and took a job as a dishwasher. Before long he moved up to become assistant baker. At night he would bring home freshly baked pies to the delight of the neighbors. He played softball with a team called the Harlem Hawks. They nicknamed him Gum because his father was called Gum.

He also had several encounters with the police, which never was a good idea for a black youth in any part of the country. Charles was moving around, a teenager essentially without roots. At 16 he was washing dishes in Miami, living with his elder brother in a rooming house with one bathroom on each of two floors. Both bathrooms were occupied when Ed came home from work. "I was about to burst," he recalled. "So I went on the second–floor porch and relieved myself over the railing. Unfortunately, the landlord was on the downstairs porch." He said he was going to tell Charles's brother they all had to leave.

Charles couldn't face his brother and had nowhere else to go. He slept in a car one night until police aggressively rousted him. He slept outdoors in a rail yard until a drenching rain forced him into a building under construction, where police found him. He spent four nights in the lockup and the judge warned him that the life he was living was leading him into deeper trouble.

He decided going back to school wasn't a bad idea after all. He moved back with his mother in St. Petersburg and told the registrar at Cardinal Gibbs High School that his records were lost when his Daytona Beach school burned the year before, and, instead of the 9th grade, he was admitted to the 10th grade. He was eligible for varsity sports and became a football and baseball star. Scouts came to watch. In the summer of 1952 the Negro Leagues were still operating, and the Indianapolis Clowns offered him a chance to sign with them.

He was barely 19 and his mother didn't want to let him go away so he expected to play in a Florida black league. But the owner of the local team was able to arrange a tryout for Charles with the Boston Braves system. Among the dozens of hopefuls at Myrtle Beach, South Carolina, Charles felt the eyes on him among the few black faces. He felt, if he wasn't signed, he couldn't go home to face his friends in St. Petersburg. If he didn't make it, he intended to live with an aunt in Harlem.

He was hitting poorly in the tryout camp. Hopeful pitchers throwing 90 miles an hour with no idea where the ball was going can do that to a hitter. The night before the Quebec City Braves broke camp to go north, manager George McQuinn summoned him. Charles thought he was going to be told to go home. The farm director said if it were up to him, Charles would be dropped, but there was something McQuinn liked so he was taking Charles to Quebec.

Young Gum Charles was going to Quebec in the Class C Provincial League. Quebec was as far from home as he could imagine. He didn't have any idea about the geography or the life in Quebec. He knew it was north.

"Quebec. Quebec. Quebec was an education," Charles recounted with affection. "It was the first time I was ever leaving the South and you have these opinions that form as a kid: all whites are bad; they're against black folks. I had never lived in a different atmosphere but one that was suppressing me all the time and telling me I was no good."

It was also cold for someone who'd never been out of Florida. And what about the rules that had been imposed all his life?

The Quebec Braves left springtime Florida and by the time the bus got to Delaware for the night it was chilly. He had Florida clothes. In Albany, New York, it was cold. By Montreal snow was in mounds beside the road. At Quebec City, "Oh, Christ," Charles said, "the wind was like a razor blade." He shivered at the recollection.

It had been arranged for him and two black teammates to live in an English–speaking neighborhood with a white family who happened to be schoolteachers. "And I'm like, 'I don't believe this,'" he said. "I'm shocked to be living with white folks."

Before there was time to learn about them, there was baseball practice on the first morning. Charles's baseball housemates were from Philadelphia and New Jersey and dressed for the weather. Charles had no such clothes. The cold overwhelmed him as much as the unfamiliar social climate. No matter how he was urged that he was missing his great chance, Charles refused to leave the warmth of his room. The owner of the team came to the house and Charles said he might as well be sent home. So the owner bought a coat and sweater for him. Another teammate said he'd teach Charles how to dress. After all, when did a kid from Florida ever see somebody wear thermal underwear beneath a baseball uniform?

"So now I'm up in Quebec City and it's an open society. And I'm very uneasy at living in white folks' home," he said. "They were lovely people but in the back of my mind I always felt like they were like the other whites I knew from the South and that eventually they were going to say something, that magic word, that put–down word. So I was always on guard and cringing. And it never did happen.

"They were such beautiful people and I said to myself, I can't condemn a whole race of people for what happened down in the Jim Crow South. Everyone is not like that. I'm seeing things. I'm being accepted. I can go places; have access to public accommodations, no problems. This is the awakening for me."

The three black teammates, Ed Charles, Bob Smith, and Stan Glenn, would walk down the hill to the ballpark and little kids who'd never seen black people before would follow out of curiosity. One day Smith impatiently turned and shouted, "Boo." The kids scattered and ran. "I said, 'Smitty, you probably confirmed what the kids already thought, that we were animals or something, that we had tails and stuff.'"

Charles was always asking himself, what would Jackie do? "Most of the guys were conscious of that," he said. "We had to present this kind of image. Like Jackie did. A lot of times, if you didn't, management would call you a troublemaker. The next thing you knew, you were out of there."

⁘⁘⁘

The hospitality of Quebec was not representative of baseball, not of the minor leagues, and certainly not of baseball in the American South. Often when Charles couldn't speak up, at risk of being labeled a troublemaking black by management, accepting teammates would speak in his defense. Southern community customs and laws were not on his side.

Once when the team bus stopped on the road in rural Georgia, Charles and a black teammate were refused entrance to the restaurant. Teammates brought food to them. Nobody could go to the restroom for him. "I was fed up and I said I'm going right in to that 'Whites Only,' and I did. I'm relieving myself and this attendant comes in and says, 'Say, boy, can you read? Did you see that sign out there saying 'White Only?'" While the attendant was laying down the Jim Crow to Charles's small act of defiance, a teammate entered and, Charles said, "got in the guy's chest." A couple of other white players came to Charles's aid and the attendant backed down.

A white player who was friendly toward black players at that time often ran the risk of being known as a "nigger lover." It didn't help his career. But any kind of sympathy or support helped Charles endure.

In contrast with Charles's experience playing in the South, Jackie Robinson was playing in mostly northern cities where the people had been somewhat exposed to blacks within the restrictions of the law. Robinson had to survive considerable hostility. The simple fact of being first was excruciating in itself. But he didn't have to deal with the extreme bigotry that the first wave of black players in the minors faced every day. Ed Charles played nine seasons in the major leagues, but it took eight seasons in the minors for him to get there. "Jackie integrated the major leagues," Charles said. "We integrated baseball."

They used to call playing in the minor leagues being part of the "chain gang." It had some validity. A hotel for blacks in Macon, Georgia, was so hot Charles is forced to laugh at the recollection. White players had an air–conditioned hotel; in the black neighborhood, it was too hot to sleep. Charles and his few black teammates would sit all night on the steps in front of the hotel so they could catch any wisp of a cooling breeze.

If any man in that league was the only black on the team, he was denied any camaraderie and support of teammates. "I know it was expected of us that regardless of conditions we had to perform at a level comparable or better than the best white player," Charles said.

When black players were hurt, the manager or the owner frequently regarded them as "lazy niggers." Charles's teammate at Wichita, the dark–skinned left–hander Juan Pizarro from Puerto Rico, limped through a workout and the coach accused him of not wanting to do the work, said he should go back to Africa. Charles, who had by 1957 established himself with some people in the organization, phoned the farm director in Milwaukee, where the Boston Braves had moved, lamenting how Pizarro was being treated and Pizarro was promptly moved to another minor–league team. Pizarro got special consideration from the Braves because he was one of the best pitching prospects in the organization.

By 1957, after six years in the minor leagues, Charles had been browbeaten and worn down by racism from management, fans, and some teammates. The Braves weren't doing anything with him, even though he was the all–star second baseman in the South Atlantic League. White players were moving up and the unwritten quota system said there were going to be only so many blacks on the big–league team. Black Ed Charles was stuck in the South. He phoned his grandfather in Daytona Beach, and said he wanted to go home and got the wisdom of a minister in reply.

"Granddaddy told me, 'Son, what I want you to do is get a good night's sleep. If you feel the same way in the morning, give me a call and then come on home.' I didn't sleep well that night. All I could think was, 'Jackie wasn't a quitter.' I couldn't deal with the guys on my block who were going to tell me, 'I told you you weren't good enough.' In the morning I had myself in control. It was my low point." He decided to stick it out, at least for a while.

Yes, black players were often started at lower levels than whites. Yes, progress was slower. Yes, there were just so many black guys on the team. "There was nothing you could do about it except try to be one of those guys," he said.

He was an all–star. He recalls a game in Knoxville, Tennessee, in which he could do no wrong. "I was a shortstop and that day everything was hit to me. I was picking it up and making the plays and stealing bases and hitting home runs. It was like every time I came to bat I got a base hit. I mean it was just a perfect day for me.

"But throughout this game there was this southern white gentleman—I don't know why I call him a gentleman—right over our dugout, calling me everything but the child of God. Some of the things he called me, I had to put my glove up to my face because it was kind of funny to me. I'm like saying, 'How in heck did this guy think of something like this to call me?' Well you never want the guy to know you're laughing at him.

"He would dis me any kind of way he could think of. So now after the game we had to pass through a little gate to enter our clubhouse. And as I was walking off the field, there is this southern gentleman standing right there. So as I got closer I'm saying to myself, 'Why is this guy standing there? If he says something else should I hit him? No, I got to be under control. I might bring my career to an end right there, okay. So now as I come upon him he extends his hand.

"I'm shocked. He said, 'Nigger let me shake your hand. You're one hell of a ballplayer.' I couldn't believe he said it and I just walked on by him.

"Sure you could be angry but you controlled anger because all your life, especially if you were born down there, you lived through that, and you come to accept that.

"And when I thought about it, I said, 'Now he caught himself paying me a compliment on my play.' He had been reared to look upon blacks as being inferior. He had brought himself probably for the first time ever to pay a compliment to a black. So I, I felt sort of good about it in a way."

Charles feels his progress was stagnated by being changed from second base to third base behind big–league star Eddie Matthews, and then switched back to second base again. The Braves sent him back to Triple A Wichita in 1958 and Charles prodded himself to play well. He and teammates were watching the Braves on television when second baseman Mel Roach, in whom the Braves had considerable investment, was carried off the field. Harry Carey, the broadcaster, said the Braves had a minor–league second baseman, Ed Charles, going great guns. "My heart jumps," Charles recalled. The other black players tell him to pack his bags. He went to the ballpark and was informed the Braves were calling up light–hitting shortstop Joe Koppe. And so it went for another three seasons.

When his break came with a trade to Kansas City, there was one more lesson, taught by owner Charlie Finley. Ed Charles finished second to Yankee Tom Tresh for 1962 Rookie of the Year. Charles started so well at the minimum salary of $7,000 that at midseason Finley gave him a $5,000 raise. Nice stuff: $12,000.

That winter he was sent a contract for $10,000. But, there must be a mistake, he told Finley, for his salary to be cut after such a good year. Finley told him, "Ed, you're looking at it the wrong way." He told Charles his base was $7,000 and the $5,000 was a bonus, so now he really had a $3,000 raise. In the words of the time: take it or leave it. And so it went. That wasn't racism, it was baseball's own plantation system in practice and it applied to blacks and whites; the players were not allowed professional negotiators. If more black players were disadvantaged in their negotiations because they weren't educated and didn't have outside professionals to consult with, then that was one more fact of life to absorb.

The system of free agency that liberates a player to learn his worth in the marketplace was a decade away. At that time the owner determined how much he would pay a player and the player might refuse to sign for a few weeks and get a slight increase, but he was effectively a slave in the system.

If good things really do come to he who waits, there was reward for Charles when he was traded to the Mets. Their growth needed Charles's experience and the easy style that got him nicknamed the Glider. He was integrated easily into the clubhouse chemistry. He gave the Mets two useful seasons at third base while they matured. He managed to make the team in 1969 and played a valuable part as the Mets turned baseball upside down by winning the National League pennant and the World Series.

The Mets and their ace pitcher Tom Seaver lost to the heavily favored Baltimore Orioles in the first game of the World Series. It looked as if the Mets might be swept by one of the best teams of the decade.

In the second game in the top of the ninth inning, score, 1–1, against the Orioles' very tough lefty Dave McNally, Charles singled and was driven home with the winning run. The Mets got the idea they could win. It was the biggest single moment of Charles's career. The next season he was gone—released—but the picture of Ed Charles's black face shining in the clutch of players when the 1969 championship was won stands for a whole era of American history. It stands next to the portrait of the first man on the moon. The integration of baseball had an impact on the thinking of people all across America. "I know it brought a lot of pride to blacks," Charles said. "I know blacks began to say, 'Yes, we got people that compete with the mainstream society.' They felt good about the experiment. They felt hope. That's very important.

"Hope, hope, hope, hope is what Jackie brought to all of us, black and white, whatever. Jackie helped bring us closer together. There was Jackie; he brought hope. He had all of us hoping for the better day.

"I looked upon him as being some sort of Messiah because of what he was trying to accomplish. Prior to his time, where was the hope?"

Ed Charles waved his fist over his head in exclaiming his emancipation. "There was Jackie," he said. "He brought hope."

❖❖❖

5

Worse than You Imagine

Mudcat Grant Dodged the Bullets

(Born Lacoochee, Florida, August 13, 1935–)

WHEN MUDCAT GRANT was a little boy—when his parents called him Timothy—his father built a trapdoor with a wooden box beneath the floor next to the fireplace. It was in the little town of Lacoochee in the piney woods of redneck Florida.

When marauding whites out for a good time would come through the community shooting into the houses just for fun, his parents would shove Timothy through the trapdoor into the box. "You'd push yourself up close to the chimney so you couldn't get hit," Mudcat Grant, the first black pitcher to win 20 games in the American League, recalled.

"You don't even know half the experiences I could tell that were so common. When you're born into this kind of hell, you know. But it sounded like it was an uncommon thing when you told it to people who had never heard of anything like that."

When Timothy Grant was about nine years old there was a teenage boy he used to play with in the woods. This boy worked at the lumber mill and in order to earn a few dollars, he carried groceries from the store for white people. "In those days you didn't go in the front door," Grant said. "Some white men saw him—or they said they saw him—going to the front door of this lady's house.

"They tied him to the railroad tracks because of what he didn't do. Killed him, obviously. He had gone in the front door too many times. It was to teach all of us a lesson.

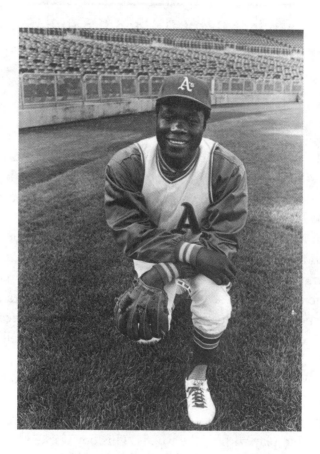

"When you see tragedy, when you know of somebody that was castrated, when you're knowing somebody that was hung from a tree, you know these are white people that did this."

Mudcat Grant, now a blues singer of some international renown, tells his children and grandchildren about what he and a whole race of people had endured. "So they might understand what went on before them," he said. "These are some of the people who died in order for you to have the freedom you have today.

"And they say, 'It couldn't have been that bad, Grampa. Why did you stand for something like that?'"

Black people, so many of them, stood for it because it was so dangerous to fight back. "They had an old saying: 'Now don't be no fool,'" Grant said. "That meant you had to be aware of all the dangers that exist. When I went away and came home, your mind had to change right away because you had to be very careful."

Lynchings of black people were treated as carnival events. And little, almost trivial slights for a man who grew up under that yoke instantly trigger whole complexes of recollections and lessons learned.

There was the night in the Cleveland bullpen that stands out in Grant's history as much as the fact that he won 21 games in 1965 and was the first black pitcher in the American League to win a World Series game.

"You always have to resist your impulses," he said, "because as a human being we all have the same kind of impulses. You were taught that when you were three years old, four, five, six. After getting to the point of playing baseball, after making sure you weren't killed for saying something, being in the wrong place, baseball wasn't nothing."

He laughed. He had learned which were the real insults and which were merely words that people used out of habit or simply naive curiosity. Fargo, North Dakota, was his first exposure to water fountains that weren't identified for black or white. There was one black couple in Fargo in 1954 and most of the kids had never seen a colored person. Grant was sending much of his paycheck home to Lacoochee so sometimes he would babysit for white families to put a few extra bucks in his minor–league pocket. Little white Sarah was sitting on his lap, rubbed his face and asked why his skin was that color. He explained that when he was her age he drank a lot of chocolate milk and she said she wasn't going to drink any more chocolate milk.

Grant's mother, daughter of a slave, a wise woman with a fourth–grade education, told him that not everyone in Fargo would be Baptist. She told him to visit every church and tell her about it when he got home. So he'd go to services and accept Bibles and medals as gifts and put them in a box to take home. "I was the laughingstock of Fargo, North Dakota," he said, "because one minister would phone another and ask, 'Did that ballplayer come by your place yet?'"

Well before his current age of 70 Grant learned to laugh at those moments and at himself. He also learned how to reflect on coming home after winning 21 games in Fargo to be celebrated in Lacoochee. The one black businessman in town introduced young Grant around. He introduced him to man who owned the filling station, which made him a man in town. The man was delighted, but he could not bring himself to shake Grant's hand. Grant accepted a hug around the neck. "Maybe next time he'll shake my hand," he reflected.

Years later Grant was in the bullpen of the Cleveland Indians. The Yankees were in town and there was a big crowd in the ballpark. Grant was keeping company with a multiethnic, all–white rat pack of pitchers: Barry Latman, Jewish; Gary Bell, a flake; Frank Funk and Bob Allen, both white and essentially conservative. The Birmingham church had been bombed, four children had been killed, and the rat pack was urging Grant to make some kind of a statement. Grant balanced in his mind the need to do something against all those warnings not to let anger get in the way of his dream.

They played the national anthem in Municipal Stadium and when they got down to "the land of the free and the home of the brave," Grant completed the phrase. "I said, 'And this land is not so free, 'cause I can't even go to Mississipp–ee." Or words to that effect he recalled 40 years later.

The rat pack applauded. Ted Wilks, the bullpen coach and an adopted son of Texas, responded. "He was fiery red," Grant recalled.

"And he said, 'If you don't like our country, why in hell don't you get out.' And I said, 'Well, if I wanted to leave the country, all I had to do was go to Texas. That's worse than Russia.'"

Of course, them was fightin' words for a Texan. Wilks advised Grant, as he recalls, that if Grant were caught in Texas they'd find him in the nearest tree. Players grabbed other players, the teams ran onto the field, people jumped out of the stands. Wilks landed a punch and Grant, out of the tangle of arms, managed to bite Wilks's ear in a prequel to Mike Tyson.

Ultimately, Grant was suspended for the last two weeks of the season. To make up the lost revenue he signed on for an all–black barnstorming tour that played a game in Yazoo, Mississippi. Grant suspected that he might be a target in the wake of the bullpen incident. A white man and his son visited the pregame dugout. Grant identified himself and the man said, "You had some trouble up there, didn't you?"

"Yes, I did."

"Well, you're gonna find out we're not as tough on niggers down here as you think we are. Can I get your autograph for my son?"

So Mudcat Grant, a nigger in the man's lexicon, signed the autograph. "Sometimes the mentality of whites is way beyond where you think they actually are," he reflected. "Sometimes it's just words they learned in the custom of 30 years before."

❖

Silence, he learned, can speak louder than words. When he was moving up the minor–league ladder, after Tipton, Georgia, he thought Reading, Pennsylvania, was going to be better. There would be other blacks in town.

He and Bell after a game in Reading early in the season went to a lounge frequented by white ballplayers and they were refused service. They left the place and Grant told Bell, a white player, to go where he wanted, but Grant was going to go back and sit all night. He went into that lounge after every home game and sat until closing and never once was served.

"If I am willing to sit there all night long and not get served," Grant said, "they have to think just a little bit when they go home at night, 'Well, maybe this is not right.' The idea is to get them to think that blacks are human beings."

Not that Mudcat Grant would put himself in Rosa Parks's category, but wasn't that what she had tried to do? It was Grant's form of non-violent protest.

His concept of protest had been evolving from Lacoochee through spring trainings in Daytona Beach at the former military base the Cleveland Indians rented. Players mixed in the lobby but the white players slept on one side and the colored players on the other. On the bus to town players sat where they wanted until the bus got onto the highway, then the driver would stop and black players had to get to the back. "Riding four blocks in the front of the bus in Florida was sort of a triumph," Grant said.

Sympathetic white players, especially Gary Bell—a "special guy" to Grant—would ask how Grant could put up with the restrictions and how he could compete and play baseball under the conditions. Grant's only response was that he had to bear it, find a laugh when he could instead of getting angry, and deafen himself to the names he was called as much as he could.

The only time in the major leagues he recalled hearing what the crowd was saying or doing was when he and Larry Doby were Cleveland teammates playing at Baltimore in 1958. They were the two blacks on the field for the Indians that day, Grant pitching and Doby in center-field. Grant was shutting out the Orioles and when the teams changed sides he'd pause on the way to the dugout for Doby to catch up so they could walk in together.

On the way in one inning they saw a man waving a long pole with raccoon tails attached—coon tails, as they were called. He was shaking it at Grant. Of course Doby saw it, and all the other Indians, too. Nobody on the bench said anything. Doby and Grant went into the clubhouse for a moment and Doby asked, "Did you see that coon tail?"

Grant said, "That's the biggest coon tail I ever saw."

The guy kept waving and Grant kept winning. "You don't hear things and you don't see things that keep you from winning," he said.

So Grant laughed. He saw humor. Doby, raised in New Jersey and with sensitivity that pushed him to touchiness, could not. "Larry got angry," Grant said. "But I said, 'Larry, hey, man.'"

Then both laughed.

Grant would wait patiently when it took too long to be served in a restaurant. He'd go in the back door at home when he had to, ignore the looks that might be thrown at him and the white bellmen who refused to get his bag. And turn away when militant blacks called him an Uncle Tom.

"They said that was giving in to the master," Grant said. "They never thought how intelligent some Uncle Toms were. They were the ones feeding the whole community, bringing food back from the master's house, playing that 'yassuh' stuff." He never forgot his mother's admonition never to let anger keep him from his dream.

"You can be emotional, but don't show a kind of weakness," he said. "If you ever believe that there is strength in being able to take the blow, you've got to play."

He found reinforcement from some white teammates and took them to his places, warning them that they might be ostracized as nigger lovers. They went with him anyway. Bell had grown up in Texas and he didn't know how dangerous it had been to be black. Grant took Bell, Sam McDowell, and Woody Held to the Apollo Theater in Harlem to see James Brown and Gladys Knight and the Pips. The show had started and the lights were down when they went in together.

Mudcat laughed at the scene he was describing. "Now the show is over and it's all of 'us' and three of 'them,'" he said. "So I get up and say, 'Hey, guys, I'll see you later.' They grabbed me: 'Oh no.' And we went out of the theater hand in hand. After that they didn't mind going among black people."

Grant took Bell to the Howard Theater in Washington and to Bill Russell's restaurant in Boston and Bell accepted it when teammates said he was crazy. "The only thing he wouldn't do is eat chitlins," Grant said with a conspiratorial laugh. (Author's note: Anyone who won't eat pig intestines when it isn't life or death is understandable. At the same time, it's to be recognized that pig intestines were the food of affliction in the American Negro tradition.)

❖

The process of opening minds worked both ways. Grant recalled that more than one white person came to him saying that for so long they had misunderstood so much about black people and had come to regret thinking and saying what they had. When Martin Luther King Jr. was killed, Grant said, "some whites said, 'Wait a minute, this is America; you can't do that. They were racists, and in just a second they weren't such racists anymore."

Like most black players, Grant held himself at the outer edge of Dr. King's civil rights movement out of fear that baseball would reject him. It was common at the time that black players who took part in anything political other than in support of the establishment were considered troublemakers. Players who served as representatives for the players association were frequently traded in order to fraction union strength and to warn other players. When Grant went to civil rights rallies he was careful not to be recognized. But he couldn't help being drawn to them; it was too important in his mind not to keep pushing for change.

People like Gary Bell taught him how difficult racism was to unlearn. White players were reluctant to protest the treatment of black teammates because they were afraid to be identified by the racists as not like them. "They bury those terrible thoughts in the back of their mind and its difficult when they go back home after the season to the atmosphere where they were raised," Grant said. "And some of them go home and say: 'Mom and dad, I know what you said, but I've been around these teammates and they ain't what you said."

❖

At the time Mudcat won 21 games pitching the Minnesota Twins to the 1965 World Series against the Los Angeles Dodgers and two more to get them to the seventh game, players—white or black—were not permitted to have agents negotiate for them. So Grant had to negotiate by himself with owner Calvin Griffith, still identified as Mr. Griffith. It went like this:

"How much money you guys get from the World Series?"

"Forty–five hundred dollars."

"How many games did you win?"

"Twenty–one."

"Yeah, you won two games in the World Series. I'll tell you what I'm gonna do. I'm gonna give you a $2,000 raise, and you take that $2,000 and you put it with the $4,500 and you've got a lot of money."

Grant recalls telling Mr. Griffith, "'You take that offer and you cut it up into little bitty pieces and you shove . . .' And Mr. Griffith started laughing and called the police and said 'Get him out of my office.'"

Grant said he didn't see that as racism. It was baseball before free agency and players' rights. "Mr. Griffith cheated all of us," Grant said. "You didn't have to be black."

What was racism was in the bigger counting house of American business. *Sport* magazine put Grant on the cover as its pitcher of the year, but Sandy Koufax, who also won two and lost one in the World Series but pitched a shutout in the seventh game, was chosen the World Series MVP. Koufax also won the Cy Young Award, which then was a single award for the outstanding pitcher in both leagues and was voted before the World Series. The next year separate Cy Young Awards were given for each league. But the greater rub was that Koufax got the endorsements and Grant got none.

"Don't we use toothpaste, too?" Grant's asked. There was little black entrepreneurship and marketing of black people then. "However, when you make statements, maybe somewhere along the line, things will change," he said. "And of course, they did."

It was his best professional season. In 1970 he pitched in 80 games in relief. He figures his 24 saves included 11 of Catfish Hunter's 18 wins. His relief helped get the Pirates to the 1971 World Series. He pitched 14 seasons.

⋯⋰⋱⋯

Instead of endorsements, what Grant did get was a lot of bookings for Mudcat and the Kittens. He worked The Embers in New York with bandleader Charlie Barnett and comedian Gene Baylos. He made more money singing, he said, than in baseball.

Still does. He's a blues singer, performing around the world.

His second wife is a white woman who grew up in Austria, where he is a popular entertainer. They were close when Grant was a young pitcher but he said, "A white wife was a no–no in baseball." He recalled playing in Hamburg, Germany, stopping at a store that displayed figurines of New Orleans jazzmen and a white boy of about seven hollered to his mother, *"Mutter, mutter, ein nigger."* The mother shushed the child. "I said it was okay," Grant said. "I put the boy's hand in mine and we went in the store. He probably had never seen a black person except on TV." No offense taken.

Of course acceptance is better now. "There are inequities still, but nothing like the slaughterhouse it was in those days," Grant said. "Today's generation has enjoyed more freedom than I ever enjoyed," he said. "I had patience but not the patience my mother would have. Kids want everything NOW. You got to keep pushing; the rolling stone can never roll back, but sometimes it's slow.

"Thank goodness for the community that taught us how humiliating it was to succeed in life if you were black. We understood the fear of what you call White Baseball. Our parents' generation was scared to death that when the owners finally got a black player they might get a player so independent he would do what he wanted to do.

"Jackie always taught me, no matter what you are, when you go on that field you better win. If you don't win, whatever you are, if you speak your mind, if you decide you're gonna date white girls, if you don't win, you're gone. If a player decided he wanted to be a little white, that was the game he played. We knew that Elston Howard was doing what he did to survive."

Above all, Elston Howard won. And he made a difference in his way. "Baseball taught us to work together. It put something in our minds of possibilities. Those possibilities grew stronger and stronger. We need to recognize that.

"It can never go back."

6

Looking Back with Regret

Ernie Banks Was Playing Baseball

(Born Dallas, Texas, January 31, 1931-)

It was always a great day for a ball game, even when Ernie Banks wasn't home at Wrigley Field, and he always said, "Let's play two." When it was raining and he said it was a beautiful day, he laughed a little laugh in recognition of himself.

And when the conversation went just a little deeper than what he called "the beautiful confines of Wrigley Field," his fertile mind found a way to hide behind the lyrics of a song lest he reveal what was really inside him. His smile was the Mona Lisa of the clubhouse. "Do you smile to tempt a lover, Mona Lisa? Or are you just a cold and lonely lovely work of art?"

He was 75 years old when we talked, a member of the Baseball Hall of Fame, an elder statesman and salesman of the game. He was the first black to own a Ford dealership. There have been black managers, although not enough, and black general managers have won the World Series with the Yankees and the White Sox. Black baseball players are no longer limited by quotas on ball clubs, nor do they have to endure the pain of isolation. Black athletes are on the playing field for universities in the once–segregated South.

He came to the Chicago Cubs in 1953 from the Kansas City Monarchs of the Negro American League as the only black on the team. Sam Hairston had played briefly with the White Sox in 1959 and Gene Baker was with the Cubs briefly beside Banks, but his departure left

Banks alone, the only black on the Cubs or White Sox in Chicago. He became Mr. Cub—still is.

⋯⟡⋯

Banks was one of 11 children growing up in Dallas during the Depression. He had picked cotton as a boy in Texas. "We didn't have much money," he said, which was likely an understatement. His father, Eddie Banks, had been a semipro pitcher in the area and used to give Ernie a nickel or a dime to play catch with him. Eddie Banks bought Ernie his first baseball glove for $2.98, which was a considerable sacrifice. His father was a porter; his mother worked as a housemaid. The grocery shopping was beans and rice. When he signed with the Cubs for $2,000 he phoned his father to exult, "We're rich."

The world had changed and Ernie Banks lamented that he had missed it. Black people had purposefully disobeyed the Jim Crow laws, had sat in at lunch counters, had refused to move to the back of the bus, had demonstrated as freedom riders, had endured the pressures of being the first blacks at white–only schools. He was playing baseball.

"That's a real void in my life," he said softly. Being earnest instead of just Ernie was a rare posture. "I see a lot of people today who struggled and went to jail and the dogs were after them, and I'd look at them and look 'em in the eyes and say, 'God almighty, I wish I'd'a been there.' My children, sometimes they think about, 'Daddy, where were you all the times that the struggle was going on?' And I could only answer one way: 'I was playing baseball.' That was the struggle."

He prefers to fit the occasion with a bit of a song. Or with bits of poetry. Or by borrowing lines from speeches with which he thinks his listener is familiar. Certainly Mr. Cub wouldn't want to be thought a plagiarist. And hiding his emotions behind a Dinah Washington lyric is hardly unfamiliar to him.

He played 19 seasons in the major leagues, beginning in Chicago when few big–league cities had ever had a black player, in a time when all black players had to endure a time of awful trial. He hit 512 home runs, and was twice named Most Valuable Player. Six years after the end of his career he was elected to the Hall of Fame. He's one of the few great ones who never got to the showcase of the World Series. They didn't have the rounds of the playoffs to display a man's talent in his day as they do today. Bittersweet is a more becoming description of him than bitter. It's better not to dwell on what he never had. Wistful is a better word.

It often seemed there was sadness underneath when he was so charming. "I never met a stranger and hope I never do," he said. Was it a put–on? "Most people think so," he said.

One of his contemporaries, a peer in the Hall of Fame, calls him "the most insincere man I ever met." The implication was that all of Banks's cheerful bantering and posturing was deliberate manipulation of the media. Of course, sometimes the face beneath the mask is the same as the mask. Putting on the same makeup for so long, a man could think the man in the glass really is him.

"Hello," he said when he answered my phone call. "My name is Ernie Banks. I'm an American. That's baseball, hot dogs, and apple pie." Then he went into a bit of "Chicago, that toddlin' town."

Then he moved on to "I Have a Dream," with due respect for Martin Luther King but also with enduring affection for long–suffering fans who took him as their own. Cubs fans haven't been to a World Series since 1945 and haven't won a World Series since 1908.

⁙

The 22–year–old Banks had just arrived in Chicago in September of 1953 after a season and a half with the Negro League Monarchs when Jackie Robinson came to town with the Brooklyn Dodgers. The Dodgers already had clinched the pennant, Robinson had the day off and he purposely went across the field to visit Banks in the Cubs' clubhouse. Banks went out to meet the man who had opened the world for him. Robinson said he was delighted to see Banks there. "And he just gave me some good advice," Banks recalled. "He said, 'If you listen you can learn.' And for four or five years in the majors, that's all I did."

Banks was a revelation, playing shortstop and hitting home runs like no shortstop before ever had. From 1955 to 1960 he hit more home runs than Mickey Mantle. No shortstop had hit so many home runs before. That he twice was voted Most Valuable Player was a remarkable honor for a player on bad teams.

He was one of the great ones who came from the Monarchs. The Yankees scouted him, but they wouldn't have a black player until Elston Howard in 1955. "My roommate in the Negro League," Banks said. "His life had a lot of championships; mine did not." In his first 14 seasons, the Cubs won more games than they lost only once. Then Banks lapsed again into a bit of lyric: "Don't look so sad; those times are over."

Sometimes laughing was a challenge. On bad teams, there was seldom an ally. "I thought my life was a constant stream of insults," he said. Three times he thought pitchers deliberately hit him: Bob Purkey, Jack Sanford, and Bob Friend. Each time, he hit a home run the next time up. It was a great day for a ball game, wasn't it?

He would never speak about how hard it was. Search the libraries and the clip files and there's scant evidence of how hard. He kept that to himself. Now he was revealing himself. There was the time bandleader Lionel Hampton and singer Pearl Bailey, black celebrities of the time, came to young Ernie Banks. Hey, young man, they said, you're playing for a whole lot of people, you gotta be the best. And we're gonna check on you to make sure you do not get into trouble.

"And," he said, "I would say in my mind, 'I don't want to do this.' I really wanted to quit. 'God! This is too much.'" The incessant scrutiny, he said, made him think, "I was a fugitive."

It's an awesome burden to feel you're carrying the hopes of a whole race, under constant scrutiny, thinking that every error, every strikeout, every failure in the clutch was taken as a reflection of inferiority in your whole race. Robinson felt it in Brooklyn and Larry Doby felt it in Cleveland. Now it was the weight on Banks in Chicago. His alternative to succeeding was going back to Dallas and working as a bellhop in the Gustavus Adolphus Hotel or the equivalent, which was no alternative at all. So Banks kept up his good nature and held his tongue along with the few other black players. "It also labeled us with the next wave of players who came into the majors and we were called 'Uncle Tom' because we didn't question anything," he said.

He remembered the time in his first spring when his Cubs stopped in Alabama for an exhibition game and, of course, he and Gene Baker, his only black teammate and a few years older, could not dress at the hotel with the white players. They stayed on the bus while the team went in to dress. They were near the Greyhound station so Banks told Baker he was going to buy some candy, "Want any?"

Baker, also a veteran of the Negro Leagues, "kind of smiled knowingly and said, 'Oh, yeah, bring me a piece.'"

So Banks went in the front door of the Alabama bus station and everything stopped. "I wasn't even thinking about segregation," Banks said. "I looked around and one guy came up to me and said I was supposed to be around back: 'You can't buy any stuff in here.'

"I went around the back, got the candy, came back, got on the bus and Gene was just laughing. He thought that was funny as the devil. I looked at him. I said, 'Man, why didn't you tell me I couldn't go in there?' He said, 'I wanted you to get the experience and to know what's going on.'

"I thought, well, I'm playing for the Cubs. I mean everybody knows the Cubs, you play for the Cubs and you can go anywhere, it gave me a free pass. But Gene already knew that wasn't the truth."

⁜

Banks listened to the speeches when Robinson was reaching beyond baseball. He followed Robinson when he was with Governor Nelson Rockefeller in New York, and went to Robinson's speeches in Chicago at Operation Push. "He wanted me to be there," Banks said, stammering a bit. "It was wonderful to be around him."

Jackie pushed for blacks to be included in baseball's high–level jobs, not only on the field. When Jackie died, Rachel Robinson asked Banks to attend the funeral. "Jackie wanted to see change and I feel that way today," Banks said. "He said we've got to stand for something—for our children, for the people who followed our career."

Robinson's urgency for progress, Banks said, "kind of drifted into my life. It drifted into Henry's."

Henry Aaron acquired some of Jackie's urgency, not in his early years but more when he was breaking Babe Ruth's home run record, and in the years since. First it was when Aaron was proving he could play the game; when he was playing in Milwaukee where there wasn't a lot of media attention. Then he was thrust into the spotlight in Atlanta when all of a sudden it was clear that he was going to set his own home run record.

Banks knew of the hostile mail and threats Aaron was getting. He and Aaron didn't talk about it until later when they were visiting troops in Korea and Japan. "Hank and I shared this later on in our lives," Banks said, "that a lot of people never come out of the dark no matter how hard anyone tries to reach them. It can be regulation, rules, system policies, wars. Certain people are just going to stay there." (*See* chapter 17 for more of Hank Aaron's story.)

In Banks's second season with the Cubs, owner P. K. Wrigley, the man who sold all the chewing gum, offered to set up a trust fund for players. Banks thinks he was the only one who took the offer. He put in half his salary throughout his career and couldn't touch the fund until he was 55. "When I was 55, I had $4 million in the bank," Banks said. In terms of player salaries of those times, that was a great deal of money. He said "Mr. Wrigley" called "Mr. Ford," and that resulted in Banks becoming a partner in the Ford dealership.

As a sportswriter, only once did I find Banks other than cheerful. "In 1969," he explained, "I thought we were going to get there." He was 38 years old that year. He was playing first base and struggling on swollen knees. When the Cubs were in first place Leo Durocher, the crusty manager, used to bray, "Mr. Cub, my ass. I'm Mr. Cub." He resented

Banks's popularity and would have preferred him gone. After the Cubs had been passed by the Miracle Mets, Durocher wrote of Banks: "He was a great player in his time. Unfortunately his time wasn't my time. He couldn't run. He couldn't field; toward the end he couldn't even hit. There are some players who instinctively do the right thing on the base paths. Ernie had an unfailing instinct for doing the wrong thing."

Some players felt Durocher deliberately tried to embarrass Banks. Banks still responds to the Durocher matter with that enigmatic smile. Banks drove in 106 runs that year, most on the Cubs, and as the Mets surged past, it was clear Banks would never get his World Series showcase.

One day standing at Banks's locker late in the 1969 season, when it was apparent that the Cubs would not catch the Mets, I used a Jewish word, *rachmones*, meaning something like "compassion" or "pity" for him. Ken Holtzman in an adjacent locker translated it as meaning, "oh shit!" The definition fit.

"I never said it's never going to happen," Banks reflected not long ago. "Many athletes didn't get into the playoffs, but they always mention my name. I'm the poster boy. As you move on in your life, you come to think you really don't have to win in order to win.

"I'd see a woman surviving with five children and no husband and wonder, how in the world could I do that? Another time, a woman in a shop or something asked me, 'What is it like to do something you love and get paid for it?' I was stunned by the thought." How could a man who made a comfortable living playing a child's game feel sorry for himself?

In 1995, Yankee Don Mattingly, after a fine career broken in two by injury, finally got his chance in the October crucible and thrived. Even as the Yankees lost in the playoffs to Seattle, he thanked his teammates for getting him there. "I would have liked to see myself in that pressure," Banks said. "I'd like to think I would have done all right. I'll never know."

Then a bit of lyric: "Don't look so sad; those times are over."

Banks doesn't sit still for age. He is hard to pin down to interview. He has to play golf with Nelson Mandela or Bill Gates or Warren Buffet. At the 1996 Democratic National Convention he introduced Hillary Clinton, who grew up rooting for the Cubs. He can drop names with the best of them.

"That's the way it is," he said. "Movin' on, groovin' on, lookin' at life on the bright side." He quoted another piece of lyric. It was about smiling so nobody knows how you feel inside, but I couldn't write fast enough to get it right.

He answered the ring on his cell phone. Sorry, he said, he had to leave our conversation. He had an appointment to buy a bank.

❖

7

The Pinstripes
Go Black and White

Elston Howard Hid the Pain

*(Born St. Louis, Missouri, February 23, 1929.
Died New York, New York, December 14, 1980.)*

JACKIE ROBINSON'S STAR with the Dodgers was still bright, a monumental figure in New York, when Elston Howard's time came with the Yankees. Early in Howard's rookie season Jackie phoned first.

The Dodgers Jackie represented were the team of the people, the ones with the dirty work shirts, the socialists, the Jews, the immigrants in the neighborhoods on the other side of the great bridge. The Yankees were of the aristocracy and were the aristocracy, the nobility of baseball wearing their pinstripes as if they were bankers' gray. The Yankees weren't part of the establishment, they were the establishment. Their fans were Wall Street and Park Avenue, season tickets held by businesses that hired few Jews, fewer Negroes, and only the "right" kind.

It had been eight seasons since Jackie proved he was good enough and tough enough to touch off the racial revolution in baseball. And still the Yankees had not been moved to join the movement. Then came Elston Howard, who was retrained as an outfielder because Yogi Berra was the Yankees' catcher. In the Yankees' policy of always having a star waiting to replace an aging star, it wasn't until Berra's waning seasons that Howard emerged as an all–star catcher.

On occasion, when both teams were in New York at the same time or during the winter, Jackie and Rachel would get together with Elston and Arlene, relative newlyweds in baseball and strangers in the city. Outcasts even.

"I do remember Jackie saying to Elston, 'I respect what you did. I consider what you did tougher than what I had to do,'" Arlene, Howard's widow, reflected after years of American social readjustment enabled black people to be heard in the crowd. "Jackie said, 'I had Branch Rickey behind me, the whole club behind me. You didn't even have your club behind you. They didn't want black players in there.'"

It wasn't the ballplayers. Mostly they wanted to keep winning, and a player as talented as Howard was another plus toward a World Series check. Berra and his wife, Carmen, were always kind even if Howard was something of a rival for the catcher position. Berra, from the poor Hill section of St. Louis, never displayed a racist thought. Phil Rizzuto was essentially free of bigotry. So, too, were Moose Skowron, Andy Carey, and Gil McDougald.

Not everyone who wore the same uniform was as open to a black teammate. Redneck pitcher Jim Coates was an irritant to Howard until one day in 1960 at the Yankees' annual exhibition game at West Point, pitcher Whitey Ford, a keen observer of people and a Yankee of considerable status, arranged to have Coates and Howard put on boxing gloves and get in the ring together. Howard swiftly flattened Coates and ended the crabbing. Coates was not an important member of the team to begin with.

Arlene Howard recalls that it was fortunate to have among Howard's teammates only one Enos Slaughter, the former Cardinals outfielder who threatened to strike in 1947 if Jackie was permitted to play. The greater obstacle, Arlene Howard said, was "basically the Yankees front office. That was George Weiss and Dan Topping. I think it was Weiss more than anybody."

Until Howard's arrival, Topping and Weiss managed to hold the Yankees against the rising tide of talented black players. Topping was the playboy owner, always deeply tanned, his hair polished as if brushed with buttered toast. He had been married to glamour actress Lana

Turner. He was an elitist. George Weiss, the general manager, was Prussian. He was also a brilliant practitioner of Yankee power. He had New York money and the Yankee aura to use in signing players in the era before the free–agent draft, and he had the money to pick up expensive players other teams didn't want to keep. He was devious enough to keep Yankees pitchers—even Whitey Ford—from being 20–game winners because 20–game winners demanded too much money.

"And it was America," Arlene said. She was sitting at home in Teaneck, New Jersey, as we spoke, in a house she and Howard had bought 40 years before in spite of the community's opposition. Teaneck had already honored him as a Teaneck Yankee, but living in the best part of town in a home appropriate to his income was not easily accepted.

Howard had been with the Yankees for five years before he and his wife found a piece of property that excited their imaginations. Howard came to the Yankees and to New York in 1955, the year Rosa Parks refused to move to the back of the bus. Elston and Arlene Howard grew up in East St. Louis, just across the river from the Cardinals, but the Cardinals had declined to take the recommendations of their scouts and didn't sign Howard.

Instead, Howard played two seasons with the Kansas City Monarchs, which Arlene fondly recalls. In July of 1950 the Yankees bought his contract and sent him to the minors in Muskegon, Michigan. He spent two years in the army, then a year at Kansas City, then the Yankees' minor–league farm, and then Toronto, where he won the AAA International League's Most Valuable Player award.

By 1955 the Yankees organization decided that Howard was the right man to be their first black player. Vic Power, who went on to be a star with Cleveland and Minnesota had shown the talent in the farm system but he was too flashy for the Yankees. He rode around with white women in a convertible. So they traded him. Elston Howard was just right. Arlene was the fiery one; Elston was quiet and soft–spoken. And the prospect of being first with the Yankees was understandably daunting.

Elston and Arlene Howard grew up together in the strictly segregated city of East St. Louis, walking past the white schools to go to Vashon High. Arlene's parents wouldn't let her go to the segregated movies. Most restaurants were closed to blacks. "The zoo was the only thing they didn't bar you from going to," she said. So they went often.

They came to New York with expectations only to be disappointed. "New York was the same in some ways," she said. "They would show us apartments in Harlem that were all horrible." Because they couldn't get a decent apartment in the Bronx they decided to buy something across the river in New Jersey.

"Elston—I don't know if he internalized it—he was very angry and very moody and of course he couldn't let it out at the ballpark," she said. "He would come home and he wouldn't talk and it was a stress. You always felt like you were on view, on stage. You had to be this perfect person."

In those times a black man knew he represented all black people. The white writers would say what a gentleman he was. "The black press would say he's an Uncle Tom because he doesn't raise the roof," she said. Others thought he was a class act, able to raise himself over the insults and indignities.

Howard learned life skills from his godfather, Reverend Baker, a minister, in St. Louis. Early in Howard's Yankees career he and Arlene were driving from home in St. Louis to spring training in St. Petersburg. They knew they couldn't stay at any decent hotels so they mapped out college campuses and homes. Howard's godfather said he had a dear friend who was the pastor of Ebenezer Baptist Church in Montgomery, Alabama. He had a son who was also a minister, Arlene said, "and you'd like him."

When they got to Montgomery the pastor was Martin Luther King Jr., and he said he'd love to have the Howards stay with him, but his home had been bombed that day. "So we stayed at some flophouse," she said.

When they got to St. Petersburg it was hardly better. The white Yankees stayed at a decent hotel or rented nice homes on the beach. Black players on the Yankees and St. Louis Cardinals had to find housing in the black section of the city, which was where the traveling secretary looked for housing, or in the homes of black families in the neighborhood. Curt Flood, with the Cardinals, stayed in a room inside a garage. And when the Chamber of Commerce ran its annual booster breakfast at the yacht club, black players were not invited.

The Howards stayed with a Mrs. Williams, who also cooked because the players couldn't go to restaurants. "So it was awful," Arlene said. But they came in contact with Dr. Ralph Wimbish, a physician who was a regional president of the NAACP in town. Ralph Junior recalls that Dr. Wimbish was known to whites as "The Devil." When Arlene was not at spring training, Howard would sleep in Ralph Junior's room. They had a swimming pool in the front yard not the backyard, which was smaller because a law prevented blacks from living within 100 feet from 15th Avenue South. Imagine such foolishness!

Foolishness, indeed. An arsonist later burned Dr. Wimbish's home because he violated the rules.

❖

"Elston opposed in his way all the rules of segregation, but he wasn't going to let it embitter him," Arlene said, "and I was happy that he didn't."

For one thing, he learned to measure what others might feel was offensive. He identified who was his enemy and who was not, Yankee manager Casey Stengel in particular. Some revisionists would tell us that Stengel was a racist. Arlene Howard does not.

Stengel was an old man by 1955 baseball standards. He was born in 1890 Kansas City, the era of *Tom Sawyer* and *Huckleberry Finn*. His language was based on what he learned as a young man there. From time to time he would refer to Howard as "my jig," and would say, "they finally got me one and he's the only one who can't run." It's true that Howard was slow on the bases, but in my time covering him as a reporter, Stengel did not treat Howard with anything less than respect. When Jackie Robinson was romping on the base paths against the Yankees in the World Series, Stengel hollered, "Throw the nigger out."

Nonetheless, Arlene said, "I really don't think he was ever this prejudiced, racist person." She counted off examples. When the Yankees were in Japan and Arlene was giving birth in New Jersey, Stengel placed the call home for Howard. When Ed Sullivan asked Howard to go on his television show, Stengel said he'd go with him. When Arlene arrived in New York from St. Louis with a toothache, Stengel, the former left-handed dental student, summoned his dentist.

In Howard's first season the Yankees stayed in Chicago at the Del Prado Hotel, which would not accept black people. The next season, Stengel threatened, if Howard couldn't stay with the team, the team wasn't staying. Howard stayed.

"When we won every year there would be this big party and I would always dance with Casey," Arlene said, "and Edna would dance with Elston."

❖

Howard thrived with the Yankees. He was the first black named World Series MVP, as an outfielder in 1958. In 1963 he was the first black elected American League MVP, as a catcher.

He had already been honored—big banquet and everything—by the town of Teaneck. They had a comfortable split-level on the north side, but Howard was the highest paid catcher in the league and in 1960 they found an exciting piece of property where they wanted to build their dream house. "The people selling it would not sell to a black, simple as that. Some kind of agreement," Arlene said.

So they got builders to buy the lot as if on speculation, and the Howards hired an architect, who happened to be a friend of the mayor. The mayor "came to the house and said, 'Oh, you don't really want to live in that neighborhood,'" Arlene said. He said there was a nice piece of property back in the other part of town.

They were determined to go ahead with their plans. One day Howard went to see how the framing was going and found a white teenager running from the shell of the house. He had scribbled, "No niggers wanted in this neighborhood." Someone also scratched the equivalent into the glass brick.

"I was angry, of course," Arlene said. "I wasn't hurt because I felt if the people were so small, I felt superior to them. They were trying to tell me, you couldn't live next to me because you're black and I'm white and I'm better."

There were some white allies in the neighborhood: Mr. Moore, the head of the high school English Department, and the Goldklangs, whose son, Marvin, today is a Yankee minority partner, "but that's about it." They had other longtime friends in Teaneck, but the prevailing attitude at the time was don't try to move next door.

"We had our own friends," Arlene said.

❖

Elston Howard died of heart disease in 1980 at the age of 51. He had wanted to manage in the big leagues but that chance never came.

Bill Veeck, the iconoclast who had owned teams before and was the Cleveland owner who brought Larry Doby to the American League, said if he could buy the new Washington expansion team, he'd make Howard the manager. But baseball gave the franchise to Bill Short. It was a repeat of 1942, when Veeck tried to buy the wartime Philadelphia Athletics and stock them with black players, only to be rejected by the commissioner.

People in baseball management, veteran observers in the media, and friends advised Howard to go out and manage some place in the minors to make himself an unavoidable candidate. The Yankees offered him a chance with their Binghamton farm team. Howard saw that any number of white men had been hired as managers without any experience. He felt he had enough credentials that he didn't need to demonstrate anything more in the minors and chose to decline the offer.

In 1977 the Yankees did make Howard batting coach. On the team flight during the World Series, Howard Cosell, the outspoken telecaster, agitated George Steinbrenner, who was always hiring and firing a manager in those years. Cosell told Steinbrenner that he should make

Howard his manager. Steinbrenner said he wanted a "better job" for Howard, that he wanted Howard in the front office. Steinbrenner was always making grand promises of some sort.

"I don't know if that was an excuse or if that's how he felt; I assume he did," Arlene said. "I don't know if he just didn't want to be put on the spot of having to fire this black manager." Howard knew perfectly well that if he ever was hired to manage, he could expect to be fired. Steinbrenner changed managers as often as he changed underwear. And managers everywhere know they are hired to be fired. That's how it is.

⁛

Times have changed in the intervening years, although they haven't changed enough. Willie Randolph is managing the New York Mets, the first black man to manage a New York team. "New York is a whole lot better now," Arlene said. "I don't know when it changed. If you have money you can buy." She and Howard paid $50,000 for their fine house and now she's told she can put it on the market for "a million–two." She could pick her spot.

"It seems so strange now; how mean and evil people were. God!" she said. "Of course, we have somebody like that now in the White House. It brings tears to your eyes that people were so evil."

Times are better, but with the progress, young people never learned what price was paid by people who paved the way. The Howards led exemplary lives, gave money to support Martin Luther King Jr.'s civil rights marches, brought up their children with pride. Arlene Howard is impatient—even resentful—that so few athletes, black or white, know how they got where they are.

"And don't really care," she said. "To me Curt Flood was a real hero and most of the players don't even remember he fought to get free agency for them. Marvin Miller was a real hero in organizing their players association and those dumb–ass people didn't elect him to the Hall of Fame. They're just not aware. All they see is the dollar.

"Where do these people come from? We came from the background where the family cared about you, where you had a mother and you had a father. Now they just spring up out of the street. They have God–given talent but there's nothing else. Latrell Sprewell making millions playing basketball says he worries about feeding his family. They're raising absolute idiots. These basketball players who went into the stands to fight, where do they come from? Where is the role model?"

When Elston Howard was on constant display as the first black Yankee, his behavior was considered a reflection on all black people. "You're a good black American and what you do is good for your race, where you have to carry your race on your shoulders," Arlene Howard said. "I don't buy that anymore. I'm not sure that I ever did. Maybe a little bit."

Elston Howard was proud of being African American. On Howard's death, broadcaster Red Barber, a Southerner once reluctant to be the voice of Jackie's arrival with Brooklyn, commented: "The Yankees lost more class over the weekend than George Steinbrenner could buy in 10 years."

Class never went out of style.

8

You Know You Go in the Back Door

Alvin Jackson Reports to Spring Training

(Born Waco, Texas, December 26, 1935-)

ALVIN JACKSON DOESN'T REMEMBER his parents telling him of the terrible thing that happened in his hometown. They didn't have to. In 1922, 13 years before he was born, three Negroes were burned at the stake in Waco, Texas.

Tales of an event like that are passed from generation to generation, person to person, older child to younger child in the oral history that stings more than any written word. Three black men were accused of the murder of a white girl. It didn't matter what a court and jury might rule about guilt or innocence. The group of angry whites grabbed the accused, piled kindling wood and doused it with fuel oil, and bound the men to poles. The grandfather of the slain girl gave the word to light the fires.

What that history imposed on a black child growing up in the 1930s didn't need to be explained. These were the first facts of life.

"When you are born and raised in an area, you know a lot about it," said Jackson, now a kind of elder statesman and a valued member of the Mets' minor–league instructional staff. "We lived in a small world, a separate world. We were part of it; we could mingle some, but it was a small world. Just so many things you were allowed to do.

85

"You always knew where you were and you knew where you stood. We did have a black community you could kind of dwell in. You knew when you were crossing the tracks and where you stayed. You didn't go to white restaurants, because I tried that and it didn't work.

"Looking back makes me angry."

∗∗∗

As long as I've known him, Al Jackson has been an infinitely cheerful man, and that goes back to the time of the original Mets in 1962. Even while he was suffering through two 20–loss seasons, he and his wife, Nadine, maintained a good–humored outlook. A left–handed pitcher at 5′10″ and 165 pounds, Jackson was a little short with a fastball but not with heart. Looking back now he trembled—not just about Waco and its in–your–face segregation but about the times that were supposed to be better for races mixing but weren't.

After two seasons in the minor leagues he went to his first big–league spring camp with the 1957 Pittsburgh Pirates in Fort Myers on the west coast of Florida. He went by train because his mother insisted. She had heard too many things she didn't like about airplanes. "So I took a train through Texas all the way to Florida. I think it was 29 hours. That's a lo–o–o–ng time," he said drawing out the distance like iron rails. He lugged a footlocker on the train because that was the luggage he owned.

The station at Fort Myers was hardly big enough to be called a terminal and, as he recalled, there were 75 to 100 people trying to get into the room. Too many. "It's raining like hell," he said. Some things a man never forgets.

"So I get my big old footlocker and I'm looking for a cab."

It's absurd that supposedly big–league organizations at that time were so unorganized. They still are in some ways. Nobody thought to make a phone call or send a note to a young black player from Texas telling him the Florida rules.

There were half a dozen vacant taxis across the street and a redcap, a black fellow, asked where Jackson was going. Bradford Hotel, Jackson told him.

"And he said to me, 'Are you going there to work?'" Jackson recalled. The redcap meant work as a porter or dishwasher. "Otherwise, what would I be doing at the Bradford Hotel? So then I knew what he meant. I wasn't going to stay there. Pittsburgh didn't tell me anything. They just said come to the headquarters; that's all I was told."

So Jackson and his footlocker still needed a taxi, there were six of them waiting right there and the redcap said he had to phone for one. "I don't think I had ever been in a white cab, but it didn't dawn on me," Jackson recalled. "I'd been in black cabs at home but not too many of them. I asked why do I have to wait for you to call? Are these taken? He says they're white cabs. I'm getting drenched."

Jackson lugged his footlocker across the street and asked a driver if he would take him to the Bradford. The driver muttered yeah and never got out of his cab; Jackson threw his footlocker in the backseat and got in beside it. And the driver took the passenger to the Bradford. "But the way he took me—down the alleys, not down the main street, so he wouldn't be seen," Jackson said.

They crossed Broad Street, Jackson saw the sign on the Bradford. "The driver takes me to the back of the hotel; he wouldn't take me out front," Jackson said. "I said I can't pay until you get around front. He would not drive me there." Jackson got out of the car in back of the hotel, the cab dropped the footlocker in front for Jackson to carry. "I paid him, knowing I'm not going to stay there," Jackson said. "But I still got to go in there, say I'm here; I don't know where else to go."

This was one of the routine indignities that confronted black players. "So I walk in and the eyes of the people sitting in the lobby, the way they looked at me was unreal," Jackson said. "And I'm carrying a suitcase, too. Daggers stuck all into me."

And the woman running the hotel front desk said he must want to know where he was going to stay, because "obviously it's not going to be here." It was mindless for the Pirates organization not to tell Jackson or any other nonwhite rookie that he wasn't going to stay at the

Bradford as part of the team. Jackson knew what segregation was all about. Telling him that he was going to stay someplace other than the team hotel would have saved him a lot of humiliation, aggravation, and inconvenience. All it would have taken was courtesy and consideration, but that was not part of the package for a black player.

Jackson stayed in the private home of a black family with five other black players, including Roberto Clemente, who was already emerging as a star. "I guess we were all strong-minded; we had to be," Jackson said. "We weren't totally understanding what was going on but we were living with it every day." They had their goal and the unspoken acknowledgment that "sticks and stones . . . but words will never kill you."

While Clemente was fulfilling his stardom and still couldn't eat in a restaurant in Florida, the Pirates rented a car for him so he and Jackson and the other blacks could find a place off the road on their own. Clemente's special talent made him a special case.

Jackson had a kind of break in his first season because he was sent to the Pirates' Big State League team in Waco, where he had been noticed in the first place. He lived at home, which was a good deal for the other black players on the team and in the league. Jackson often invited teammates and rival players to his home. "His mother cooked some ribs," recalled Ed Charles, who played for Corpus Christi. "We were strictly competitive on the field," Charles said, "but that was a good place to eat."

It was a refuge. One of Jackson's teammates was Roberto Sanchez, a Cuban who had played the season before in Batavia, New York. He was 19 and this American segregation and second-class status was new to him. "He had it tougher than me," Jackson said. So he moved Sanchez in with mom and dad, too.

Jackson rejected an invitation to be the exception. The general manager of the Waco team owned a white restaurant in town. One Sunday Jackson and Nadine, then dating, and another Waco couple not involved with the team stopped by the restaurant after a game. The general manager said the Jacksons could eat there but the other couple could not. "That didn't sit right with me," Jackson said. They all left.

On the road he couldn't eat where the team ate or sleep where the team slept. The bus would drop the black players off and come back and pick them up, which meant they had to do everything in a hurry. Once the bus stopped at a diner on the way home from Austin. Sanchez and Jackson went in with the team and were told they would have to go in the back door, pick up their food, and get out.

Don Rowe, a Californian who pitched briefly with Jackson on the Mets, rebelled. "No, no, no; if they can't eat here, we can't stay," Rowe said. In Jackson's retelling Rowe convinced everyone to leave. "I took a ribbing. A good ribbing," Jackson said. He had some strong–hearted allies, which was not always the case.

It was a touchy situation with so many minor–league teams based in the South. The Pirates' Double A team was in New Orleans but Louisiana law didn't permit whites and blacks to play against each other. So Jackson was assigned instead to Mexico City and had a good year. Since he still couldn't go up to New Orleans the following year, he was sent from the minor–league spring training camp to Lincoln, Nebraska, in another Class A league.

Every morning he moped. "I was pissed," he said. "I just wanted to quit. The day I pitch, I pitch three innings; that's all they let me do. I think I did that three times. As soon as I pitched, I'd shower and leave: 10 o'clock game in the morning and I wasn't staying for the rest of it." Monty Basgall, the manager, said nothing.

When the season opened, Basgall told Jackson he was the fifth starter. "I didn't give a damn; I was just there," Jackson said. He pitched three scoreless innings in his first start and got his butt kicked in the fourth inning. The manager said nothing. The next time Jackson pitched four good innings and was pounded in the fifth. Two losses. "The third time I'm in the seventh with a two–run lead, pitched pretty good, and I'm tired as hell," Jackson said. "I'm looking for help."

Basgall went to the mound and said to Jackson, "You just screwed around all spring, didn't get ready for the season. You're going to stay in this game. I don't give a shit if you give up a hundred runs, this is your game to win or lose."

"I said, 'OK,'" Jackson recalled. "I got 'em out in the seventh. A guy hit a home run off me in the eighth and now I'm winning by one. I give up a home run in the ninth; now it's tied. I end up losing in the tenth. But it taught me a lesson. It taught me about preparation; I've known about that all my life. I didn't do that. I learned my lesson.

"From then on I just took off. I became the number one pitcher on that club." Jackson's 2.07 earned–run average was the best in the Western League.

Moving up to Columbus, Ohio, put him into Triple A, the highest category in the minor leagues, but also back to the road trips in the segregated South and beating his head against the color barrier. Also fighting to keep his temper. "One time I got totally angry," Jackson recalled. Perhaps fans and spectators don't appreciate the handicap of living separate from teammates who are given every opportunity to succeed, and how Jackson and the other black ballplayers weren't given the same opportunities as whites. There were countless obstacles that appear trivial 40 years later but constantly impeded their progress.

Richmond in 1959 was still the product of its history as the capital of the Confederacy. Black players never stayed in white hotels in Richmond. "Our hotel was B–A–D," Jackson said. "Zero–grade hotel. It was hot as Richmond summer can be and the air conditioning was a big wall fan. If you don't turn on the fan it's so hot you can't sleep," he said. "If you turn it on, it makes so much noise you can't sleep. And it just really pissed me off."

In steamy Richmond it was Jackson's turn to pitch. "They come by to take us to the ballpark the next day—the whole bus," he said. "And I'm exhausted. The manager thought I had been out all night. I told him I thought it was horseshit. I hadn't slept all night. I said nobody could sleep there; try to change places with me and see how unfair it is."

The manager, Cal Ermer, said he was trying everything he could to ease Jackson's living conditions—in addition to jumping to the stereotype conclusion that Jackson had been out all night partying.

From time to time Branch Rickey Jr., the Pirates' farm director and son of baseball's great emancipator, would come around, often when

Jackson was most discouraged. He'd take Jackson to dinner, maybe just for a hamburger—the elder Rickey was known in Brooklyn for his thrift—and they'd talk a long time.

Mostly, the advice was keep on keepin' on. Don't be discouraged.

⋯⋯⋯

Unfortunately, not all the teammates were as supportive as Don Rowe, who led the team out of the restaurant that wouldn't serve Jackson. On the field Jackson generally was able to ignore the names he was called by the spectators. "They call you names to distract you," Jackson said. "I guess my skin was too thick for it to affect me. As long as men were doing it, it didn't bother me."

But right behind the visitors' dugout in Richmond one day there was this woman. "She got on me so bad. I took it for seven innings and I couldn't take anymore," Jackson said. "I can't really repeat what I said to her because I really didn't care at the time." Remember, the culture of Texas or Virginia in the 1950s said a black man certainly didn't speak harshly to a white woman.

"Everybody in the dugout got real quiet," Jackson recalled. "They weren't expecting me to do that because she had been shouting things since the third inning. She was saying I shouldn't be on the field with their white players, calling me 'pok' chop' and all kind of nasty names. Just crazy, crazy. After I came out of the game I just walked down the dugout steps, came back up, and called her a few names. I couldn't have cared less if she called somebody."

He walked down into the dugout and all the players who had listened in silence, accepting the baiting directed at Jackson, were still silent. "Everybody was looking at me and I said to my players, 'That was meant for everybody in our dugout, too,'" Jackson said. "All of them were white. They never said a thing."

There could have been consequences. There were none. But if a batter, followed by teammates, had rushed Jackson on the mound, would Jackson's white teammates have rushed to his defense? "You never know," he said.

Of course, the big leagues had to be better. Jackson was one of the Mets when the team was formed in 1962. The Colonial Inn in St. Petersburg, Florida, was integrated for the first time by the Mets; all the players were housed there. They all ate in the private dining room. I covered that training camp for *Newsday* and didn't recognize until I was told later that, for the black players, being in the Colonial Inn was a mixed blessing at best.

Veteran players had the option of renting houses on the beach. White veterans did, anyhow. Jackson, the first black person ever to register at the Colonial Inn, checked in and went to his room. The phone rang. The manager asked Jackson to come to the office. He said the guests weren't used to seeing blacks in the hotel; would Jackson do him a favor? Do not go into the bar, the restaurant, and especially not the pool.

"I thought, I'll be damned," Jackson recalled.

Lou Niss, the traveling secretary whose baseball career began back with the Brooklyn Dodgers of Jackie Robinson, "raised hell" with the hotel to no avail. "That's when they came up with the private dining room," Jackson said. "That's when the club told all of the players not to go in the bar."

Living at the Colonial Inn was a step for desegregation that had to be taken, but it didn't mean the black players—Charlie Neal, Sherman Jones, and Sammy Drake—had to like it. There was no fun for them in relative isolation on the beach. They couldn't buy anything to eat or drink out there after practice. Fun and welcome waited on the other side of town. They'd need a car to get there.

"We were just immobile," Jackson said. "So we bought this car, a beat–up Mercury, I think." When spring training was over the four players gave the car to a man who worked in the kitchen and had done favors for them.

"When we came back the next year we saw that same car," Jackson said. "He fixed it up so well we wanted it back."

Nadine, Jackson's wife, would play Scrabble with the writers' wives poolside at the Colonial Inn, but she never went in the pool.

Jackson raised his family in suburban Long Island. Every year he went Christmas shopping with Larry Bearnarth, a white teammate; neither was concerned about the color of the other. At home, Jackson talked to his kids about real life outside the cocoon of the team. "I didn't say they had to know," he said. "They asked questions and they understood." The boys, Reggie and Barry, went through the suburban school systems. "Very few blacks there," Jackson said. They went to black colleges, Fisk and Howard, "for identity."

So much has changed for the better during Jackson's time. Now he lives in Port St. Lucie, Florida, where the Mets have spring training and a minor–league team. It is the rare community that never had a black side of town and a white side because there was no Port St. Lucie of any consequence until the 1980s. The Mets moved training camp there in 1988 and Jackson bought a home on the golf course next to the tee box on 18. "I did not want to live on a fairway," he said. "I hit too many houses myself."

He must be rich. "Rich?" he railed. "I live comfortable." He laughed out loud. "It makes my head spin to live on prime real estate. I never thought about this when I first got to the big leagues; I thought it was too far–fetched. First, I didn't have the money, but if I had the money they wouldn't have allowed me to buy it."

Some things, he has noticed, have not changed so much. Even today when players are compared, which scouts and coaches do, it's always a white player compared to a white player and black to black. "I'm sure there got to be some things we have in common," Jackson, a former left–handed pitcher, said.

When he goes to play golf, however, he goes in the front door of the clubhouse.

❖

9

I'm No Jackie Robinson

Too Much Bigotry for Charlie Murray

(Born Cary, Mississippi, September 8, 1943-)

"Of all of us brothers, Charlie had the most talent. He also had the best disposition. It was hard to make him angry, but when he was . . ."
> —*Eddie Murray, Hall of Fame 2003*

"I never saw anybody in our organization hit the ball farther than Charlie. He was an awesome talent. He was a great guy, just great. Some people say he was a better prospect than his brother and his brother is in the Hall of Fame. The period called for adjustments; there's no denying it was a difficult time."
> —*Tal Smith, president of the Houston Astros, then farm director*

CHARLIE MURRAY FEELS that he's a pleasant enough fellow, not too hard to get along with, reasonably adaptable, slow to take offense. But how much does a man have to take?

More than Murray was willing to accept. He didn't need to be a baseball player that badly.

"I'm no Jackie, I'm no Jackie Robinson," Murray said, looking back nearly 40 years to the time he decided he wasn't going to turn another cheek. "You can't walk in my shoes unless you are black."

There are layers upon layers that go into the way he looks back at the time he tried to be a baseball player. No, at the time he tried to endure the insults that lay in the path of a black man who wanted to be

a baseball player. He wouldn't give in to the indignities, whether they were real or perceived.

"I was a different type because I didn't grow up playing ball," he reflected. "I worked before I signed, so it was no big thing to go out and get a job. It was not as if, if I didn't play baseball my life was over. I would have loved to play in the big leagues."

In 1963, his second season in the minor leagues, Charlie Murray of the Moultrie, Georgia, Colts led the Georgia–Florida League with 15 home runs. The next season he hit 37 home runs for the Modesto Colts of the California League and drove in 139 runs in 140 games, a remarkable accomplishment. A future in the major leagues lay ahead. The big team was known as the Houston Colts then.

❖

Charlie Murray, one of five brothers, all of whom played professional baseball, grew up in Los Angeles without the Little League experience. Not playing in the Little League can be a mixed blessing. He didn't play organized baseball until he was 17 years old and a senior at Fremont High School. He hit an impressive .417, which did attract the attention of the scouts, but there was a gap in his baseball education.

He had his own ideas about what being a newcomer to the game meant. "I didn't have the rah–rah of Little League," he said, looking back. "With my brothers, when the coach said something, that was it. I obeyed the coach. I just didn't understand why he had to put his hand on me. The coach wasn't like my dad."

Racial relations among young people growing up in Los Angeles in the 1950s were far ahead of much of America. Murray could go to integrated schools. He could go downtown and go to the movies or buy a hamburger. His money was perfectly good in the shoe store.

He went off to play with the Modesto Colts, California League at the bottom of the professional ladder. Some good major–league players came out of that league: Hal Lanier, Jim Lefebvre, and Darold Knowles. It was California. There was some lingering prejudice of the 1950s, but when he got a big hit, he could be rewarded with a steak dinner like anyone else. The power he showed the next season with Moultrie, Georgia, was reason for the Colts to move him up a rung on the ladder.

The scout's adage is that you can't teach power. Murray struck out too often, but that often goes with power hitters, especially ones as young and inexperienced as Murray was. But a .263 average with 37 home runs and all those RBI wasn't bad. He could learn to hit for a better average. "Everything I learned, I learned in the pros," he said. "At one time they thought I could be a big–league player."

He was a left–handed hitter, a right fielder with a great arm and good speed. "At that time I thought he would be better than Eddie was," said longtime major leaguer Bob Watson, who played junior varsity the year Murray was varsity at Fremont. "At that time he had no idea of segregation and he was one of those guys who could not take it." Watson understood how to take it in his way. He developed into a 19–season big leaguer and became the first black general manager to win a championship.

Unfortunately, Moultrie was too Georgia for Murray. He wasn't welcomed to the steak dinner rewards when he earned them. Too bad. "You stayed in the black neighborhood where people were nice to you," he said. "You didn't come in contact with whites until game time." That's when he was immersed in the culture of separate but equal white water fountains and black water fountains, and all that suggests, especially after night games. "You couldn't be downtown after games," he said. "Blacks had to be off the street by midnight."

That was the law. More offensive to Murray was the fact that when he walked downtown in broad daylight women would fold their arms and clutch their purses to their chests. "Just crazy," Murray said. They felt the only reason he was in their downtown was to steal from them. That's how they perceived him because he was a black man in their town, where a black man's place had never been on the ball field with whites before.

The black community found a place for the five players of color to stay at a minister's home. "They got that for us because the black people were proud to have an integrated team in town," Murray said. There were some allies among the white teammates, particularly two men from California who were married and had rented houses. "One of them invited us to dinner and they threatened to get him kicked out of town for having those niggers over," Murray said.

"It really upset him but we told him, you don't have to invite us if it's a hardship for your family. Then the manager was called nigger lover because he played two or three of us at a time."

Jim Walton was the manager, a man from Oklahoma, and Murray still thinks the world of him. Walton got off the bus from one road trip and "nigger lover" had been painted on his white 1963 Oldsmobile. "How do you hate somebody you don't know?" Murray said. "I couldn't understand the animosity against me."

Road trips were seldom comfortable for any player in the bus leagues of the low minors. "We didn't have a good bus, either," Murray said. On the longest trips, to Brunswick or Waycross, the white players on the team stayed overnight at a hotel while the black players were dropped off to stay with black families. They were left in the middle of the night to find a black–operated restaurant that was open, if there was such a thing, to eat alone, and find their way back—perhaps through a white neighborhood—to where they were sleeping. When they walked back to the house, townspeople would throw rocks at them. "At night you can't see the rocks coming," Murray said. "It made me an angry person."

If they wanted to eat at the same time as their white teammates, the black players had to wait on the bus for someone to bring something for them while the others had a hot meal. Charlie Murray's anger was building. He refused to eat on the bus. He preferred to go hungry. "I decided, if they won't feed me through the front door, they will not get my money," he said. He's a good–sized man, 6'2" and more than 200 pounds, built as big as his major–league brothers Eddie, who slugged his way to the Hall of Fame, and Rich, who played briefly with the San Francisco Giants. "He had a thicker body than we did," Eddie said. It did not help Charlie's progress to go hungry.

Jim Walton worked on the problem. At one restaurant he told the restaurant manager he had the Moultrie ball club with four black players and would like all his players to eat dinner there as a team when they bused through town. The restaurant arranged to put all the players in the back room and screened them off so the white patrons wouldn't be offended by the sight of black athletes. That was acceptable when they stopped at the place the first time. All the players were together as teammates.

The next time the Colts stopped there and put in their orders—ballplayers do like to eat steak—the restaurant manager said he had a large party coming to the back room and the black guys would have to leave. "Jim waited," Murray said, "until the dinners they ordered were about to be served, stood up, and said, 'Everybody out, Charlie can't eat here.'

"My teammates were glad to do that."

It was Murray's first real confrontation with racism and he talked to teammates about standing up to it. His father had warned him when he went off to play ball in the South to be careful and keep his eyes open because people "might do anything to you." Murray remembered being 11 years old in Los Angeles and reading about the brutal lynching of Emmett Till in Mississippi 1954. "I was a kid myself," he recalled. "I couldn't believe they did this to this kid."

Here he saw the hatred for himself. "It was in my face and I'm supposed to do nothing," Murray said. "That's not me." Teammates who had been raised in the South warned him not to make a strong response, as he had discussed. "Hey, man, you do that and you'd be dead a long time ago."

Their message was repeated by the little old black lady who cleaned house for them. The banker where Murray went to cash his checks on payday always sat, as Murray recalled, in the cheap outfield seats near the home bullpen. "He kept calling me the N–word," Murray said. He was leading the team in home runs, but he was in a batting slump and his self–restraint was strained. One more "N–word" jarred him past his patience and Murray started over the fence with a bat in his hands before teammates in the bullpen held him back.

The little old cleaning lady heard the story quickly on the player's grapevine. "The lady, like a grandmother, said, 'Charles, I heard you went up there after one of those white people last night. Please don't do that. They came to my house one night and took my son, just walked in, took him out of bed, and I never saw him again.'"

That's when Charles Murray from Los Angeles bought a gun to keep under his pillow.

❖

Next stop, with the Amarillo Sonics of the Texas League, Murray thought there would be more integration and playing would be more comfortable. Instead he found that Jim Crow still was the star of the league. "It's so hard to be by yourself in a strange place," he said. Even black people in the black neighborhood were often hostile because they thought the black players were making a lot of money. Murray's white teammates were on the other side of town and essentially off limits to him.

When a black player would come to town with another team, he was welcome new company for Murray. Here was somebody who was paid to do the same job, who faced the same challenges, and who knew what it was to be black and in Texas. "We'd bring him home to our place, cook together, and sit down and just talk," Murray said.

When he and teammate Aaron Poynter were looking for a better apartment, they found a vacancy over the phone. When the landlady saw them, there was no vacancy for them. So they swallowed their pride and went to the movies with their black teammates.

Murray was still replaying in his mind the indignity with the landlady and paused a moment in the line to buy tickets before stepping to the window. "The ticket seller," Murray recalled, "snapped, 'Well, black boy, do you just want to stand there?' I said, 'What did you call me?'

"You know what that did to me inside. When I requested team-mates to get out of the ticket line with me, I was told, 'Charlie, don't ruffle nobody's feathers.'

"I was happy to be playing ball, thinking I was moving up, making a reputation for myself, and maybe one day I'd get to play in he big leagues. But I couldn't swallow my pride any longer, and I still can't."

Durham, North Carolina, in the Carolina Leagues was a comfortable spot but it was a step back when Murray felt he should still be higher up in the Texas League. He had a fight with a southern teammate on the Bulls who admitted he threw the first punch. Dave Philley, the manager, took both players into the clubhouse and said he'd fine both if they didn't shake hands. "I knew the other guy didn't mean it but I shook hands because I wasn't making any money," Murray said.

His progress was breaking down. By this time the Astros were assigning a coach to help the manager at each level, and Murray, with that great power potential, was struggling. Buddy Hanken was the coach at Amarillo and he wanted Murray to slap the ball to left field. Murray thought of himself in terms of power and was uncomfortable doing it Hanken's way. He said he couldn't. Hanken grabbed him.

"Nobody grabbed me like that," Murray recalled. Teammates had to pull him off the coach.

As his status in the organization was breaking down and his animosity toward bigoted society was building, Charlie Murray was drafted into the army. Harry Truman ordered the army integrated in 1948, but no presidential order could integrate attitudes. "The army didn't make me any better," Murray said. Fourteen months as an American soldier in Germany made him only angrier.

"The Germans treated me better than the people I worked with and slept with," he said. "The rednecks tried to make trouble with me. They said I should be in Vietnam on the front lines because of my color. In this German country town I'd be dancing with everybody. And when it got close to midnight they became distant. White soldiers told the people that after midnight blacks grew tails and became mean. I had Germans tell me that."

He came back with his interest in baseball diminished and an attitude he described as "I don't care what you do because I don't need you." But his brothers Eddie and Richie were involved in baseball and he was careful not to let his anger hurt their chances. "I didn't want my brothers branded," he said. "If I did something, I was a black militant, they said. I wasn't militant; I did something stupid."

After serving his time in the army he was optioned to the Phillies, went to spring training camp with the Triple A team, and that was the end. He didn't want to be moved around anymore. He was ready to quit, went back to Durham for a while to satisfy his father, who didn't want him to give up. In Durham, Murray saw the end. He wasn't going any further and it was time to leave. He was 27.

"When I got out of it," he said, "I had to tell my brothers it's not about if you're good enough; it's a whole different thing." Perhaps that partially explains why Eddie, as good as he was and as popular as he was with the Orioles, always presented a suspicious—even hostile—front to the media. He still took that stance in his short time late in his career with the Mets.

Murray moved to Baltimore when his brother Eddie was there displaying his Hall of Fame stuff. He was a security guard with FEMA. He was a corrections officer. He says he talks to young people in the neighborhood about things he learned and they don't want to hear what he came through. "I tell them, back in the day they wouldn't have done this or that," Murray said. "I say, 'you got so much more and you don't know where you got it.' Worse, they don't care. As a corrections officer, I was trying to get next to them and get them to understand why they did what they did and what to do when they get out. They carry guns and they won't listen; the shame is they don't want to know.

"I don't take crap from them. I tell them my kid brothers would never be in here."

It sounded as if talking about it made him angry again. "I'm all right," he said. "I just don't like talking about it. That anger is nothing to be boasting about. God put me here for a reason. I'm sorry I never got a chance to let people know I did improve and could run and had a good arm and could play."

But was it anger that clouded his ambition and his talent, or was it really something as big as dignity? Was there some greater nobility in saying nothing was so important that I would lower myself to bow to your bigotry?

"No," said Frank Robinson, who endured those same trials and overcame them. "He wasn't strong. He didn't pursue what he wanted to do in his life. He let it be a barrier. If it was dignity, there would be no blacks in baseball."

10

Recognition 50 Years Later

Chuck Harmon Gets His Own Street

(Born Washington, Indiana, April 23, 1924-)

CHUCK HARMON IS A MILESTONE figure in baseball, especially in Cincinnati. He is hardly a household name. Except in his neighborhood on Chuck Harmon Way over on Rosedale Avenue.

The City of Cincinnati renamed a six–block stretch of Rosedale in August of 1997 to commemorate the day Harmon became the first black player with the Reds. It was part of the 50th anniversary celebration of Jackie Robinson's entrance into the big leagues.

The amount of social guilt involved in recognizing Harmon is difficult to measure. Harmon's time with the Reds began in 1954 and in many ways reflects just how unwelcoming baseball was to colored, Negro, black, or African American players—however labeled—for so long. The fact that Harmon was signed to his first minor–league contract in 1947, hit .300 or better his first five seasons in the minor leagues, and took seven years to get to Cincinnati is one symptom.

He amassed four major–league seasons from 1954 to 1957. Was he cheated, I asked. "I'm going to say yes," he responded. "I thought I could be playing more and got more time in the big leagues. They had guys who couldn't chew gum and run at the same time, and you go two or three weeks without getting an at bat, and you knew you were better."

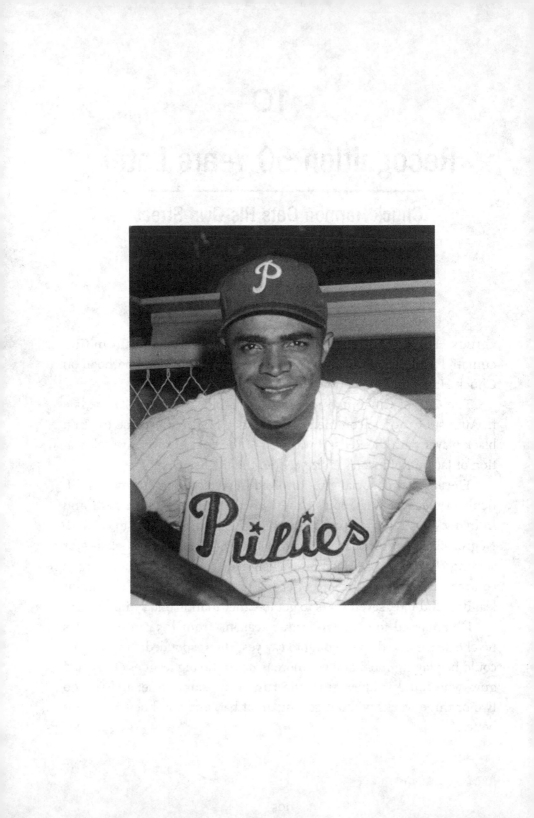

Chuck Harmon is a cheerful man, a valued administrative assistant with the Ohio District Court of Appeals. He laughs easily at himself. His calm bearing, instead of displays of outrage, enabled him to get as much out of baseball as he did. It was a time for not speaking out.

Harmon was an all–American basketball player at the University of Toledo in the early 1940s, a college career interrupted by an interlude in the segregated U.S. Navy. He starred at Madison Square Garden in 1943. He scored 22 points in the semifinal game when Toledo went to the finals of the National Invitation Tournament, then the premiere college tournament. Before that, he starred for Washington High School on consecutive Indiana state basketball championships when there were communities that felt high school basketball had as prominent a place in their lives as segregation. Southern Indiana was the northern headquarters of the Klan, but basketball was basketball.

The love of the game is evident in Washington, Indiana, where a street is named Harmon Drive. Chuck was raised there as one of 12 children, and in 1930, when he was six years old, two Negroes were mutilated and lynched by a mob in upstate Marion. Photos of the event were sold as postcards to a public that was thoroughly entertained.

Schools didn't dwell on unpleasant things like that, but the oral tradition carried the story from generation to generation. "You heard about those things," Harmon reflected, an understatement, more than 70 years later. By this time his identity in Cincinnati had been officially acknowledged by that city.

When he was the high school star, there was no black neighborhood in Washington—it was too small. There were restaurants in town that would serve the three black players when the basketball players ate as a team. Otherwise the restaurants served whites only. Before the team traveled out of town, the coach would take the trouble to search out restaurants that would serve his black players. At tournament time, when the team stayed in the big cities of Gary and Kokomo, Harmon and his black teammates had to stay apart at black hotels.

"We used to run around with the white kids all the time, stay at each other's house, camp out in the backyard," Harmon said. Every once in a while when the kids would get together for their innocent games of tag or the improvised child's games of the time, some adult would observe them and be offended by the mixing of races. The adult would blurt, "What are you doing playing with that nigger?" Harmon recalled. The children, as he recalled, did not let those adult ideas get in the way of life. When they were older, Harmon said, one of his white buddies would grab a collar and say, "Keep your mouth shut or we'll beat the soup out of you."

At that age big–league baseball was not in the genetic code of his mind. The Cincinnati Reds played 150 miles away. The two teams in Chicago were closer than that, but there was no role model to be seen, no picture in the *Indianapolis Star* of a black player in their uniform. "You may say when you're out in the backyard that you're Babe Ruth, but you're just saying it because everybody else was saying it," Harmon said. "As far as visualizing yourself playing big–league ball, it was so far–fetched it wasn't funny. Where there's no hope, you don't think about it."

What he did think about was a college scholarship. Black kids could go to college in Indiana. Indiana University won the NCAA championship in 1940 and set the style for high schools in the whole state. That was Harmon's first choice. But that was out. Indiana University had black football players, but Hall of Fame basketball coach Branch McCracken would have no blacks on his team.

When Harmon served in the navy, which was fighting for America, the rules were hardly different. Black sailors and white sailors at Great Lakes Naval Training Station lived in separate barracks. Black men Buddy Young and Marion Motley, former college football stars who later became professional legends, could play on the navy football teams coached by Paul Brown. Harmon and Larry Doby played on both the navy basketball and baseball teams, but they had to be black basketball and baseball teams. It was not explained by the navy why football could be integrated while baseball and basketball were segregated. Call it the uniform code of military injustice. But those were the rules; go fight the navy. Harmon could only watch the white men he'd played beside on college all–star teams. "Funny how one day you can do something and the next day you can't," Harmon said. "Hard to understand today, isn't it? If you said something in the navy, it was mutiny and they could put you in the brig."

After the navy Harmon played baseball briefly with the Indianapolis Clowns of the Negro Leagues. He played under the assumed name Charlie Fine in order to protect the remainder of his eligibility at Toledo. After Robinson's debut with the Dodgers opened the door, the St. Louis Browns signed Harmon to a minor–league baseball contract.

Between baseball seasons, he even came close to making the Boston Celtics of the National Basketball Association in 1950. As he recalls it, he was doing fine until the Celtics picked up some guy named Bob Cousy, who was available after the original Chicago team went out of business. Cousy became a Hall of Fame basketball player and so there was no room for Chuck Harmon on the Celtics.

Harmon went with the Utica team in the Eastern League, the minor league of professional basketball and was player–coach. It has been written that he was the first black man to coach a mixed team in professional sports. Early records are so limited that it is all but impossible to determine if that is so.

Baseball, however, was his ambition and each season in the minors encouraged him. He hit .351, .374, and .375 in his first three minor–league seasons and kept being sent back to the Class D Pony League, the lowest of categories. One year he led the league in RBI and another year he led in hits. Every place he went, he was the only black in the ballpark. "It's tough fighting alone," he said.

The Reds bought his contract and sent him to Tulsa in the Texas League, which was in the throes of painful integration. If Harmon was ready for the league, was the league ready for him? He and Nino Escalera, a dark–skinned Puerto Rican, would take a blacks–only taxi to and from the ballpark. In cities where it was a long ride from the black accommodations, Harmon would leave tickets for people who'd drive him to work. One time he and Escalera were banging hits at Shreveport, Louisiana, and they heard some loudmouth holler to the home manager, "Hey, when are you going to get yourself some of those niggers?" Harmon said he almost fell on the dugout floor to keep from laughing out loud. Wouldn't that have gone over big in Louisiana?

Life in Tulsa was complicated by the fact that Harmon's wife, Daurel, is light skinned. Would they make her sit in the black section or with the wives in the white section? One of her first visits to the ballpark, she was in the section reserved for whites and some people stood up and pointed her out. Did she have to use the outhouse in the Negro section and drink soda from a cup dipped in dirty water? The obvious solution was to tell Harmon to take his wife and play elsewhere. Daurel said she'd go home if her presence meant Chuck would be sent out, or she'd go sit in the section with the black people. He was hitting well and Gabe Paul, from the home office, said Chuck wasn't being sent down. The Harmons managed to cope.

There were devious schemes in those years when there were still 16 teams and talent was so abundant that standards were unreasonably high for a black player. The Reds could finish sixth with the likes of Sammy Meeks, Bob Usher, and Eddie Pellagrini doing little more than taking up space on the bench. Harmon played third base, first base, and the outfield in the minor leagues and hit well enough no matter what position he was playing, but everybody concerned knew that there was no place on the bench for a black utility player.

In 1958 Harmon was playing winter ball in Puerto Rico and chatting with Branch Rickey Jr., who was working for his father, the boss of the Pirates. "He said he had Roberto Clemente and Donn Clendenon and so many good black players, 'but there's a quota. We can't bring them up because we can have only so many,'" Harmon recalled.

It shouldn't have been shocking. "It was the same thing for Buddy Young playing college football at Illinois; maybe you're a running back and you never get to run," Harmon said. "In basketball you go for a layup and they call a foul. The ref says the foul was before the shot; no basket. Another guy, a white guy, they say the basket is good.

"They write scouting reports in baseball and say one guy has a little better arm and how does anybody know? They see one guy is doing good and write that he's not actually doing that good because he doesn't score from second base. He's hitting home runs but they write he still hasn't hit a sacrifice fly, or he doesn't get a guy in from third base. If they want to hold you back, they can hold you back."

Add that to the demands of eating and sleeping and getting a taxi. "The white players didn't know we weren't staying at the same hotels with them and eating where they did," Harmon said. "They'd get to the ballpark and ask, where were you guys last night? We'd laugh."

That was until one day in Dallas when the white players saw all the cabs lined up to take them to the train station. The train was being delayed until the Tulsa team arrived. Escalera and Harmon and the team athletic trainer got into the last taxi in the queue and joined the procession down the wide street. Then a police car overtook them and the cop peered into their vehicle at them. They heard the siren.

"He waved us over, made us get out of the cab and called us everything but the son of God," Harmon recalled. "The cab driver said we were part of the Tulsa ball club. The cop said he didn't give a damn, 'Get these damn niggers out of the cab.' The cop calls headquarters and tells the cab driver to get going, but here's the ticket and tomorrow morning 'You be at the station house.'"

Tulsa players, waiting at the railroad station for the last of their group, asked for an explanation and Harmon gave them one. "You mean you guys can't ride in cabs?" a surprised teammate asked. Like so much of white America, they had never noticed.

In looking back 50 years, what irritated Harmon the most was that teammates didn't know what he and Escalera had to go through—they couldn't stay at the same hotels or eat in the same restaurants. That's the reason why his teammates didn't see Harmon and Escalera after the ball game. Perhaps they didn't notice because they didn't care to see.

At the age of 30, Harmon concluded that the only way up from the minor leagues was not to give the Reds an excuse to send him down again. However much bigotry was involved, baseball teams were ultimately selfish. In spring training in 1954, he didn't give the Reds a choice. "If a guy is going good, they'll find a way," he said. He played very well all spring, and, ultimately, playing well overcomes all but the most severe racism; management wants an attractive team to sell more tickets.

He made his debut on April 17, 1954, pinch-hitting as the Reds' first African American player. Birdie Tebbetts, the manager, had warned

Harmon and Escalera that if there was an incident on the field, they were to walk away and fold their arms. Otherwise, he said, "You'll get beat up or get blamed for starting it."

Tebbetts's role in the integration of the Reds is clouded by uncertainty. In 1956 Brooks Lawrence won his first 13 decisions for the Reds; he was 15–2 at the end of July. Some players say that Tebbetts said, "I bet you he doesn't win 20." Harmon says he was told the manager declared that no black pitcher was going to be a 20–game winner for him. Memories can be imprecise. Harmon was traded away in May of that season, before Lawrence had come close. George Crowe, who was there, said Tebbetts offered precisely that bet when Lawrence returned from the All–Star Game. And Frank Robinson, who was not there, says such an attitude would have been entirely out of character for Tebbetts. Lawrence and Tebbetts are both dead. Lawrence did win his 18th game on September 3 and was starting pitcher only once more during the last three weeks of the season. He finished the season 19–10 and the Reds finished third, two games behind Brooklyn.

Cincinnati was one of the major–league cities most resistant to integrating its team. In 1957 when it stuffed the fan balloting for the All–Star Game with Reds players, the only starter omitted was first baseman Crowe, a black man. Obviously, Robinson couldn't be left off even if he was black.

About 20 years later, Harmon was visiting the Hall of Fame at Cooperstown, New York, with his son, Charlie, when they encountered former Reds general manager Gabe Paul, who had been helpful in the minor leagues. Paul told young Charlie, "Your father and I went through a lot of stuff." Harmon said that was the first he heard of the threatening calls and the volume of hate mail the club received.

He did know of the death threat when he broke up a no–hitter by Giants pitcher Jim Hearn in New York in 1955. "I got a letter saying that when I came back to New York, they were going to shoot me," Harmon said. The FBI stationed agents at the Reds' hotel and at the Polo Grounds when the Reds returned.

Fifty years later, Harmon recalls a minor–league teammate, his name lost in time, coming to a sudden understanding of what Chuck

Harmon had to overcome as a black player. "All we got to do is worry about the damn curveball and you guys . . . " the player said.

The names of those black players who had to overcome are also unknown in the greater freedom of black players today. "It makes a lot of older black players mad that if you ask some modern–day players, they never heard of so and so," Harmon said. "They think they started everything. They think it was a piece of cake for us."

11

Sometimes People Live and Learn

Maury Wills Finds a White Ally

(Born Washington, D.C., October 2, 1932-)

DEEP IN THE HEART OF TEXAS, Maury Wills was honoring Bobby Bragan for his 60 years in baseball. Here was Wills, who had grown up so poor that reaching the poverty level would have been a step up, paying tribute to a man who had tried to keep Jackie Robinson, Wills, and all the others whose skin wasn't white out of organized baseball.

Actually, Wills's participation was a celebration showing how much two men could grow. "He was a great man to me," Wills said. "And we are best of friends. He was responsible for me getting to the big leagues."

Wills spent eight discouraging seasons in the minor leagues before Bragan's personal guidance boosted him to the Los Angeles Dodgers. Bragan was born in 1917 and grew up in Birmingham, Alabama. His nickname was "Nig," a handle other whites frequently pinned on dark-skinned white men.

Bragan was one of the Dodgers who signed the failed petition in 1947 to keep Robinson out of baseball and the color barrier in. "If there is no Jackie Robinson, there is no Maury Wills," Wills pointed out.

❖

The ghetto walls of the 1930s and early 1940s were so impenetrable around the Parkside housing project where he grew up in the Anacostia section of Washington, D.C., that he didn't even know there was a major-league team called the Senators in the city. Making a way out of that small world was unlikely.

Wills was seventh born of a minister's family of 13 children who moved to the government housing project from the Garfield area, which suffered worse poverty. The problems then were not so much of the violence that infects impoverished neighborhoods today, but of greater isolation than that of today. There was no television, and what was in the newspapers rarely concerned the people in the neighborhood. At the age of 8 or 10, Wills recalls, a player from the Washington Senators came to the playground near his project. "We didn't even know there was a team in town called the Washington Senators from the major leagues," he said. "The word never got into our neighborhood."

It was in the 1940s, before television offered an eye to the world for the poverty-stricken. So a visit from a major-league player was not a big deal because the major leagues didn't mean much in the neighborhood. "Our heroes were these old guys who played on weekends and called themselves semipro," Wills said. They probably didn't get paid anything except when they won a game and a bet from the other team.

"These guys wore argyle socks under their stirrups and they wore mix-and-match uniforms and caps on the side of their heads. And they all had a half-pint of whiskey in their back pockets. If they didn't get too drunk on Saturday night and if enough guys showed up on Sunday, they would have a game. Those guys were our heroes, the guys we wanted to emulate."

They were so isolated that kids Wills's age did not know that the major leagues were closed to them. "We didn't know anything about major-league baseball at that time," he said. They didn't know of the Negro Leagues, either, where a number of those semipros had once played.

One player in the full uniform of the Washington Senators came to give a clinic. The fact that he was white caused a stir among the people. The Senators weren't developing black players, but the team did want more black people to buy tickets. Wills remembers from his time with the Los Angeles Dodgers in the 1960s that players really didn't want to be sent out into the community to give their time at clinics teaching eight– and nine–year–olds how to field a ground ball, but the team said they had to go and stay at least 15 or 20 minutes and wing it if they had to.

"If they told us that in the 1960s, I can imagine what they must have told those players back in that time," Wills said. "I'm sure he wasn't looking forward to coming there. But he didn't stay a half hour, he didn't stay 20 minutes, he stayed at least two hours.

"His uniform was immaculate, nice and pressed and color coordinated with the piping around the collar and belt loops and down the side of this leg. His shoes were clean. And his eyes weren't all red. And he spoke like he was used to trying to get a message across. He had compassion. I looked behind him to see if he had a bottle in his back pocket, and he didn't. He was white and him spending time there was unheard of."

The player from the Senators was Gerry Priddy, who had grown up in the Yankees organization as second baseman to Phil Rizzuto's shortstop. The Yankees didn't care for his gift of gab in the taciturn clubhouse, and it was one good reason for them to trade him. But he took the grooming style of the pinstripes with him. He could look as elegant as any Yankee and act as proper in public. Wills spelled out the name: "P–R–I–D–D–Y." The fact that Priddy, years after his baseball career, was convicted of trying to extort a shipping company by planting a bomb on a ship, does not diminish his inspiration to the young Wills. Wills had various problems of his own.

"Right then and there I was so impressed with Gerry Priddy that by the time he left, I knew I did not want to play on Sundays with those guys I thought were my heroes," Wills said. "I wanted to play with them guys, wherever he played on Sundays. That's when I knew I wanted to be in major–league baseball. For the first time in my life I had direction."

But there was still no Jackie Robinson in major–league baseball. Five years later, 14–year–old Maurice Wills heard the people in the neighborhood buzzing about this black man in Brooklyn so he asked who was that Robinson? And why are people making a fuss about him? That's when it dawned on him that there had been no black players in the big leagues. Until that moment all black baseball players had played in the Negro Leagues.

And then where is Brooklyn? Wills had hardly ever been out of the projects and didn't know where Brooklyn was, but it didn't matter where Brooklyn was. It was in the big leagues where people were paid real money to play baseball. "They told me and I already knew because of Gerry Priddy that I wanted to be a major–league player," Wills said.

The players he saw on the ragged baseball fields in his projects he now recognizes as being drunks, but they played baseball the way the Negro Leagues played. "That's where I got my style of play—running, bunting, base stealing, running the bases, playing aggressive, being a good fielder, knowing how to throw the ball, where to throw it; good inside baseball is the way the game should be played," he said.

While we spoke at spring training in Vero Beach, Florida, Wills was studying a Dodger hopeful, Joe Thurston, a second baseman who had become his protégé. Wills is trying to impart his tools to young players in an era that has forsaken them. To Wills, today's young players are playing a version of baseball because they aren't interested in fundamentals. They have greater physical skills but, he says, they don't have an interest in playing better.

The generational attitude is comparable in the National Basketball Association, where Larry Brown, the master coach, wears out his welcome because he wants to make players better. Not so many of them want to get better. Wills always tried to get better, even after he was MVP and stole a record 104 bases, breaking the record Ty Cobb had set generations before. In an adaptation of the title of a movie from an earlier generation, Wills established himself as "The Thief of Bags, Dad."

He studied pitchers and catchers and was out stealing only 13 times when he stole those 104 bases. By comparison, when Ty Cobb set the previous record of 96 steals, a half century before, he was out 38 times. Defensively, in his first full season, Wills led both leagues' shortstops with 40 errors. In his second and third seasons he won the Gold Glove Award as the best defensive shortstop in the National League.

He quotes Lew Burdette, a successful pitcher of the time, as saying Wills took all the fun out of pitching. "And that was my intent, to keep that pitcher ill at ease," Wills said. "I had to get better because I made the opposition better in trying to stop me." Wills wears those comments as medals. He quotes Henry Aaron as writing in his biography that Wills came into the majors trying to do things Aaron hadn't seen before.

He believes he can pass along some of his baseball skills and make young people understand the harshness of his life growing up. He didn't learn the rules of life in the big world because his world was essentially his neighborhood; it was uncomfortable when he passed through another area. "Even though nobody told me what was different out there," he said.

When he signed his first contract in 1951 and headed off to be a baseball player like Gerry Priddy, Wills packed his glove and spikes in a cardboard box and boarded a train at Union Station for Vero Beach, where Brooklyn's minor leaguers trained. But first he told his brother and playground buddies that in three years he was going to be in Brooklyn with Jackie. When they laughed, so what!

At Vero Beach he was immersed in the oral tradition of the Dodgers, the "Boys of Summer." When the players on the big team walked through the dining room they'd leave the young ones in awe. Robinson, of course, was bigger than life.

But Holman Stadium, where the Dodgers played their home exhibition games, was segregated—blacks seated in the far corner of the right-field stands, black and white fountains, and all the trappings of segregation. After three seasons of playing in the North in the low minors when Wills recalls he had no sense of being a man apart, he was sent to Fort Worth in the Texas League. From there, if a man had a good year he could jump to the big leagues. But there had never been a black player in that league. "I crumbled," Wills said.

A trip to Shreveport, Louisiana, was especially devastating. When the team got to its hotel, the white traveling secretary, who was responsible for making housing arrangements and who had been there the season before, had his own idea of proper arrangements. He told Wills there was no key for him and he didn't know where Wills would stay. Wills recalls walking down the street with his bag at 3 a.m. with the sympathetic trainer trying to be helpful, knocking on doors to find a place for Wills to stay. The place he found for Wills was a cot on the back porch of a black family.

Breakfast was Oreo cookies and milk from the drugstore and by the time the one black taxi came for him, Wills arrived late at the ballpark. Tommy Holmes, the manager, reprimanded him. In Fort Worth, Wills stayed near the railroad station where the loud banging and switching of boxcars rang all night. The bathroom was down the hall and a neon light kept flashing in the dark. He couldn't stay with his teammates; he couldn't go in taxis with them. "I couldn't go on a bus with them without sitting in the back," he said. "The thing that got to me was fighting the feeling of being less than, of being not as good as . . . then having to go out there and perform. It just tore me up."

It was his worst of times. He almost didn't hit at all. "I just wanted to go home," Wills said.

He had spent five seasons in the minor leagues and his career had hit the wall. What saved him was that in those years the Dodgers had 15 minor–league teams and keeping a marginal shortstop who could run was cheap.

The Dodgers loaned him to the Tigers and the Tigers sent him back. The Topps Company, the company that makes baseball trading cards, passed on him.

When times were bleakest, he was 26 years old and playing at the Dodgers' Spokane farm team in the Pacific Coast League. The great northwest was not all that great either. It was all right to have white friends, but he shouldn't expect to buy a house near them. When he had a real estate broker buying a home for him, the question the broker was asked was how black Wills was. Wills is a light skinned black man, for whatever that's worth.

He was also light hitting, which was worth less in the baseball marketplace. Wills's nickname was Mouse, which identified his physical size. He was not a slugger. As fast as he was, he couldn't steal first base. But speed always fascinates; it can't be taught. Above everything, speed was Wills's asset.

Bragan was fired as Cleveland manager in the middle of the 1958 season and soon after became the Spokane manager. He understood the difficulty of surviving as a light–hitting shortstop because he had been one himself with the Phillies in the war years of the 1940s. Later in Brooklyn he was remade into a backup catcher. As one of his last acts as an executive, Branch Rickey hired Bragan as manager of the Pittsburgh Pirates. In Brooklyn and as a catcher, Bragan's view of baseball and of life had broadened.

One thing he observed was that a left–handed hitter gained two steps toward first base. And he noticed Wills fooling around in the batting cage, swinging left–handed.

On his good advice, Wills became a switch–hitter. No, he couldn't steal first base, but he wouldn't be driven off the plate by a right–hander's curveball, and batting left–handed he could beat out a lot of ground balls to the infield. His speed would make infielders play a step closer to the plate and he could rush them into making errors.

"Bobby and I have been so close since 1958 when he put his arms around me and said the one thing that was keeping me from the big leagues," Wills said. "We corrected it and—boom—I went out and had an outstanding year. Otherwise I would have withered away in the minor leagues."

By June, the middle of the 1959 season, Wills was moved up to be the Los Angeles Dodgers shortstop. When the Dodgers played in Cincinnati he and veteran black teammates Jim Gilliam and John Roseboro didn't join the white players when they went across the river to Kentucky, where hot times were cooking in Covington. "I heard about it, but I could never go," Wills said. "I knew that I did not want to try to go. I was at home with my teammates and we did not want to get into trouble. We did not get exposed to a lot of stuff."

In the meantime he was leading the league in stolen bases the first of six seasons in a row. He ran the Dodgers to the 1959 World Series championship against the Chicago White Sox. Luis Aparicio was the celebrated thief of the White Sox and Wills turned the series into man against man. Wills redefined the modern game of base running. He was an intimidating force. He made the pitcher and the defense constantly concerned by his presence.

In the four–game sweep of the Yankees in the 1963 World Series, he stole only one base but it led to both Los Angeles runs in the first inning of the second game and was the likely turning point of the series. He singled and took an audacious lead off first base and broke for second while pitcher Al Downing still had the ball. Downing threw to first and first baseman Joe Pepitone's hurried throw to second was wide. When Gilliam singled, Wills's bold turn around third base drew a throw that enabled Gilliam to advance to second. In the manner of Jackie Robinson, Wills threatened to steal home, forcing Downing to rush his motion, and Willie Davis doubled two runs home. It was the kind of running game Wills had learned from the red–eyed men with the hip–pocket bottles in those Sunday hangover games he watched as a kid.

For the opportunity to take that game to the big leagues, Wills gives credit to Bragan. "Bobby is a great man," Wills said. Bragan, longtime president of the Texas League, founded a youth foundation in Fort Worth that gives scholarships to young people of all backgrounds. One year he honored Rachel Robinson, Jackie's widow; Charlie Pride, the first black in the Country Music Hall of Fame; and Wills, Fort Worth's first black player.

In August 2005 Wills served as coach for Bragan's one–night celebration as manager of the Fort Worth Cats of the Central League. At 87, Bragan became the oldest man to manage in professional baseball. Wills, at 74, walked onto the field with a *Seeing* Eye dog, mocking Bragan.

"He is a great man," Wills said. "History says he was one of the guys who signed the petition against Jackie. I do know Bobby said he didn't know any better at the time. He thought that was how he was supposed to feel. I know he put his arms around me. He had come to peace with himself, to terms with his previous thinking."

What Bragan saw in Wills and what his encouragement produced for the Dodgers was a revelation. *Los Angeles Times* columnist Jim Murray wrote that watching the Dodgers hit was "like watching paint dry." Watching Wills on the bases was pastel paint. The Dodgers' offense meant a run manufactured out of Wills's legs, good clutch hitting—probably by Tommy Davis—and the pitching of Sandy Koufax and Don Drysdale. The impact of Wills's running was such that in 1961, when the Dodgers and Giants tied for first place in the National League and were forced into a league playoff, the Giants watered the area around first base in San Francisco into a bog to prevent Wills from getting a lead. The Giants won the playoff but Wills was the league's MVP.

Contract negotiations with the Dodgers and Buzzie Bavasi, the general manager, didn't have a racial component, but they did demonstrate circumstances that ultimately led to the official arbitrator granting free agency. "I was the Hickok Athlete of the Year," Wills said, "I stole 104 bases. And I figured now I can get that raise. I came out of Buzzie's office happy I was still on the team. He gave me a $20,000 raise and told me I better not tell anybody."

Sometimes to settle an argument Bavasi would write numbers on pieces of paper he held, one in each hand, and ask a player to pick one. This was in the time before players were permitted to have an agent negotiate. The player would pick the content of one hand, which would be his salary. Bavasi would destroy the other. The player would never know whether the two hands held identical figures. "Buzzie got over on us and we still liked him," Wills said.

The racial issue, however, had not disappeared. Wills and Sandy Koufax, known as the Jewish Walter Johnson, would open each other's hate mail in the clubhouse. When Koufax chose to honor the Jewish holiday of Yom Kippur by moving his turn to pitch, Wills wished him "Good *yom tov*, Sandy." Koufax replied, "Happy New Year, Mouse." They had a common bond. "Sandy understood," Wills said. "We kind of knew his deal, too."

Wills was playing for Pittsburgh when Bobby Kennedy was assassinated in 1968. It was a national day of mourning and most major-league teams canceled their games. The Pirates were in Houston, which was one of the places that did not cancel. Wills grew up as a Democrat and had high regard for what John and Robert Kennedy had done for young people and black people. "I felt they had been there for me," Wills said. He asked the manager for permission to sit out that game and was refused. He sat out anyway. Wills and Larry Shepard, the manager, had harsh words about that, and the club fined Wills. It was an early bit of Wills's insight into himself as a black man.

⁂

Wills's brief term as the third black manager in the major leagues did not help the Seattle Mariners in the pennant race. Neither did it promote Wills as a manager. He took over the Mariners in last place late in the 1980 season, called them the "Maury Wills Mariners" and promised they would steal into contention. The Mariners did not pay attention to Wills's unorthodox concepts in spring training and often it appeared that Wills was not paying attention to much of anything.

The man who was lauded for the nuance of his game, once submitted a lineup card with two men listed at the same position. Another time he went down the bench and called to pinch–hit a player he had sent to the minors. Once Tom Paciorek hit a home run only to be called out for batting out of turn. Wills's time as manager was so unpleasant that he believes his clubhouse man purposefully told Oakland manager Billy Martin of that mistake, and that Wills had illegally elongated the batters box. Wills was fired 24 games into the 1981 season.

During the period between his stardom as a player and his chance to manage, Wills began to take his first steps into addiction to cocaine. He says in his book *On the Run* with Mike Celezik that what really distracted him and led to his failure as a manager was a disastrous love affair. In the aftermath of being fired, his cocaine use cost him a chance to rebuild his managing career, his fortune, and almost his life. In his fog he lost his Most Valuable Player trophy, the Hickock Belt, and an estimated $1.6 million. He was sleeping on a mattress on the floor, waiting for his pension check so he could buy more drugs.

As hard as getting to the big leagues had been for him, overcoming his addiction was harder. In 2002 he was honored as Man of the Year by Baseballers Against Drugs for his involvement in Hugs Not Drugs.

The years of being consumed by playing the game are typical of many athletes who lose sight of their roots. Perhaps for Wills, stardom after the long struggle was his path to addiction. With his celebrity in Los Angeles, Wills sought and found what used to be called wine, women, and song.

"Life got better in the big leagues, I have to admit," Wills said. "It was a kind of utopia. I had been so sheltered. I had a better living than I ever imagined, people were making a fuss over me. I was comfortable, pampered as a star, celebrated. I kind of lost touch with reality.

"I couldn't understand the Watts riots of 1965; I stole 94 bases that year, had 11 hits in the World Series; everything was fine. I had no idea what was going on. I kind of grew up after that."

When Curt Flood refused to accept being traded and went off to live and paint in Europe, Wills said he didn't understand how Flood had the courage to defy baseball. "I think that was a shortcoming of mine," Wills said. "I never had that inner strength; that's why I didn't make it at Fort Worth in 1955." He said he had been late coming to involvement with anything beside himself. The civil rights movement was not his concern.

Yes, he conceded, "I do feel guilty about that. You bringing that up. I'm getting a chance to dump that by talking about it. That's some inner stuff. I never had anybody I did want to talk to about it."

12

Forever Is Not Too Long to Wait

Emmett Ashford Umpires Alone

*(Born Los Angeles, California, November 23, 1914.
Died Venice, California, March 1, 1980.)*

IT COULD ALMOST BE FUNNY if it wasn't so cruel. Emmett Ashford umpired in the minor leagues summers and winters for 15 years—a lifetime in real time—believing against reality that his chance in the sun would come. At 55, the age most big–league umpires have established themselves in their lonely calling and have begun to think of retirement, he was a rookie. Opening Day 1966 in Washington, D.C., was going to be his Opening Day. The Washington Senators were opening at home and embattled president Lyndon Johnson had sent the vice president, Hubert Humphrey, to throw out the first ball. But just a moment.

Ashford, who had survived a route that would have sent most men back to private life in tears, was up for the game. His smiles were real smiles of joy. He had never given up, and he had made it. He was dressed in a suit and tie. Even in the dusty minor leagues he was known for always dressing for the occasion.

He was about to enter RFK Stadium when he was halted by the vice president's Secret Service detail. They knew there was no such thing as a black umpire in the big leagues.

Not until then. Eighteen years after Jackie Robinson gave dawn to the time of the black baseball player, no black man had been accepted as a major–league umpire. Ashford had umpired since 1951, getting

as high as Triple A in the Pacific Coast League. That was a pretty big thing for an umpire before the big leagues moved west, but it wasn't the big leagues.

"He never did give up; he never showed discouragement," his daughter Adrienne Ashford Bratton said. Her biography of her father, *Strrr–ike!!,* is a loving piece of work. A man can constantly show his hopeful side to his daughter and even to the public, but how does anyone know what he feels when he lies in bed in the dark?

"It took me a long time and often I did get discouraged," he conceded years later. He was most discouraged when he was closer to the top than he knew. He had been chief umpire in the Pacific Coast League for four years. He was 50 years old and that appeared to be his last stop. "After 15 years you have to figure you're licked," he told his wife, Margaret. "Maybe it's time to quit. I can't go on umpiring in the desert for a few hundred dollars a month."

And, as he told it, she said, "I didn't marry a quitter. You'll make the big leagues." Late in 1965 the American League bought his contract. After all the discouragement, he was going to be a major–league umpire.

It was harder than outsiders cared to know. "Even though players have been boiling over at me," he said many years later, "there's never been a racial slur." Do we believe that, too? He did always show joy for his work, and joy hides a lot of insult.

Unlike Larry Doby, who was new and tender to the lash, Ashford knew about bigotry from the first day he tried to be an umpire. But does a man ever become inured to that kind of thing? And unlike the player who has some support from the framework of the team, being an umpire is the loneliest work.

Ashford's tryout was at Mexicali of the Class C Southwest International League in a game between the home team and Yuma. The umps who were assigned to work with him walked off rather than work with a black partner, and umpires had to be found in the local semipro league. Before that, he had chosen to work in the postal service for a number of years because a colored man had a good chance of promotion there.

He gave up the security of the post office and was rewarded with this insult.

⸰⸰⸰

Ashford's first assignment after being hired as the first black umpire in organized baseball was in El Paso, Texas, in the midst of a long–lasting feud between teams. There were two cops on the field before the game began and eight more were summoned before the first inning was over. And one fan—a black fan at that—yelled, "We don't need you around here doing a white man's job."

To which the new black umpire responded: "Sir, if you go home and put your brains, manners, and shoes on and come back, I'll discuss it with you."

Umpires are still umpires—men in darkest blue, no matter what color they are. Ballplayers, whatever their stripe, have the companionship of winning and losing, and they have the comfort of home stands when they can live in their own homes with their own families. Umpires have only enemies on both sides, and they're always on the road. What traveling companions they may have are other umpires. Sometimes, for various reasons, they have no companions. There were always those who felt the profession should be kept white and grim. Ashford was neither.

"Nobody's in his corner," one perceptive white American League player observed back then. Umpire Ashford had no PeeWee Reese, no Joe Gordon, no Gary Bell with him in the foxhole.

As delighted or vindicated as Ashford may have felt to be elevated to the biggest time, the reality of his position was yet to come to him. It was reasonable for a man who had been around for 18 years, and who had witnessed the gradual acceptance of black players, to think he would be accepted as well by his fraternity of peers—the other umpires. "They froze him out," Frank Robinson contradicted. Robinson had been a most steely competitor in a Hall of Fame career. The umpires did not escape his fury. However, he observed what went on around him. He saw how the umpires treated their own, which hardly included Ashford.

"They wouldn't really work with him as part of the team on the field," Robinson said. "They made him kind of an individual out there. In the dressing room they wouldn't talk to him. On and off the field they wouldn't associate with him. When they walked on the field he was always the last one behind. If he was involved in an argument, they wouldn't come to his defense. He was on his own."

Managers—all of them were white then—were faced with accepting the authority of a black umpire, which they had rarely experienced. They insisted, as one manager said, "I see a bad call and I argue. I'm not thinking if the guy is white or colored." If all the managers who railed at Ashford were indeed color–blind, it would be contradictory to all the history of whites and blacks in baseball to that time.

Ashford was, like all umpires, subject to the anger of players and managers who always perceived plays as they wanted them. People give guff to people who take guff. Players and managers criticized Ashford with comments they wouldn't dare make to other umpires because he was slow to throw them out and never carried a grudge. Some black players felt Ashford tried so hard to appear fair that he gave an advantage to white players.

Black players could be cruel to their own in the way black players in the National Basketball Association referred to a black referee as "Ray Charles," and then "Stevie Wonder," sightless black entertainers. One important black player at the time—a stand–up man (who asked not to be identified on this issue)—maintained that Ashford had "terrible judgment, one of the worst."

Players and especially umpires resented Ashford's style. He was a cheerful little man, small as umpires go. His disposition stood out among those who wear a scowl as routinely as the protective mask. He was flamboyant in a job that traditionally called for its practitioners to be as cheerful as undertakers. Perhaps he was a product of the generations of black comedians who made a living playing to white audiences.

When the young female groundskeeper in Baltimore gave him a playful pat on the seat of the pants with her broom in the 1970 World Series, as she had with visiting third basemen and third base coaches for several seasons, Ashford jumped up in the air in mock surprise.

"It's been said that I add something to a game and that it makes the fans happy," Ashford said. "Just because we're dressed in blue doesn't mean we're in charge of a funeral. And nobody has more fun than I do."

The fans liked his sense of humor, going back to the earliest of minor–league days. All the world, it is said, loves a clown. It is also noted that baseball is a game except for the players. Add the self–important umpires.

One time in Anaheim, after the umpires' pregame meeting at the plate with the managers broke up, Ashford raced down the third–base line, leaped onto the bag and bounded out to left field as he did every day. Then suddenly John Rice, a member of the umpiring crew, leaped over the mound, jumped on second base and waved his arms wildly as he darted about on the outfield grass. The umpires weren't smiling among each other. Rice was putting down Ashford for his style and his enthusiasm. The next season Rice and Ashford were placed on separate umpiring crews.

"When you're black and do the things he does, you're a clown, a performer," an insightful black player said. "If you're white, you're colorful." In Ashford's time, Ron Luciano's flamboyant umpiring style was considered colorful.

But was Ashford the worst umpire? The player who thought he would be courting the wrath of the other umpires if he was identified, named several he thought worse. "I think Ashford hurts himself by being noticeable. He takes too much guff from everybody," he said. When one manager showered Ashford with vulgarity in front of a full dugout, the umpire responded, "You shouldn't talk like that."

"I just wish I could run into him away from the field," the star player said. "I'd tell him to kick guys out—kick me out—but get tough."

❖

There was a more tangible price to be paid for living the six months of the baseball season as one black umpire with three white umpires. If they were equal, they were also separate. There were whispers that he did not seek the help of the others on difficult calls, his black experience teaching him to rely only on himself. Or was it really the other way around?

Frank Robinson, an honorable man then in his Hall of Fame playing career, recalled that when Ashford needed a little help, the other umpires turned their back to him and left him unprotected.

One time he was involved in a scene with a furious third baseman who called Ashford some things only a saintly black man would absorb. Ashford took it, even after the second–base umpire strolled into hearing range. Rather than try to calm the matter, the newly arrived umpire just listened to the abuse. When the third baseman demanded, as ballplayers will, what business was it of his, the second umpire responded, "I just like to hear you talk."

Ashford was 5' 7" tall and about 185 pounds, and he wore cufflinks peeking from under his dark blue sleeves. Cufflinks?

His uniform was always pressed, his shoes spit shined. On the south side of Los Angeles he learned which polishes made the best shine and which brushes were right and which neighborhoods provided the most business.

His father had left when Emmett was a year old, and Emmett had to earn money to go to college. He learned attention to detail and a sense of bearing in the midst of what often was a hostile environment. They were the foundations of the skills that enabled him to build a career in the midst of a crowd screaming that he was wrong. Like Harry Truman, Ashford decided early that he didn't want to be a ballplayer; he was an umpire.

He ran to and from his position on tiptoes. He ran to be in position to make his calls. When he had to evade a ground ball, he did a little bunny–hop. When he had to dodge a line drive, he did a pirouette. He brushed the plate with élan, ending up on one foot.

He had three distinct signals for called strikes: He swept his right hand out to the side and up, and when it got straight overhead, he brought it down like a cleaver. Or he reached up and gave his fist two short tugs as if pulling a train whistle. His classic stroke was for a third strike, reaching out to the side with that right fist and yanking it swiftly as if slamming a taxi door.

They were stylizations he polished in those years paying dues in the minors, charming away the hostility of fans and often players, too. Once he was faced with no place to stay in a southwestern minor-league city. So he called at the best whites–only motel in town. "Sir," he said to the owner, "I'm that barefoot and uncultured Negro man you have been reading about. I wish to seek lodging in your handsome establishment." He got a superior room. He knew how to play ball when others were making the rules.

Life in the minor leagues demanded that Ashford be assertive. He was a black man and he was an umpire in a distinctly vulnerable position. He recalled that first assignment with the teams and fans roiling all night in El Paso, Texas. It was his first confrontation with the South. Ashford called both managers together. As he described it, he said: "I know where I am," I told them. "And I know what I'm up against. But if I have to leave this field, I'm going with my boots on. The guy that makes me leave is going to lose, 9–0, on a forfeit."

"The next day the El Paso papers were very kind to me. And when I returned to the park for the next game, I got a standing ovation."

In the Pacific Coast League, distinctly not in the South, Ashford was involved in a lingering conflict in a game in Portland. The next day the manager, who was convinced Ashford's call had cost him the previous game, handed him the lineup card and said: "It's not you I'm mad at, Emmett, it's those two other guys."

The crew chief, Cesar Carlucci, who worked nearly 1,000 games with Ashford, interrupted. "What are you talking about?" he said.

"Not you, those other two," the manager said.

"Who the hell are those other two?"

"Abe Lincoln for freeing them and Branch Rickey for bringing them into baseball."

Bill Valentine, who worked two years with Ashford in the Pacific Coast League and another year on the same crew in the American League, recalled that most of the veteran umpires had no use for him.

Some players thought he was too small to call balls and strikes over the catcher and that he often anticipated a call when a curveball was still breaking. Some managers thought he missed calls in the outfield or on tag plays in the infield because he was constantly in motion. Over–hustle, they called it.

Some said he was held in the minors so long because he was black and others said he reached the big leagues only because he was black. In either case what suffering he did was in silence. "The league is maybe not concerned about him," a black player of great stature said. "Look at his age [51]. The heat is on him for four or five years, then the league figures it won't have to hire another black umpire."

He had worked too long and too hard to consider any negatives about his elevation. From the years of his youth he had been preparing to be more than ordinary. Shining shoes earned three years of college for Ashford. He was the first Negro president of the student body of his high school in Los Angeles. He liked to say he was the first Negro cashier in his neighborhood supermarket. Others were janitors and box boys; he handled money. He was determined to rise above the obstacles.

⋯⋮⋯

Ashford umpired five years in the American League, the retirement age pushed back a year so he'd qualify for a pension. On Ashford's death in 1980, when other black men had followed as umpires, Commissioner Bowie Kuhn's printed statement noted Ashford, "was sternly tested, but he was unshaken."

In his last season, at 56, Ashford worked the 1970 World Series, and he whitewashed the seasons of bitterness. "I look back on all that, on the people who told me they'd never let one on the field," he said. "Now here I am at the World Series. It has to be a source of satisfaction."

Emmett Ashford, big–league umpire, is buried in Cooperstown, New York, the home of the Baseball Hall of Fame. It's where he always wanted to be. Only he knew how difficult the road had been.

⋮

13

Most Valuable Attitude

Frank Robinson Made Them Better

(Born Beaumont, Texas, August 31, 1935–)

AT THE AGE OF 70, after 54 years in baseball, battling his way to the Hall of Fame, Frank Robinson is still an idealist, still the pioneer.

He is the only man to be voted Most Valuable Player in each league. However much the superstar he was, he may be the most underrated player in baseball history. He had the most profound influence in transforming a team into a winner—the Baltimore Orioles—in his half century. He was the first black manager; he was the Jackie Robinson of writing a lineup card. In his first time at bat as player–manager, he hit a home run. Nobody ever did that. He was also the first black manager to be fired.

He wasn't allowed into the movies in Ogden, Utah, in 1953. In 1966, the year he won the Triple Crown with the Orioles—with the best batting average, most home runs, and the most RBI—he was not recognized as a local baseball hero and was turned away as just another black face at a Baltimore movie house and told, "Your money's no good here."

He wore a bulletproof vest in the dugout when he was the manager of the San Francisco Giants because of sniper threats on his life. He has been fired three times as a manager and he did his best job when the Montreal Expos became the Washington Nationals in 2005, a most difficult job, guiding a bankrupt team moving from Montreal to a city

that had not had baseball in 30 years and holding it in contention until the last month of the season.

And still he spoke for more opportunity, not specifically for himself. "We will have gone full circle," he said, "when a black person is hired to manage a ball club and there's no reference to his color. We're still not even close to where we should be."

Willie Randolph was hired in 2005 to manage the Mets and the fact that he was a black man was an inescapable issue in the news. The ideal, as identified by Frank Robinson, would be for the stories to say: Willie Randolph was hired to manage the New York Mets. "End of story," he said.

Robinson's impact on the Orioles, one of the great teams of the last half century, was immediately demonstrated in spring training of 1966, his first spring after being traded to the Orioles. That was after his skills and his contributions to the Reds were denigrated by Cincinnati general manager Bill DeWitt, who engineered the trade. It was one of the most one-sided trades in modern baseball history. Robinson brought his star with him to Baltimore. He didn't wear it but that wasn't necessary. In a very early spring exhibition game he slid hard to break up a double play, and Hank Bauer, the hard-bitten manager from the Yankees tradition, noted with admiration: "He does that and pretty soon they're all doing it."

After finishing third the previous two years, the Orioles won the American League pennant and swept the World Series from the Dodgers. Frank Robinson was voted Most Valuable Player. In his six seasons with the team they won four pennants. He was the judge and chief prosecutor in the Orioles "kangaroo court," with which the players made fun of their own lapses in order to force themselves to pay attention at all times. They ridiculed mistakes they made on the field as well as blunders in tipping at the team hotel or wearing a garish wardrobe combination. He was the very rare athlete whose force of will and his example made others around him better. That this newcomer was put in charge indicated the respect his teammates had for him.

Consider that the Reds traded Robinson to the Orioles in a lopsided deal for a creditable but not outstanding pitcher, Milt Pappas, with the comment by DeWitt that Robinson, who was voted National League MVP at 26, was "an old 30." Five years earlier DeWitt had sought to cut Robinson's salary with the accusation that he didn't always hustle. In his 1988 book *Extra Innings*, Robinson said that Reds management regarded him and Vada Pinson as "a Negro clique" that was damaging to the morale of the team. It was overlooked that Pinson and Robinson had been treated coolly by their white teammates.

Cincinnati was one of the last National League cities to accept black players, even a superstar. Robinson's problem likely came from the fact that he was not a white superstar. He was Rookie of the Year in 1956 and the youngest starter on the National League All–Stars. As was the standard in Cincinnati, he and black teammates lived in a hotel for black people. And he spent his time in the company of those teammates who were older and some who had played in the Negro Leagues. They'd all go to a black club, drink a beer or whiskey, and young Robinson would peer through the haze of smoke, listening to their tales, and drinking Coke until his eyes burned. "I don't want another Coke in my life," he said. Those wise old heads taught him baseball and the facts of life.

At the same time Birdie Tebbetts, who was accused of saying no black pitcher would be a 20–game winner for him, gently tutored Robinson. Tebbetts held Robinson out against some of the better pitchers, sat next to him, and told him to study how they worked. He quietly corrected Robinson's mistakes. He pointed out to the press that pitchers knocked down Robinson "because he's colored," as they did with other blacks they knew wouldn't fight back.

Robinson became a formidable player with the Reds. In 1961 he batted .323 with 37 home runs and 124 RBI to lead the Reds to their first pennant since 1940. Robinson was elected Most Valuable Player. They clinched the pennant in Chicago, and Cincinnati was dancing in the streets when the Reds got off their plane and headed to a downtown club for a team party. Robinson and Pinson got out of their taxi at the club and as they went to the door the owner intercepted them. They couldn't come in. Negroes weren't welcome. It was 1961 in Cincinnati.

A woman in the crowd outside told the owner, "That's Frank Robinson and Vada Pinson." The owner decided those Negroes were all right for that night and could go in. "We walked in and we walked out the other door," Robinson recalled. "I wanted to be at that celebration with my teammates and there was nothing I could do about it except mess it up for the others. We went to a club where we knew we were welcome and celebrated by ourselves."

No teammate went to the door to welcome them. No white player on the Reds ever invited Robinson and Pinson to join him for a meal or a drink. To the contrary, it was Robinson and Pinson who invited Pete Rose, the brash rookie who was being shunned by the other Reds because he was taking the second–base job of their friend Don Blasingame.

⋯⋮⋯

Robinson was born in Beaumont, Texas, but grew up in Oakland, California, going to integrated but mostly black McClymonds High School, playing basketball with Bill Russell, and playing baseball for George Powles, the white American Legion coach who saw no color. When Jackie Robinson arrived in Brooklyn it had little impact on Frank Robinson because at 11 he wasn't aware that baseball had been all white.

Fourteen of the 25 players in Robinson's two years with Powles played professional ball. Robinson signed with the Reds and was sent to Ogden, which wasn't exactly the south but the Utah Mormons did not exactly welcome blacks either. In the reverse of other leagues, white players were housed with families in private homes while Robinson and Spanish–speaking Chico Terry shared a hotel room. Essentially, Robinson was 17 years old, away from home, and alone. "No white player reached out to me at Ogden," Robinson said, and he was determined not to tell his problems even to his mother. "I didn't try to mix with the white teammates at the time," he said. "I just wouldn't let anyone get close to me because I didn't want anyone to hurt me."

He just hit so well that the Reds advanced him, his experience and ability as yet unproven, to Double A the next season, mindlessly tried to convert him to a gangly and awkward second baseman, and quickly dropped him to Class A at Columbia, South Carolina. Columbia had never had a black player before, but it was a better place to be than Ogden. Trips to Georgia were not good, though. Each trip there meant going to Negro restaurants and eating in a hurry, unsatisfactory meals on the bus, beds too often at the YMCA, and hostile fans crying, "Nigger, go back to Africa."

Robinson had another terrific season worthy of promotion, but he hurt his shoulder in spring training with the Reds and was sent back to Columbia. He couldn't throw and he couldn't swing, and when his batting average fell to .190, three home fans became drunk and abusive. When the last out of the game was made, Robinson grabbed a bat and ran toward those fans before older and wiser Marv Williams, the other black Columbia player, held him back.

"I couldn't understand why people were this vicious," Robinson recalled.

Ernie White, the manager whose language suggested, deceptively, that he was racist, was furious when Robinson repeated what the drunks had said. He ran into the parking lot in pursuit and noted their license plate. He wrote a letter to the owner of the car, saying that if they ever doubted Robinson's courage White would arrange a meeting with him. Those people were not seen in the ballpark again.

The hostility of the community and the depression from staring at the walls, virtually isolated in his room, built to the point shortly afterward that when the team left for Charlotte, North Carolina, Robinson decided he was going home. Marv Williams decided he wasn't going to be the only black and said he wasn't going with the team either.

After considerable thought Robinson concluded he would be throwing away his whole life if he walked out. Both men decided to join the team and since the game they missed had been rained out, they hadn't officially missed anything. "No white player ever said to me, 'There is nothing we can do about it, but we want to let you know we think this is not right,'" Robinson recalled.

But this manager, Ernie White, had. And Frank Robinson had steeled himself to carry on. "You have to understand," he said. "This is why some blacks made it and some didn't—other than talent. If you could not overcome, you were going to fail. It made you angry inside, but you could not let it control you. We used to talk and say we had to be twice as good as the whites to be successful."

Actually, he was twice as good a player as almost anybody. He had a lifetime major league batting average of .294 over 21 seasons. His 586 home runs were fourth on the all–time list when he retired. As monumental as that was, his greater impact was described by Cincinnati relief pitcher Ted Davidson when Robinson was sent to Baltimore. Davidson lamented how he'd miss the feeling of coming in from the bullpen in a tight situation, looking toward right field, and seeing that guy shake his fist.

⬥

Going to Baltimore was another kind of revelation. It was a southern city that was closely tied to the Baltimore Colts and the great quarterback Johnny Unitas. In baseball season the team and the city belonged to Brooks Robinson, from Little Rock Central High School in Arkansas. Brooks was an incredible third baseman, a very tough out, and a charming fellow. He was MVP in 1964. How would Brooks and the players and fans who loved him accept the intrusion of this black star from the other league?

Frank recalls that he and the Orioles players were immediately comfortable with each other. He also recalls that some of the news people who covered the team were not. "The community accepted me as a player at the ballpark," Frank said pointedly. Barbara Robinson had a broker look for a condo for her, Frank, and the two kids, and when she showed up it seemed the owner had thought it was for Brooks and not Frank Robinson. No deal.

Owner Jerry Hoffberger, a first–class person, found a fine place, but it was in a black neighborhood. In another year, a builder's agent refused to sell to the Robinsons in an upscale white neighborhood because "the people across the street" objected to a black family. So Frank got an attorney to buy the house and turn it over to him. Barbara asked "the people across the street" if they objected to black neighbors. They said, not at all, and turned out to be fine neighbors. The builder's agent, who lived next door, did not speak with the Robinsons for the six years they owned the house.

The Orioles were a remarkably varied and compatible group of athletes, thoroughly receptive to Frank's aggressive National League transfusion that transformed them into the best team in the American League. Frank thinks that Brooks's influence was why, for the first time in Frank's baseball life, black players and white players had meals together and drinks together when they were on the road. Often.

Frank was unfamiliar with the cities in the American League and white Brooks would tell him where he and Boog Powell, or any of the other players were going. Frank and the other black players, Paul Blair and Sam Bowen, always knew where the white players were going and knew they'd be welcome. They liked talking baseball and they liked being Orioles together. It was a shame, he thought, that it had never happened to him before. And it would never happen to him on another team after Baltimore.

The tragic aspect—perhaps it was still part of the lingering 1950s thinking—was that the black players and white players never did get together socially in Baltimore. They never went together to a restaurant or to another player's home. They were close, Frank said, "but not that close."

Perhaps it was Frank's role as a leader on that team for him to arrange for teammates and wives to go out with him to a restaurant or to invite them to his home, but that was not what he had ever done. "I would have been afraid to," he said. "If one of the white players or his wife did not show up, it might have affected the Orioles as a ball club. I was always a team man above all else."

❖

Today, when a black player, a Latino such as Alex Rodriguez, or an attractive mixed–race player, such as Derek Jeter can be a marketing bonanza, it's noteworthy that when Robinson won the Triple Crown and was MVP in 1966, he made one television appearance and made only two speaking engagements, each paying $500. The next season, when white Carl Yastrzemski of the Red Sox won the Triple Crown and MVP, he had commercials worth more than $200,000.

As he was playing out his career, Robinson was maturing into something beyond the white lines of the baseball field. He is highly articulate and insightful. In Cincinnati, with the encouragement of then general manager Gabe Paul, he became a member of the NAACP. In 1968 Earl Weaver, the Orioles manager, encouraged Robinson to replace him as manager of Santurce in the Puerto Rico winter league. He took the job and began to look at his own future.

In the late 1950s, while he was blooming as a star, he made it his business to visit Jackie Robinson. "Just to pay my respects," he recalled when he was managing the San Francisco Giants. "Out of pure respect for what he had allowed me to be able to do."

The Robinsons—Jackie and Frank, elder and younger, icon and disciple—talked about how black Americans and black athletes conducted themselves, and how they always had to give it all they had. "I could never have done what Jackie did," Frank Robinson said, "I think I'm a very strong person, but I couldn't have put up with what he did."

Jackie's last public appearance was at the 1972 World Series in Cincinnati. He made an emotional appeal for baseball to finally name a black man a manager. Three weeks later he died at the age of 53, nearly blind and his body ravaged by diabetes. When Frank Robinson was named the Cleveland Indians manager in 1975, he wished Jackie could have been there.

❖

Opening Day against the Yankees was a great media event in itself. Then it rose to near–fictional dimensions. There were 58,000 fans in the stands and at the introductions Robinson received a greater ovation than any he could remember as a player. With one out in the home half of the first inning it was his turn to bat. He hit a home run. He called it aptly a "fairy–tale home run." He identifies that moment as his all–time thrill.

Managing the Indians was not quite so thrilling. To begin with, he had to be a player–manager at his playing salary because the Indians had to save every dollar they could and management knew he couldn't say no. "Somebody had to open that door; barriers need to be addressed," Robinson agreed. Give owner Ted Bonda credit for hiring him and recognition to general manager Phil Seghi for thrift; the Indians were not a team with deep pockets.

During his managing experience in Puerto Rico, Robinson's thorniest issues were with black players, namely Juan Pizarro, Joe Foy, and George Scott. At Cleveland he quickly had problems with Rico Carty, Blue Moon Odom, and Larvell Blanks, all three black, and Gaylord Perry—all cranky and white. Robinson thought those black players expected special consideration because their manager was black. That wouldn't have been true to Frank Robinson, the baseball man.

Perry had his own motives. Henry Aaron, once a teammate of Carty's, called another man "a ballplayer's ballplayer," meaning that he'd do anything to win. "Carty," Aaron said, was "his own ballplayer and would do anything to boost his own batting average."

Barbara Robinson said she and Frank had death threats before he managed his first game. "I was scared for him when he went to the ballpark, I was scared for him when he was sitting in the dugout, scared for him when he went to the mound because I didn't know what some nut may do," she said.

As a manager Frank Robinson changed what he could. For example, he had the identification of a players' race stricken from the Indians' scouting reports. His conflict with umpires was sharp as ever and most rancorous with Ron Luciano. Robinson says he now regrets his implication that their conflict was racially based.

Managing the Indians was inevitably a thankless job. It was also a painful job when Robinson felt he had to fire Larry Doby as coach. He thought Doby had not sufficiently supported previous manager Ken Aspromonte with the black players. Doby and Robinson did not speak again.

In 1976, his second year, Robinson led the Indians to their first season in 17 of winning more games than they lost. The third season got off to a stuttering start and Ted Bonda, the owner who had the nerve to hire the first black manager, noted that "anything that went wrong was blamed on the fact that he was black." The owner's support, however, did not override the influence of general manager Phil Seghi, once a minor-league manager.

When Carty stood up at a booster club luncheon, ripped the manager, and the general manager did not come to his defense, Robinson knew he was out there all alone. Then he became the first black manager to be fired.

He was afraid he'd never get another chance. It was the first time he'd failed in baseball. There were coaching jobs offered and even a managing job in the Baltimore minor-league system, but he regarded them as a step in the wrong direction. Fifty games into the 1981 season he was hired to take over the San Francisco Giants, he says, over the opposition of general manager Tom Haller. Robinson traded some players and reasoned with some others. He broke up the clique of evangelists who were known as the God Squad and sometimes explained a loss as "God's will." The manager maintained that religion was their conscience but the clubhouse was inappropriate for their sermonizing. He pushed the Giants up to second place in 1982, exciting management's expectations, and was fired in the middle of 1984 when the team didn't climb in the standings.

He felt he had been treated most unfairly by black umpires in the National League. He thought he was no harder on them than on white umpires but he believed black umpires expected him to go easier on them. He says he never regarded umpires as black, only as umpires, and he was doing his job. There is much of this theme throughout his career. It is still impossible to read men's minds to confirm or deny.

Robinson never stopped calling for managing opportunities for black men. A number of candidates were interviewed but almost all of the considerations were clearly eyewash. He thought the Reds deliberately lowballed Willie Randolph, knowing he could not accept their offer. The only sincere participants were the candidates themselves.

Robinson was given one more chance to manage in Baltimore in 1988, where he was still a magnetic name. The Orioles lost their first eight games of the season and Robinson replaced Cal Ripken Sr. as manager. The Orioles went on to lose a record 21 in a row. The next year, however, they stayed in the race until the last weekend of the season, finishing second, and Robinson was named Manager of the Year.

In 1990 he was named assistant general manager. The only black man to hold a higher position was Henry Aaron as minor–league director with the Braves. Robinson was on track to go on to become the first black general manager. Five years later the team was sold and Robinson was reshuffled out of the Orioles' front office and hired by the office of the commissioner. He was to be what he called "the lord of discipline." He was in charge of taking care of the bad stuff that happened on the field. "I liked the job; I didn't like disciplining the players," he reflected.

When Major League Baseball, the big corporation, took over operation of the financially failing Montreal Expos in 2002, Robinson was assigned to manage. It would never be that he was named to manage a team that had a chance to win from the beginning. But it was managing and that was important to him. He did breathe some life into the franchise, and when the Expos were moved to Washington, D.C., and renamed the Nationals for 2005, he somehow manipulated them into first place for a long period and kept them in the division race until the last weeks of the season. He accomplished that with a team that struggled to score as many runs as it allowed.

It's likely that he is a better manager now than he used to be. "That happens," he said. He sees that in this era of great impatience as a double–edged sword. "When we got to Washington, we weren't expected to win, but we were close for a long time," he said, "and then they expected us to win. Nowadays you have to win right away."

He's 70 years old and he'd love to get his first chance to be a general manager and make personnel evaluations and decisions for himself. He has interviewed for that role before. "An owner said to me, 'Well,

Frank, you're not well rounded on the player development side,'" Robinson said. "'Another thing is you don't have the experience in the front office.' Well, I was assistant general manager for five years. There's something wrong there."

Bob Watson has already been the first black general manager and he won the World Series with the Yankees in his first season in 1996. Robinson applauds George Steinbrenner for recognizing Watson's ability. When Robinson took over the Expos, Watson replaced him in the commissioner's office.

"I'm probably passed by for general manager now because of age," Robinson said. "You need five years and nobody's going to want a general manager who's 75 years old. Today they're in their 30s and 40s." And some are in their 20s.

Managing the Nationals is probably his last job in baseball. He's not going to walk off willingly or silently. He stood up for his ethics, against the cocaine epidemic of the 1980s and against steroid use today. He opposes reinstatement to baseball and admission to the Hall of Fame for his old friend Pete Rose because Rose broke the gambling rule—the first rule of the game.

Robinson still pushes with all his heart for black opportunity. "If I don't speak up and speak out, who will?" he said. "I think I owe that. I'd like to say I left the game a little better."

He was inducted into the Hall of Fame in 1982 on the same platform with Henry Aaron, the home–run king, and Happy Chandler, the commissioner who stood beside Branch Rickey against the 15 owners who sought to block Jackie Robinson's way. Roy Campanella, Jackie's teammate almost from the beginning, was there on that day. Aaron pointed him out and said Jackie and Campanella "proved to the world that a man's ability is limited only by his lack of opportunity."

Frank, in his acceptance speech, recognized Jackie's widow, Rachel, a glowing presence wherever she goes. "Without Jackie," he said, "I don't know if the door to baseball would have been open again for a long, long time. I know I couldn't have put up with what Jackie put up with."

Frank Robinson may have questioned his own ability to withstand the outrages of Jackie's time. Frank was a teenager with little experience in life when he set out into the baseball unknowns, which were only partly improved from Jackie's time. The evidence of a long and honored career says Frank Robinson, inspired by Jackie Robinson, would have endured to open his own doors.

❖

14

The Best of Them
Don't Always Understand

Tommy Davis Reminds the Dodgers of Their Heritage

(Born Brooklyn, New York, March 21, 1939-)

THE BROOKLYN DODGERS were the best of teams for a black kid think-ing he was going to be a baseball player. To begin with, they had Jackie Robinson, didn't they? And just as important, the Dodgers understood that the black players they signed after Jackie would probably mature better in the farm system if they weren't assigned to play in the hostil-ity of the South.

Not that the Yankees were chopped liver winning their champion-ships up in the Bronx, but Tommy Davis was a baseball player and he was a Brooklyn kid.

He was an exceptional baseball player at Boys High. He hit .480 as a senior, but high school baseball wasn't a big deal in New York, not nearly as big as basketball. Davis and Lenny Wilkens, who went on to the Basketball Hall of Fame, were stalwarts on the Boys High basket-ball team that went to the New York City semifinals in 1955 and 1956, played in "the world's most famous arena," Madison Square Garden. The city basketball championship was a big deal.

Black athletes in New York competed with and against white play-ers—no problem. The newspapers picked their all–city teams without distinction by color. Colleges in New York, which included Brooklyn,

had black players as stars for years. "In Brooklyn we went everywhere we wanted—no problems anyplace," Davis recalled.

Even the Yankees, who were late in signing black players and still had Elston Howard as their only nonwhite, wanted Davis. The Dodgers were the beloved team, having won five National League pennants in the previous nine seasons, but the Yankees kept beating them in the World Series. The Yankees were the Yankees.

It was in the years before baseball instituted its draft of young players and the Yankees courted Davis in his high school senior year. He worked out with the Yankees after school whenever he wanted, before night games or on weekends so regularly that the Yankees reserved a locker for him among Mickey Mantle and Yogi Berra and all those greats. Davis loved Moose Skowron, the Yankees' muscular first baseman. "The Yankees made me feel good," Davis said. "They weren't going to give me a lot of money but they did give me a lot of attention. They had me."

But Al Campanis, the Dodgers' top scout, kept coming around the house. It wasn't until many years later when the Dodgers had moved to Los Angeles that Campanis, as general manager, created the firestorm with his unfortunate remarks on television about blacks not having all the "necessities" to be managers and baseball executives. Obviously, blacks could play the game but Campanis was saying, essentially, that they didn't have the intelligence to meet the demands of a manager or general manager or third–base coach. At that time Al Campanis was a highly regarded judge of talent.

Davis had concluded that he might have been a fine high school basketball player but he was neither tall enough at 6'2" nor had the outside shot for big–time college basketball. Wilkens, his good friend, was going to Providence College, and Birdie Tebbetts, the Cincinnati Reds manager who was a Providence graduate, was offering Davis a scholarship to Providence if he signed with the Reds. He could play minor–league baseball after high school graduation and the Reds would pay for his college education in the off–season. He could go to school with his friend Lenny, if he accepted Tebbetts's offer to sign with the Reds. No way, Davis thought, was he going to play baseball in Cincinnati.

He had agreed to sign with the Yankees on a Tuesday night, but Campanis, who wouldn't give up on his pursuit of Davis, had Jackie Robinson, playing his last season, phone on Sunday night. Davis recalls the moment almost 50 years later as if he were still a 17–year–old fan. He answered the phone. The Yankees had Mantle and championship rings, but in Brooklyn Jackie was like a figure out of mythology, especially to a black family. "He had that high–pitched voice," Davis said. "He talked about the advantages of the Dodgers organization. All he had to do was say three or four words and I was gone."

Everybody at home wanted a chance to speak with their hero. Davis passed the phone. "Hey, Pop, it's Jackie Robinson. Talk to him." And his mother had her input.

"I wasn't going to get that much money from anybody so my mother said, what the heck, you're a Brooklyn boy and you love Jackie," Davis said. Tuesday afternoon, the day he was expected to sign with the Yankees, at age 17, he signed with the Dodgers in 1956. Tommy Davis was going to play with Jackie Robinson's team. (Davis lives in the Los Angeles area, where we talked, but he sounded wistful when he spoke of growing up in Brooklyn and said he missed the New York sense of humor.)

❖

The Dodgers treated black players, young and old, with some understanding of their special circumstance. Universities in the South were still stiffly resisting black athletes at the time, knuckling under to the pressures of racist alumni and segregated communities, and so much of baseball's minor leagues played in the South. With the Dodgers' integrationist history, owner Walter O'Malley converted an available naval air base in Vero Beach, Florida, into a spring training base and called it Dodgertown.

They were housed together, white and black, but there wasn't much to do. The only available movie house for the black players was in a town called Gifford, which was hardly the Brooklyn Paramount. What

Davis thought he knew about segregation was what he read about or saw in the movies. "I sort of understood I was going to the South, but Jackie had already integrated the game so I thought it would be a little more easy."

Robinson's integration into Brooklyn was at the far end of the rainbow. What young Tommy Davis experienced was the real–life tradition of the South. Real life was as explained by Ed Charles, who had been through the minor leagues: "Jackie integrated the major leagues; we integrated baseball."

The big team worked out on the same fields as Davis and the minor leaguers in Vero for the first weeks and then moved to segregated Miami for most of the exhibition schedule. Then the minor leaguers filled the Vero Beach facilities. During the exhibition schedule, the big team played a handful of games in Holman Stadium in Vero and the young ones basked in the aura of seeing the Dodgers seated among them in the dining room.

The town of Vero Beach had its own separate customs and the northern snowbirds only reinforced them. Davis recalls that on his own he might have refused to go to the back of the bus and might have had trouble. But older black players taught Davis lessons about survival in the South he still recalls: "Don't be too rambunctious out there because you never know. If I'm in a situation where I'm going to get hurt, get out of there real quick. This is their place; you do the things you have to do. Your thing is to play ball; don't let anything distract you."

Few players quit the Dodgers and went home because they couldn't or wouldn't cope with the indignity of segregation. Davis gives credit for retaining players to the Dodgers. "Because of Jackie, they had a special feeling toward black people," Davis said. "They made it more comfortable."

Among other things, owner Walter O'Malley recognized that black players had to go as far as Stuart to play golf because, as Davis remembers, the snowbirds didn't want them on the course. "So Walter built a golf course for us," Davis said. Knowing that the black players had difficulty getting around when they left the sanctuary of Dodgertown, Buzzie Bavasi, the general manager, rented cars for the black players.

The Dodgers recognized that America still accepted black players grudgingly in 1956 so Davis was sent to begin his career at the Dodgers' farm team in Hornell in upstate New York. Black players had been there before without incident. Davis's introduction was as smooth as a 17–year–old just out of high school could have it.

The next season at Kokomo, Indiana, in the Midwest League, however, was the initiation to harsh reality. Davis and teammate Willie Ivory, who had played in the Negro Leagues, went to a restaurant and were ignored for a half hour. When Davis questioned the wait, Ivory said they'd better leave. Davis remembers that the cook had a cleaver in his hand. Indiana, it should be recalled, had been the northernmost outpost of the Klan.

On the road in Dubuque, Iowa, where a black person was a rarity, a little boy asked his mother if Davis was what she called a "nigger."

The value of the words of wisdom at Dodgertown from the older players about not being distracted was clear as Davis led the Midwest League with a .357 batting average, 115 runs scored, and 104 RBI. He also stole 68 bases on sheer speed with no base–running technique.

That earned him the mixed blessing of promotion from Class D to Double A Victoria in the Texas League, and the advice from Bavasi that he would have to control himself in the face of an often racially hostile atmosphere.

Almost all black players introduced to Texas or other stops in the South had the experience of having to eat on the bus and sleep in awkward places. Each had its subtle distinction, sometimes laughable.

Nat Peoples, then 40, another veteran of the Negro Leagues was still the fastest thing in the league and was romping in a three–game series against Davis's team in Victoria's intimate little ballpark. It was small enough for individual voices to be picked out of the grandstand. As Davis recalled, Peoples was rapping out doubles, triples, and stealing bases. "Peoples is hitting, he's standing behind the back line of the batter's box," Davis said. "And you could hear loud and clear some guy shouting: 'Mr. Umpire. Mr. Umpire. Can you please keep the nigger's foot in the box.'" Davis, with a New Yorker's sense of humor, remembers laughing like anything.

Another time in the Victoria outfield Davis let a ball go through his legs—admittedly, he was not at any stage a Gold Glove outfielder—and was chasing it back to the fence. "And I could hear somebody in the stands yelling, 'Nigger, don't even come back. Jump over the fence and don't come back,'" Davis recalled.

Another incident he recalls that was less than funny was when there was a disturbance in the ballpark in Houston and police were on the field. "The home–plate umpire says to the cop, 'It was the nigger in the red sweater up there; he's the one. Get him.'"

The authority on the field, which was the umpire, had now acted as judge and jury and sent the police authority to single out and punish "the nigger in the red sweater." It was racial profiling before the term was coined.

This was what black people in Victoria, Texas, lived through every day of their lives. "Oh my God!" Davis remembered as his reaction. "It was the first experience of my life like that. My thoughts were that I was going take what they were going to give me and hit the ball so good that they'd remember my name."

The better he did on the field, the sooner he'd be out of Texas, he thought; when he was in the big leagues, Victoria would see his name in the newspaper and remember him. In the meantime, he was living in a room over a nightclub in the black part of town with a rag stuffed around the door because it had no lock. Often fights spilled out of the club. "I didn't like it, but I enjoyed myself among my people," he said. "Other times I was scared, too."

When white teammate Don Miles invited him to join him and his wife at the movies in Victoria, Davis said thanks, but he couldn't go to the movies in town. "He was willing to take me to the movies," Davis said, "but I said I was not going to put him in that position."

Just how wide bigotry was spread in 1958 was apparent while Davis was playing winter ball in Venezuela. Davis and manager Pete Reiser and his wife went to the popular Del Lago Hotel. The hotel manager happened to be a Texan who said in no uncertain teams that Davis could not use the swimming pool. "And this was a brown country," Davis said. "Reiser said, 'If he can't go swimming, then we can't go swimming because my wife is Jewish.'"

He also laughs at himself telling how this streetwise New Yorker with a false sense of security was conned into a three–card monte game—which one is the red card? He was walking down the street, comfortable in the black neighborhood in San Antonio when a black fellow asked Davis where he could find girls.

Another black fellow arrived and, Davis recalled, he had "a big roll of money, a Texas roll, looked like a lot of money. The guy says, 'Hey, man, did you ever play three–card monte?' I'm crazy. I'm young." A black man, he thought, wouldn't cheat another black man, would he?

"We go behind this building," Davis said, "and he says, give me $20 to get started. After I'm down about $60, I realize, these guys just did a thing on me and I want to get out. I go back around the corner and a big black guy—about that big [Davis spread his hands as wide as a doorway]—appears in case I started something. I was never so scared in my life and I learned my lesson. I got away clean."

One of the things to be learned is that people who take advantage of other people can be white or black and there is no sympathy afforded to the victim, white or black. Davis swears he later saw the guy with the Texas roll in Times Square in New York.

Perhaps Davis remembers his time in the Texas League as reasonably comfortable because he did so well on the playing field. The next season he led the Pacific Coast League in hitting. In four seasons in the minors he twice led the league in hitting. He was going to the Dodgers. In 1960 they were in Los Angeles, leaving Brooklyn to its aching nostalgia, but they were still the Dodgers. In his third and fourth seasons he was the National League batting champion. He was able to separate the job of being a baseball player from the insults around him. If the real estate ad in the good Los Angeles neighborhood turned out to be for an apartment that "was just filled" by the time he showed up, he went to work and hit.

In 1962 he had 230 hits and drove in 153 runs, the most in 25 years, with only 27 home runs. "Every time Tommy came up with a man on second, he drove him in with a single; when he came up with a man on first, he drove him in with a double," said pitcher Sandy Koufax, who was often the beneficiary of Davis's hitting.

In spring training when the Dodgers moved their quarters from Dodgertown to Miami and a whites–only hotel, the black players stayed in another part of town at the Sir John Hotel. Black entertainers who came to Miami to perform for white audiences stayed at the Sir John. Cannonball Adderly and his jazz group stayed there, and Davis went to the concerts. There was no real curfew and the players were treated like royalty.

"Then we had to go through this integration thing," Davis recalled. The team said it had worked out a plan with the downtown hotel and told the black players the Dodgers would now stay together as a team in the previously whites–only McAllister Hotel. Davis felt they were losing out on a good thing and their first impulse was to say no thanks. "We said, 'That's OK, we'll stay here,'" Davis said. He and the other black players didn't want to miss the welcome freedom they'd enjoyed at the Sir John and in the black neighborhood. "But we knew we had to go there because of the fact of it." They knew, like it or not, it was an important thing for black players to be staying where no blacks had been accepted before.

In 1961, when the Florida segregation laws were breaking down, Walter O'Malley's son, Peter, was coordinator of spring training. All the time Jackie had been there, Holman Stadium was segregated even though it was on a military base. There were separate bathrooms and black and white water fountains, and all the black fans sat in the most remote right–field corner.

So Tommy Davis, John Roseboro, Jim Gilliam, Maury Wills, and Willie Davis went to Peter and pointed out that it had been nearly 15 years since the Dodgers blessed the debut of Jackie Robinson and there was still a black–white separation in the stadium. "Peter said, 'What?'" Davis recalled. "Like it had never dawned on him. The next day all that crap was gone, whitewashed away.

"When people came to the next exhibition game, we [Davis, Rose-boro, Gilliam, Wills, and Willie Davis] bodily walked through the black people and told them to go sit in left field. They said, 'No. No.' I took them by the hand, said they should sit in left field or anyplace they wanted. All the guys did that; we sat them all over the damn field. And that was the integrating of Holman Stadium."

Like many well–meaning people, the Dodgers management just hadn't understood how oppressive the rules had been. And the black fans that had been relegated to the distant corner of the stadium and accepted it had been down so long they couldn't grasp that they had been given a way up.

❖

Tommy Davis's career was on a path straight up. In 1963 he won his second batting title and hit .400 in the World Series, and the Los Ange-les Dodgers pulled off a stunning four–game sweep of the Yankees. Unlike many of the best hitters, Davis stole bases and was noted as one of the hardest sliders in the hard–sliding National League.

Early in 1965 he severely broke his ankle and a career that appeared headed for the Hall of Fame was suddenly restricted. He could never run again as before. The stride of his batting stroke was altered. He was never a .320– or .340–hitter again. As it was, his career lasted 18 years with nine teams and Davis left his mark as a remarkable clutch hitter.

He remembers that the most severe racist incident he experienced came after his playing career, when he was scouting for the Dodgers. In 1988 he went to see 19–year–old wunderkind Ken Griffey Jr. play-ing at Bakersfield, a throwback of the redneck Old South in northern California. "These hillbillies were on Junior pretty good and these guys were saying, meet them in the parking lot after the game," Davis said. "I saw what was happening and after the game—I'll be damned—these guys were there looking for Griffey."

If Griffey had ventured into the parking lot alone, those guys were waiting to beat him up. Who knows what weapons they were ready to use? Davis went back to get help and Griffey emerged with four teammates. "Those guys went back to their cars but they were ready to do something," Davis said.

⁘

After all of it, a half century after the Brooklyn Dodgers were kidnapped and taken to California, Davis still flushes with the enthusiasm of a fan. It is said that a man remembers best the events that occur when he is 17. "You know, he's Sir Jackie Robinson, the Knight of Brooklyn," Davis said, bubbling at the days of his own youth, of watching on television and going to the shrine of the community that was Ebbets Field. "You should have seen Jackie play. He brought electricity and people from all walks of life came to see him play.

"The Giants and Dodgers: Sal Maglie would throw very close to Jackie and it got to be a thing. One time Jackie bunted to first base, hoping Sal would cover. Whitey Lockman fielded it, and Davey Williams covered, and him and Jackie got to first base at the same time. I don't think Williams played after that year—not because Jackie tried to hurt him . . .

"Next inning Alvin Dark hit one in the gap that normally would have been a double but Jackie was playing third. Dark kept going and slid so hard he ripped Jackie Robinson's shirt off. Jackie didn't say anything, just went back to his position."

In his mind, Tommy Davis was still as drawn to the Dodgers of his youth and to Jackie Robinson as he had been the day Jackie phoned.

Campanis's blunder on television in 1987 implied that he welcomed black athletes for their strong backs but felt they didn't have the mental agility for the front office, and so he was fired by the Dodgers. Tommy Davis had never seen a racist side of the man who died in 1998. What Davis preferred to remember was the man who started him on a notable 18–year career that began in the same uniform of Jackie Robinson. Knowing his own experience with Campanis, Tommy Davis said, "I feel bad for him."

⁘

15

Living Up to His Own Image

Bob Gibson Overcomes the Stereotype

(Born Omaha, Nebraska, November 9, 1935-)

BOB GIBSON FOUND HIS PARADISE in a St. Louis Cardinals uniform in the mid–1960s, on the ball field or in the clubhouse, wherever he and his teammates were. There was no prejudice to be overcome, no color, only common respect and the common goal of winning. Gibson was admired—even revered—for his single–mindedness when he was at work, and the sharpness of his wit when he was at rest.

He could make the Cardinals his island and feel he belonged with them, as much as he felt the Logan Fontanelle Project where he grew up was his heaven in Omaha, Nebraska. Wearing that red St. Louis baseball cap, he was free to create his own image as a hard and fearless man and an unyielding competitor. Even the image was something of a deception and a self–deception as well, but he used that image to make his own island in the midst of that team.

And when the time came, as it does for all athletes, to move on, where could he find such completeness again? Where would he find such an absence of color? And who would want him?

Gibson was the paragon of a single–minded pitcher and he culti-vated that image of meanness because he thought it made him a more effective pitcher. Undoubtedly it did. Once he had established himself as a big–league pitcher, no hitter was ever comfortable batting against him.

"My thing was winning," he reflected years later when he could look back on a Hall of Fame career. "I didn't see how being pleasant or amiable had anything to do with winning, so I wasn't pleasant on the mound and I wasn't amiable off it."

He was one of the great pitchers of all time. What he accomplished in 1968 remains a landmark for the record book. As players, press, and fans recall, it was the season when he got everybody out. Pitching, particularly Gibson's, was so dominant that the rules were changed to lower the mound and reduce some of the pitcher's effectiveness. Gibson's peak evolved at the time when the Cardinals were the most racially comfortable team in baseball history. Players joined the group with notions formed in childhood, and if they stayed, either remade their mind–set or had it remade for them. White players were respectful of blacks both on and off the field and the other way around, too. Gibson, stung as he had been by earlier racism in the minor leagues, formed close friendships with both black and white teammates that he has cherished throughout his life.

The racial insults Gibson suffered, however, formed hard knots in his mind that he now suspects worked against him when he wanted to stay in baseball.

He established a barrier between himself and the media. He is a witty and insightful man. To a baseball writer or columnist, he was obviously a good man; whether he was also a good guy was not so apparent. He does not suffer fools easily, and sometimes he made misjudgments.

One of the first things a newspaper guy learns in covering a team or an event is who to talk to so precious time on deadline is not wasted. Early on—and he and I are contemporaries—I found interviewing Gibson a prickly matter. Once I picked a way through his barbed wire, he was rewarding. First I had to establish myself according to whatever standards he set. Forty years later I enjoy our contact.

He has fixed in his unforgiving memory a line from a magazine story in 1959 when he was struggling to make the team. He isn't sure which magazine but he's sure how it quoted him: "I don't do no thinkin' about pitchin', I just hum dat pea." Think what that says about an articulate man who had four years of college but happens to be black. That became the core of his wariness. He was going to protect himself. "I did not want to be hurt," he reflected.

"My relationship with the press might have hurt me in the long run," he conceded in *Stranger to the Game*, his 1994 autobiography, "because to this day I carry the reputation of being angry and hard to deal with, but it helped my pitching and that was all I cared about at the time."

At the time of that still–unforgiven incident, the Cardinals were not all that comfortable with being integrated. Gibson was 23 years old, had been a college basketball star at Creighton University, had played with the Harlem Globetrotters, and was still unsure whether his future belonged in basketball or baseball. He was trying to cope with Solly Hemus, who was managing the Cardinals at the time. Gibson felt Hemus would constantly ridicule black players. Hemus had suggested that pitcher Gibson should go back to basketball. He would demean Gibson's intelligence. When he would meet with the pitchers to go over the opposition before a new series, he would say, "You don't have to listen to this, Gibson. You just try to get the ball over the plate."

Of course, growing up in the 1950s, even in Nebraska, a black man absorbed stuff he would carry the rest of his life. Gibson was the seventh child and the baby of his family. His father, Pack Gibson, died of tuberculosis before Bob was born, and he was largely raised by his big brother LeRoy, known as Josh for Josh Gibson, the star of the Negro Leagues. His mother cleaned other people's homes and worked in a laundry, and when the family moved from what he called a shack to the project with brick walls, electricity, and heat, this home became what he came to regard as a "golden ghetto."

The project was a square with a playing field in the middle. More whites than blacks lived in the project; they were all poor. "Our side had blacks and whites mixed and we were all friends," he remembered. "If there was a fight there would be blacks and whites on our side and whites on the other, and we'd kick the hell out of them. I don't know what the fights were about. It was probably racial, but the guys on our side didn't notice that."

Brother Josh was also coach. And Bob was a star. When he was 14 and 15 years old people were picking Bob up in a Piper Cub, flying him to play with teams in places where there wasn't another black for 500 miles. After a game in Maryville, Missouri, the hosts took the players to the town square for cold watermelon. On a hot and dusty day, the players attacked the watermelon while the hosts took pictures.

Josh directed his players to ask for forks. It was his rule. He knew what was going on. His players ate watermelon with forks. Except Bob; he would have none. He thought it was demeaning to be given watermelon   and to have pictures taken.

He was the first black basketball player at his high school in Omaha. When his coach wrote to Indiana University, the 1953 NCAA champions, recommending a scholarship, the denial letter said "because we have already filled our quota of Negroes." The quota was one per class. "They picked the wrong Negro," Gibson said with a ring of sarcasm.

So Gibson became the first black scholarship basketball player at Creighton University, not far from home in Omaha. Early in his first season Creighton traveled to the University of Tulsa. It was not until they were on the train that the coach informed Gibson he would not be allowed to stay or eat with his white teammates in Oklahoma. It was a painful jolt and Gibson says he would have stayed home if he had known in advance.

When the team went to a restaurant, Gibson was told he had to eat in the kitchen. White teammate Glenn Sullivan, who didn't have Gibson's star potential but had the courage to stand up to cruelty when he saw it, went to the kitchen with Gibson, but Gibson walked out of the place. When the team went to its hotel, he went to a black rooming house. Sullivan accompanied him and offered to spend the night but Gibson sent him back to the team. He preferred the privacy to cry in pain. "I wasn't ready for that," he reflected.

Gibson, the competitor looking to pay back Tulsa, scored 18 points and was Creighton's leading rebounder, but Tulsa won, 69–54. By the time Gibson completed his three varsity years—freshmen weren't eligible at that time—he was the leading scorer in Creighton history with an average of 20.2 points a game. He had enough course credits for a degree but, he explained, not enough quality points.

❖

When he was most stung by Cardinals manager Hemus, who suggested he go back to playing basketball, Gibson stormed into the clubhouse and began packing. First baseman Bill White, sage beyond his years, advised Gibson, "Don't burn yourself out on things you can't change. Your time will come." Coach Harry Walker, once a staunch opponent to Jackie Robinson, assured Gibson that he'd be around long after Hemus was gone, which, of course, was true.

Hemus maintained Gibson would "never make it as a big–league pitcher. He throws everything the same speed." Years later when Gibson's fastball was the scourge of the National League, catcher Tim McCarver agreed: "Yeah, hard!" Hemus's implication was that Gibson was incapable of learning to mix his pitches.

Obviously, the manager did not know Gibson very well. Once Hemus patted Gibson on the back, mistaking him for teammate Julio Gotay, called him Julio and complimented him for his play at shortstop. Gibson flung about the contents of his locker. Of course, all black men look alike.

Gibson refuses to rehash the Hemus experience "because I don't think he deserves the ink. In all these years since 1959, almost 50 years, he's had a chance to say he was sorry, he was wrong. And he says, 'Are you still mad at me?' What I want to say is fuck 'im!"

Midway through the 1961 season Hemus was fired, to Gibson's delight, and replaced by Johnny Keane, who had been Gibson's manager and his refuge as manager of the Cardinals' minor–league team in Omaha. Keane had studied for the priesthood and had managed young players for 21 years in the minor leagues. Gibson says Keane was the closest thing he'd seen to a saint in baseball. To Gibson he was "part father."

Keane promptly took Curt Flood off Hemus's bench and made him the regular center fielder. He told Gibson he was going to start every fourth or fifth day. "I don't want you to worry about anything else," he said. "Just go out and pitch."

Gibson says it was hard for white players then and also for contemporary black players to understand how much Keane's attitude meant to black players of that team, and how much they trusted Keane. He didn't care about color.

Out of that concept the Cardinals of Gibson's blessed memory were built. "It wasn't limited to the clubhouse and the field; we spent our time off the field together, too," Gibson said when he was feeling the nostalgia of his final season. "I've known a few guys I've learned to love as brothers."

They had a collective spirit. There is chicken–and–egg disagreement about whether team chemistry brings about winning or whether winning creates chemistry. There is no disagreement that team atmosphere makes it a whole lot easier to survive the long season. Racial attitudes of the Cardinals were out in the open. Gibson, Flood, and White were intelligent and articulate black men. When unthinking words were uttered by white players, they were called to task. Those three black players had northern sensibilities and would not back down on racial issues. White players on the Cardinals respected that. They openly discussed their disagreements. When Lou Brock arrived, southern but equally sharp–thinking, he was added smoothly to the mix.

Flood wrote in *The Way It Is*, those players were "as close to being free of racist poison as a diverse group of 20th century Americans could possibly be."

Gibson, Flood, and White had suffered the insult of being closed out of the team's Florida hotel. Gibson disliked living in a boarding-house in St. Petersburg and disliked the overbearing black woman who ran it. Among other things, he thought she charged too much and was exploiting other people's pain and humiliation. Years later when Gibson drove to spring training, he and his wife and two small girls would sleep in the car because no convenient motel would take them. They were scarred by being relegated to grimy restrooms.

When the Jim Crow rules were breaking down in Florida in the early 1960s, general manager Bing Devine and white stars Stan Musial and Ken Boyer pushed for breaking down any team segregation. In 1962 the Cardinals bought a large, comfortable motel in St. Petersburg and there would be none of the pretense of the team being cloistered in a separate dining room and told to stay away from the pool.

Musial and Boyer gave up their personal comfort to live with the team. Players and wives and children mixed comfortably at their motel, in playgrounds, at barbecues, and at the pool. In addition to respect for ability, players liked each other. They enjoyed each other. Gibson wrote in *Stranger to the Game* that they were the Rainbow Coalition long before Jesse Jackson adopted the term.

And Dr. Ralph Wimbish, a bold NAACP leader in St. Petersburg, took White and Gibson to formerly all–white restaurants in town so no black person would have to suffer the anxiety of being first.

After Musial's retirement, Gibson was the Cardinals' towering personality. In the heat of the 1964 pennant race, Gene Mauch, the manager of the Phillies and the master of doublethink, said the Cardinals would never win with Gibson as their number one pitcher. What Mauch, whose team's collapse is now legend, had in mind is not known, but he was known for trying to plant a seed of doubt. What Keane had in mind was clear when he let thoroughly fatigued Gibson work through the ninth inning—despite giving up two solo home runs—to beat the Yankees in the seventh game of the World Series. "I had a commitment to his heart," the manager said. To Gibson he said afterward, "Nothing will stop you now." And he was right.

⋄

Gibson was perfecting the impenetrable shell of personality as part of his pitching repertoire. He would be a dark mystery on the mound. He wanted the hitter to know nothing about him. He worked at not making a friend by accident among opponents. To outsiders he was a stunning man, 6'2" and slender. "Nobody wears clothes like Gibson," said Cardinals teammate Joe Torre. And Gibson's skin glows a regal black.

Teammates, however, became friends by Gibson's personal standards, regardless of color. He was close to Flood and White, both black
men. He became close to white Joe Torre, who grew up in Brooklyn after Torre was traded to the Cardinals in 1969—and white Tim
McCarver, who grew up the son of a cop in segregated Memphis. From
the beginning, Gibson recognized something in McCarver beyond the
prejudice of his background. McCarver credits Gibson with helping
him grow and eventually become a sought-after broadcaster.

McCarver giggles fondly when he tells of the time he went to the
mound and Gibson told him to get back behind the plate where he
belonged: "The only thing you know about pitching is that it's hard to
hit." That is one of the best examples of heat-of-battle wit of our time.

It was challenging for McCarver to get that far with Gibson. "Tor-
turous years," McCarver recalls, not the worst of which was the way
Gibson's moving fastball tore up the catcher's hands. McCarver never
played with or against black players in Memphis and he was all of 18
when he first joined the Cardinals briefly and became a regular at 22.
"Gibson mistrusted me absolutely and It wasn't only me," McCarver
said. "The way he looks. The way he dresses. His charisma can turn
you on and turn you off. There was a fervor and passion about things
close to him that most people aren't willing to go through."

One day in McCarver's first spring training he was sipping an
orange soda on the bus. "Can I have a swig?" Gibson asked with deliberate intent. McCarver had never been asked or ever considered such a
thing, as Gibson fully understood. Young McCarver stammered. "I'll
save you some," he said. Gibson had made his point. He had made
McCarver think, just as Gibson made hitters think about the inside
fastball.

As they played together, the gap became smaller and, more of Gibson's wit and insight came through to a maturing McCarver. Once
Gibson asked him, "Do you know how a white boy shakes hands with
a Negro?" McCarver bit at the question. Gibson, playing the part of the
white boy, extended his hand to Curt Flood and they shook. Gibson then
looked at his own hand and wiped it on his pants. He asked McCarver
if that looked familiar. McCarver recognized Gibson's accuracy.

Just because Gibson would refuse to speak to Joe Torre at all–star games in order to avoid forming a friendship with a good hitter he'd have to get out did not mean that Gibson did not sense a common bond. When Torre joined the Cardinals, Gibson broke the chill immediately. "Hey," Gibson said, "it took me long enough to get you over here." Torre, Gibson explained years later, "is just a good person."

The three teammates, Gibson, McCarver, and Torre, became constant companions, often visiting together during the off–season. By the time McCarver was traded to the Phillies, and thus was an opponent, Gibson's shell had softened somewhat. Besides, McCarver knew what Gibson was beneath the shell. In one game against Philadelphia, Lou Brock had exploited McCarver's fading arm and had embarrassed him; the two had a fight at the plate. After the game Gibson wrote a reassuring letter to McCarver, still his treasured friend. Gibson had never done anything like that before.

In contrast, Gibson found the barrier impenetrable between him and reserve infielder Phil Gagliano, who also came from Memphis. Perhaps Gibson had judged that it wasn't worth his effort to penetrate the barrier. As Gibson recalled it, the night after the Cardinals clinched the 1968 pennant, the more they drank the more Gagliano maintained that white people were better than black people. Gibson does not forgive or forget easily. He says that when Gagliano was hospitalized the next year, only one Cardinal did not visit.

In early 1960s Cassius Clay, who had not yet changed his name to Ali, was staying at the same segregated motel as several Cardinals and became friendly with them. He went with Gibson and Curt Flood to a Black Muslim meeting. Flood recalled that much of the meeting was talk about vengeance against whites. Gibson emerged with the observation: "Sounds as if black power would be white power backwards. That wouldn't be much improvement."

Gibson's sensitivity to prejudice was not limited to black and white. One winter he visited military hospitals in the Far East with a group headed by Arthur Richman, then traveling secretary of the Mets. Graig Nettles, then the Cleveland third baseman, made an anti–Semitic comment about Richman and Gibson recoiled. He said he wanted nothing more to do with Nettles and warned that if they ever met at batters box and pitchers mound, Nettles should beware.

❖

As a pitcher, Gibson's Hall of Fame accomplishments are there in black and white. He won 20 games five times, 19 games twice. His 1.12 earned-run average in 1968 when he was 22–9 was the lowest since the dead-ball era. How he lost nine times remains a mystery. He completed 28 of his 34 starts and over one stretch of 95 innings allowed only two earned runs. He was arguably the greatest pitcher of his time. He concedes that Sandy Koufax over five seasons before he retired in pain was unmatched in history, but Gibson's dominance was over 13 seasons. A good argument.

From his position with the Cardinals he observed how the world was evolving around him—and how in some ways it was not changing much at all. As a rookie he couldn't find a decent place to live in St. Louis or a bank that would give him a mortgage in Omaha. Thirty years later, he notes that both would be available to him. It used to be that if there were a black man on a team, he would be playing or he was gone; now there are blacks in utility roles.

There have been black managers and successful black general managers, but not enough of either. "Some people still feel the same as they used to, but they're more sophisticated and able to conceal it," he noted in his last season. "I just want to be respected, not liked. People used to come up and call me names and that crap—not just kids but adults. If they don't say those things to your face and say it behind your back, that's a kind of respect."

He used to insist that it was the money that drove him to excel. Teammates knew otherwise. "He says it's money, money, money," shortstop Dal Maxvill said after Gibson beat the Red Sox for the third time in the seventh game of the 1967 World Series. Maxvill formed a circle with his fingers over his chest. "There's a big heart in there," Maxvill said. "He's a world champion again. He's always like that."

After Flood left America, having abandoned baseball in the wake of having lost his suit in the Supreme Court against the reserve system, Gibson searched Copenhagen for him. He did not find Flood. "I don't dwell on the thought that I won't see him again," Gibson said. "I remember the friendship we had."

Of course he cherished the warmth of relationships. "It's not that I cover it," he said of his heart. "I just don't go around with it in my hands. If you do, somebody will knock it out." He is forever wary.

For years after retiring as a pitcher he lamented, sometimes angrily, that there were so few jobs in baseball open to him. Twice he was a coach for manager Joe Torre. His identification was as an "attitude" coach as much as anything else. He felt he had earned more opportunity in baseball—not "a job, a position," he once said. Perhaps there weren't more offers to be a coach or to be someone who could use his mind in the front office because he was black and the traditionalists of the front office—owners and general managers—still were uncomfortable with black men. Perhaps they were uncomfortable with the thought of Gibson because they believed his intimidating front really was him, and they, too, were intimidated. Perhaps it was both. He had a brief experience as a broadcaster, but that was not his element.

❖

Without a doubt he missed baseball after 17 years of being Bob Gibson on the mound with the baseball in his hand. Once when he was at the brink of retiring he showed me how the years of throwing hard had left him unable to straighten his right arm. I asked if he would miss pitching. "I don't love pitching," he said. "I love winning."

Wendy, his second wife, mother to their 20–something son, is a charming, bright woman with special qualities. She is also white and blonde. Once at a baseball gathering she noted to her husband, "We're the only black couple here." Joe Torre relates that story.

She recognizes the real loss an athlete suffers when his time has gone and he's still a man with a life to live. "Nothing will ever be enough for him now," she said to Roger Angell, *The New Yorker*'s poet laureate of baseball writers.

Gibson takes his motor home for his nearly annual trip from Omaha to Cooperstown for the Hall of Fame induction. He does love to kibitz with his peers and to compare arthritic knees with the likes of Frank Robinson. On one trip in his motor home in the late 1970s, traveling with his wife Wendy and Cardinal trainer Gene Gieselmann and his wife Rita—a black man and three white people—Gibson was pulled over by a California state trooper. They were detained, questioned, and then followed for several miles. That, Gibson said, was a small taste of what life was like for most black people in America.

Gibson's experience explains to me why my dark-skinned friend and neighbor on Long Island, George Ramos, makes sure he never leaves home without identification.

Gibson ran a restaurant for a while near the Creighton campus, which further softened his hard image. He insisted on quality, as if he were working on his pitching. However, he was not so much boss and taskmaster as counselor to young people who worked for him. On occasion he'd babysit the children of his staff because somebody had to. Their children enjoyed his pool.

⁙

He is still a formidable person. He still looks the part. Sometimes he plays the part.

"What do you think I am as a person?" he demanded over the phone.

"A chocolate-covered marshmallow," I said.

He laughed. "Wendy," he called. "He said I was a chocolate-covered marshmallow. What do you think about that?

"She said that was just about right."

For a long time there was a lot of Tabasco inside it too.

⁙

16

Joan of Arc of Baseball

Curt Flood Sacrifices His Career

(Born Houston, Texas, January 18, 1938.
Died Los Angeles, California, January 20, 1997.)

EVERY NOVEMBER WHEN the date for baseball players to file for free agency comes around, each player owes a moment of silent thanks to Curt Flood for what he did for them.

In the simplest of terms, Flood gave baseball players the right to earn the millions that they have come to see as their right for having been born with hand–and–eye coordination, perhaps fleetness of foot, and what the players call good hands.

Flood gave his career to win their freedom. "Very few guys have ever had an appreciation for who he was," said Frank Robinson. "A guy with a whole load of guts."

It wasn't quite the Emancipation Proclamation. Flood didn't even win his own freedom. He did set in motion the thinking that overturned the rule by which teams owned players forever. Until December 23, 1975, baseball players worked in a kind of employment slavery. At age 17 or 18, young men chose which organization they would sign with, and never again had a choice where they would play. A player could be traded with no consideration of his needs. How much he would be paid was determined by his owner—take it or leave it. (When the draft of amateur talent was instituted in 1966, players didn't have even that original choice.) They weren't permitted to have professional agents represent them in negotiations with ball–club officials until years later

That was the reserve system. It was based on a provision that automatically renewed a player's contract from one year to the next, which was known as the reserve clause. It was the system that had been the foundation of baseball's mastery over labor relations for nearly a century.

Today every player after six years of service is bound only for the length of his contract. Once that has expired, he is free to negotiate with any team willing to bid for him. So after the 2000 season Alex Rodriguez, the classic example, was able to move from the Seattle Mariners to the Texas Rangers for a contract worth $252 million over 10 years—$25,705,118 a year—a salary that could not have been imagined in Flood's time.

"I really don't think the average player understands anything about it," said Bob Gibson, whose Hall of Fame pitching career concluded before he had a chance at the riches Flood's struggle uncovered. "I don't think most of 'em know who Curt Flood was—they don't even know that Curt Flood was the guy to challenge the reserve clause. They have it pretty good today, but I don't think they spend time wondering how this came about, I really don't."

That's a shame. In order to challenge the reserve system, Flood, at 32, in the prime of his career as a marvelous center fielder and a .300–hitter, was willing to walk away from a contract offered by the Washington Senators that would have paid him $110,000 for one season. He was likely to have several productive and lucrative seasons after that. He had played 12 seasons with the Cardinals already, had established friendships and business in the community. He liked it there. When the Cardinals traded him to Philadelphia, his choice was to go to Philadelphia or quit. He said he wasn't going to Philadelphia. He was going to court.

It was in the 1960s, which gave birth to a new sense of empowerment to challenge authority, when protests against the war in Vietnam were common and heated, and black awareness was building. Baseball players, to the contrary, accepted what the system gave them. Either they thought they were happy with the system or, when they weren't happy, they felt powerless to do anything about it. When Flood's intention to challenge the reserve system was disclosed to the members of the not yet powerful players association, Tom Haller of the Los Angeles Dodgers asked, "This is a period of black militancy. Do you feel that you're doing this as part of that movement? Because you're black?"

No, Flood insisted to the day of his death, he was railing against the injustices that affected every player, whatever color. Of course, there is no measuring the effect of Flood's experience as a black man, including his early times with the Cardinals. Can any man completely ignore the sources and causes of injustice in his life?

❖

Curt Flood came out of the ghetto in Oakland, California, at the age of 17 with an innocent heart and the dream of being a baseball player. He grew up with enough to eat and clothes to wear because his mother and father worked three and four jobs, but the family was intact. "I truly did not know, I did not know in my bones that I had been discriminated against from birth," he reflected years later.

He didn't recall discussion among friends or family in 1954 when 14-year-old Emmett Till was lynched in Mississippi, and when that same year the Supreme Court outlawed segregation in schools. Flood was 15 years old and no more aware of the big picture than any 15-year-old whose life was playing baseball.

Flood got his high school diploma, took his first airplane flight to spring training in Tampa with the Cincinnati Reds organization, and found there were water fountains designated "White" and "Colored." He hadn't seen such a thing in California. In Tampa the first door was slammed in his face. When he got to the Floridian Hotel, the team's headquarters, "this boy with the ball team" was directed to a taxi with a black driver who was told to take him to "Ma Felder's," where he would stay with Frank Robinson, Joe Black, and Brooks Lawrence, black veterans of the system.

After that first spring training he was alone, the only black man on the team for his introduction to professional baseball in America in 1956 at High Point–Thomasville in the Class B Carolina League. He heard himself called "eight-ball" and "black bastard" and "jigaboo" so relentlessly at home and away by fans and people in the street that he would retreat to the solitary confinement of his blacks–only rooming house and cry. There was little warmth in his relations with his white teammates.

That was a painful contrast to his experience with George Powles, the welcoming white coach in Oakland at McClymonds High School, whose mind and sensitivity were open to his young players, as was his home and his refrigerator. Flood's exposure to Powles and the mixed society at McClymonds had left him unprepared for what he found in North Carolina.

"If I now see whites as human beings of variable worth rather than as stereotypes, it is because of a process that began with George Powles," Flood reflected years later in *The Way It Is*, his often bitter autobiography. "I was prepared for High Point–Thomasville, but the peckerwood communities were not ready for me."

One night in Fayetteville, North Carolina, he heard a voice from the stands snarl, "There's a god damn nigger son of a bitch playing ball with them white boys. I'm leaving." When the team traveled, he had meals on the bus and more than once was forced to relieve himself against the rear wheel because only whites were permitted to use the restroom.

More than once he considered purposely missing a catch because it would cause a hated racist teammate to become the losing pitcher. Instead, he drove himself into scorching the league statistics. He burned himself down to 135 pounds by season's end and led the league with a .340 batting average, 190 hits, and 128 runs scored; his 29 home runs were second. For those accomplishments he was named 1957 MVP. The fact that he sacrificed himself to challenge the system should not obscure the fact that he was a terrific player. That he had star status and a star–level salary made his commitment to fight the injustice that much more remarkable.

Reward for his first–year performance was promotion for 1957 to the Class A South Atlantic League with Savannah, which happened to be in Georgia. Integration of the Savannah schools had stimulated racial hostility among the whites in the community, which resisted change. The Reds, with the lack of understanding typical of baseball executives, showed no thought that such an environment might retard the development of a major–league talent.

Georgia law prohibited black and Hispanic people from dressing in the same clubhouse as white people. Flood's widow, Judy Pace Flood, described it on ESPN:

In the Savannah clubhouse they had partitioned off a space for him. It was outside. It was with a dirt floor. And it was made out of corrugated tin, like a little shed. During a doubleheader, you wore the same uniform. Between games players put their clothes in a pile and the clubhouse guy washed them between games. The clubhouse guy started screaming and yelling, "This nigger put his clothes in here. My God!" And he took a long stick with a nail on the end of it, plucked Curt's clothes out of the pile of dirty, sweaty uniforms and dumped them into a paper bag. Then he called a colored taxi company, told him to take the clothes to the colored cleaners, while Curt sat there, naked.

As Flood recalled the season, most players were offended by the fact of his presence and would not talk to him when they were off the field. Few teammates would let him know they sympathized. A rare exception was Buddy Gilbert, who would bring food to him and Leo Cardenas, a Cuban black, saying, "I wish it wasn't like this." Flood commented that he felt sorry for Gilbert and his shame at being helpless. Perhaps some teammates were afraid they would be shunned by the other white teammates if they appeared sympathetic. Or maybe, as Flood thought, they didn't give a damn about his discomfort. "My teammates," Flood wrote, "despised me and rejected me as subhuman."

One more indignity was that the best accommodations available to him were in a dormitory at Savannah State College, a black school. The students were his own age, but Flood was a ballplayer, not a student, and not one of them. When Gilbert invited black teammates to his home, some white teammates called him "nigger lover." Gilbert later said he'd never seen anybody as lonely as Flood.

"I don't know how you stand it," Gilbert said to Flood. Gilbert's big–league career was seven games with the Reds in 1959. Flood was good enough and especially tough enough to get through the minor leagues.

In Savannah Flood's closest companion was Leo Cardenas, who was lodged with a Spanish–speaking family. They fed Cardenas, which was better than what Flood got. Cardenas spoke little English and, coming from Cuba, which did not have segregation, was baffled by the American laws. Isolation pushed him and Flood together.

They'd walk down the street of a Southern town and Cardenas would suggest a pleasant–looking restaurant, "We go there."

"We can't," Flood would reply.

"Why?"

"They don't like us."

"Like?"

"They don't want us."

"Why they no want us?"

"They don't want black people."

"Why?"

Isn't "why?" at the root of everything? Don't those experiences shape the thinking of any man? Flood did maintain his own sense of balance. He rejected the pull of the Black Muslims as just another face of bigotry.

⁕

His first taste of professional comfort came when his 1956 MVP season in the minors earned him a few days playing with the Reds in New York. The entire team stayed at the Biltmore Hotel "as if," Flood wrote, "blacks were members of the human race."

Flood said he came to write *The Way It Is* after a phone call from a businessman, Dave Oliphant, who had pitched in the Yankees farm system. Oliphant signed after a strong high school career in New York for a bonus of $3,000 and was shuttled around the lower farm clubs.

Flood said the treatment was similar to his own in the Cincinnati organization because Oliphant is Jewish.

The Yankees assigned Oliphant to a team managed by a rabid anti–Semite who ostracized him—except when threatening to get rid of "that Jewboy." Oliphant asked for his release to seek another organization and his father had to buy his contract for $2,000. Oliphant came close to making the Dodgers and maybe he could have made a lesser team; he'll never know. Eventually his father threatened to expose the anti–Semitism of the Yankees and they refunded $1,000 of the ransom money.

⁘

Flood's rapid climb left the Reds with the prospect of an all–black outfield of Frank Robinson, Vada Pinson, and Flood. That would have been a marvelous outfield on both offense and defense, but the Reds didn't think Cincinnati was ready for such a thing, and neither were they. There was this very real quota of black players. "It wasn't a written rule," Robinson reflects. "We knew it was there on a lot of ball clubs. I don't think any major–league baseball team wanted more than four blacks, and usually when they would get up to four, one of those black players had to go."

So Flood was traded to St. Louis, where he got no warm welcome from manager Solly Hemus, who was still a part–time player. For the most part, Hemus thought Flood would never be a big–league player.

Flood wrote of the time Hemus was knocked down by a pitch from Benny Daniels of Pittsburgh. On the next pitch, Hemus swung and missed and his bat sailed toward the mound. The third pitch from Daniels hit Hemus in the back. As he headed to first base, Hemus shouted at Daniels.

The next day Hemus called a clubhouse meeting and, according to Flood, said: "I want you to be the first to know what I said to Daniels. I called him a black so–and–so."

End of meeting. Hemus said no word of regret or heat–of–combat excess. Flood said he, Bob Gibson, Bill White, and George Crowe "sat with our jaws open, eyeing each other. We had been wondering how the manager really felt about us. Now we knew. . . ."

In 1962, when Flood had become a star and Hemus was a coach for the Mets, Flood had a big day in New York and Hemus tried to pay a compliment. "I never thought you'd make it in the league," Flood quotes Hemus as saying. Flood did not repeat his reply, which he said was "lengthy and venomous."

With a letter, Hemus tried again to make amends, the purpose of which was in his mind. "If I ever missed on evaluating a ballplayer, it was you," Flood quotes Hemus, "and I admire you for all of your determination, guts, and pride in your work."

In the years following Hemus, Flood was exposed to the unbiased chemistry developing among the Cardinals. Players cared for each other—white or black. Tennessean Tim McCarver was tutored away from his roots in segregation. McCarver and Flood were co–captains. Genuine friendships were formed. Flood's wit reached all of them. He told Gibson he was the luckiest pitcher in the league: "When you pitch, the other team never scores any runs."

Those Cardinals were victorious on and off the field. Flood said it was "a beautiful little foretaste of what life will be like when Americans finally unshackle themselves." Those Cardinals felt their mutual respect was a key ingredient in winning. In 12 full seasons with the Cardinals, Flood hit .300 six times. He was never bigger than 5'9" and 165 pounds. Only Willie Mays was his equal as a center fielder.

Flood's reward as one of the stars in beating the Yankees in the 1964 World Series was that when he and his first wife were so bold as to venture out of the familiar inner city they found suburban northern California not so eager to accept them. Some of the suburban neighbors outside of Oakland welcomed them to the home they bought. Others tried to drive him out; some of them burned a cross on his lawn.

Television news showed him haggard and worn in front of the house. He said, "Due to the notoriety that is undoubtedly going to be involved here, it will make people aware, if nothing else, that prejudice is not confined to the southern part of our United States. And if they move their mustache and look under their nose, they'll find it right here at home, too. It's unfortunate but it's true." So it was.

And Flood's unremitting resentment was further fixed in his heart. "To be sure," Flood wrote, "black experience teaches that the American white is guilty until he proves himself innocent." That was after years among a Cardinals team that Flood called an ideal, and after the support he acknowledged from George Powles and poor Buddy Gilbert.

The unprejudiced Cardinals beat the Boston Red Sox in the 1967 World Series and lost to the Detroit Tigers in the seventh game of 1968. It's more than a painful footnote to Flood's glowing career that he did not catch a fly ball that cost the seventh game. "If Curt Flood can't catch that ball, nobody can," Bob Gibson, the losing pitcher, maintained. Flood was his best friend on the club and it pained Gibson that Flood should be blamed. "To me he personified what the Cardinals were all about," Gibson wrote. "As a man and teammate, he was smart, funny, sensitive and, most of all, unique. As a ballplayer, he was resourceful, dedicated, and very, very good. Hell, the little guy was us, through and through."

Owner August Busch, the baron of Budweiser, didn't feel that sense of attachment. He concluded it was time to break up the team and reduce his payroll. Before the season Flood and Busch had a contentious contract negotiation. Busch had helped Flood with financial problems before and they had once enjoyed good relations. Flood had even painted a portrait of the owner. But now Busch was disappointed. Flood would be the first to go. He was traded to the Phillies.

He had made good friends—white and black, in and out of baseball. He had an art studio in St. Louis and was developing a reputation as a portrait painter. He had gone into a high–level engraving business with a white partner, John Jorgensen. When Flood's first marriage was breaking up, he lived with Jorgensen and his wife, Marion. They had a relationship beyond business until Jorgensen was brutally murdered. An emotional link with the world outside of baseball was broken and Flood was staggered. For years prior to this, Flood's stability had been stretched thin by his brother Carl's repeated trips in and out of jail.

Flood thought Carl was a better baseball player and a better artist than he was, but Carl never gave himself a chance to display his talent.

And now the team Flood had called home didn't even care enough about him to tell him he had been traded before the news was released to the press. "If I had been a foot–shuffling porter, they might have at least given me a pocket watch," Flood wrote. He said the trade "violated the logic and integrity of my existence. I was not a consignment of goods."

What choice did he have? He could retire, threaten to retire and perhaps get a boost in salary, or he could sue. He was convinced he was right even if the court ruled against him. He would not be bought for a few hundred thousand dollars. He met with Marvin Miller, who was then just gathering the strength of the players association when the owners still thought its primary issues concerned the length of the grass and bathrooms available to the dugouts.

Miller had sought to reform baseball's labor relations since taking over the union in 1966, but he thought it was too soon for him and warned Flood it would likely cost him a fortune. Flood thought if the Cardinals didn't want him, he should be free to find his place.

Baseball Commissioner Bowie Kuhn vowed, never! "I asked, how about at age 65?" Flood recalled years later. "They said no. They said then we'd be asking for it at age 60, and then 59." And that surely would be the ruination of the game.

In December 1969, represented by former Supreme Court justice Arthur Goldberg, Flood filed suit, went off to Copenhagen to study art and to paint, and let the lawyers practice law. By agreement with Kuhn so it wouldn't prejudice his lawsuit, Flood came back to play with Washington in the spring of 1971 but he didn't have any baseball left in him. He batted .200 in 13 games and went back to Europe. Not one player took his side in court. His wife was seeking support for their five children and he had no money. He went to Majorca, ran a bar, and became an alcoholic.

He lost his first round and eventually his case went to the Supreme Court in 1972 where he lost again, the court repeating its 1922 decision that baseball was sport and not to be regulated as interstate commerce. But it was a split decision, five to three. The voice of dissent changed the world. Justices William O. Douglas and William Brennan wrote, "Were we considering the question of baseball for the first time on a clean slate, we would hold it to be subject to federal antitrust regulations." They said the "unbroken silence of Congress should not prevent us from correcting our own mistakes."

Flood lost his suit but the dissenting judges' argument raised the consciousness of everyone concerned with baseball—other than the commissioner and most of the owners, that is. Two days before Christmas 1975, official arbitrator Peter Seitz, chosen by both labor and management, ruled a player was bound only for the length of his contract. It was precisely what Flood sought.

Player's salaries multiplied. A year later, Reggie Jackson went to the Yankees for $2.9 million over five years. Pitcher Bill Campbell went from $37,000 to $180,000 for one year.

Flood got deeper in debt. "He did something that was courageous, and paid for it—financially, mentally, and physically," said Bill White, the former president of the National League and a longtime teammate of Flood's on the Cardinals. "He changed the thinking, and the change of thinking is much of the reason why we are where we are."

In 1979 Flood returned briefly to broadcast for the Oakland A's, but he didn't have much zest for that job other than for the paycheck he needed. His spirit was gone. "You seldom see a man's basic character change, especially a strong character like Flood, a genuinely thoughtful rebel," said Mike Epstein, then an Oakland player. "But when you see Curt Flood today, you see a man who has been tied to the mast and has taken one lash too many."

Flood paid his own price beyond the dollars he lost. He drank and chased and caught women, and lived hard. He lost his first marriage and his family. By 1993 it had occurred to Flood that the pendulum that was unconscionably so far on one side might have swung too far to the other. "If that's my legacy," he said, "I'm proud to have been a part of it. It turned out to be not that bad: attendance is better; television revenue is greater. I can't see where free agency has been so negative."

He did wince at the thought that a mindless mentality had arisen, not to be the best player but to be highest paid. "We created the $5 million star," he said. "We started back when he was 11, didn't we? When he should have been learning morality and standards, somebody was taking care of him and doing his homework for him. Now he acts like a spoiled brat, and we don't know why?" Flood thought about things like that. His voice was hoarse then. He thought perhaps he needed to have his tonsils removed.

Flood died of throat cancer in 1997 at age 59. His second wife, actress Judy Pace, said Flood did not die a bitter man. "This is not Greek tragedy," she said, "although some people would like to portray it as such. He had a giving heart."

He gave away so much of his life. Joe Torre, who played on Flood's team in St. Louis and was a strong force in the players association, identified him as the "Joan of Arc of all this." Joan of Arc was burned at the stake, and Flood lost his suit. But look at what came of it.

17

Breaking That Record
and Bigoted Hearts

Henry Aaron Sets the Record

(Born Mobile, Alabama, February 5, 1934-)

HENRY AARON'S HATE MAIL had become a torrent of anonymous cruelty
and bigotry. It spread to telephone calls and death threats and phone
calls to his parents warning that they'd never see their son again. The
FBI went to daughter Gaile's dormitory at Fisk University to protect her
from a threat of kidnapping. The other Aaron children were watched
carefully at school in Atlanta. The threats were too numerous and some
too detailed and too chilling for Aaron to block out of his mind.

In 1973 he was a black man on the verge of breaking Babe Ruth's
sacred career home-run record. Aaron was playing left field for the
Atlanta Braves that night in Olympic Stadium, Montreal, trying to keep
the thoughts that lurked in the back of his mind from interfering with
what he was trying to do. President Kennedy had been shot; Bobby Kennedy had been shot; and black people felt those men had been trying to
help them. Martin Luther King Jr. had been shot and nobody needed
an explanation of why the bigots targeted him.

From time to time Hank Aaron, Number 44, would tell his team-
mates not to sit too close to him in the dugout and try to make it a joke.
And from time to time there was too much tension to make a bad joke.
He was crouched at his outfield position, hands on his knees, when he

heard a bang ring out in the grandstand and echo around the concrete oval.

Alive and well, he described the moment: "It sounded like a gun-shot, and I thought, uh–oh, this is it. I kept my eyes straight ahead and didn't move a muscle until I realized I was still in one piece and breathing." It was a firecracker. But oh, what it seemed to be! Imagine how it felt to be in the crosshairs every minute of the day.

No athlete since Jackie Robinson had been so tormented and threatened, and America—white America where all men were created equal—was supposed to have grown and opened its arms in those 27 years since Robinson's debut. Baseball was a game, wasn't it? Whether the home team won or lost didn't put a quart of milk or a loaf of bread on a fan's table or ease his burden at the factory.

But this was Babe Ruth that a black man was challenging. Ruth was the colossus. He was the image Japanese soldiers cursed, hoping to infuriate American troops in World War II. Ruth hit 714 home runs in his career, reconfiguring the game with his power hitting and rising to the level of mythology. Dethroning such an icon of society could not be considered merely a game.

⁙

Challenging society began, however unintentionally, for Aaron as a 17–year–old infielder with the Indianapolis Clowns of the Negro Leagues, having a meal in a restaurant in the nation's capital in 1951 and hearing the white kitchen help smash the dishes the black players had used. At 19 he was in "so–called organized baseball," playing in Jacksonville, Florida, of the South Atlantic League. Blacks had played in the league before, but never for Jacksonville. People would get to the ballpark early, the better for this black man to hear their vile slurs. That while Aaron's bat was tearing up the league.

Many times on the late–night bus rides there were tears. "Why, Joe, why?" he asked first baseman Joe Andrews, the white player who almost always sat next to him. "The only thing I want to do is play ball.

I don't want to hurt anybody. I just want to play ball. They don't even want me to do that."

Aaron's 1953 season with the Jacksonville Braves summarizes the lingering grip of segregation, and the strength of the righteous whites like Andrews to stand up and say it was wrong. "Joe was our protector," Aaron wrote in *I Had a Hammer*. "We couldn't talk back to the fans calling us names, but Joe could, and he damn sure did." Andrews talked back, brought food back to the bus, and ate with the black players and, when he had to, came to the rescue with a bat in his hands.

Manager Ben Geraghty, a sensitive man from New Jersey and a longtime cultivator of young players, made it his business to visit the black players often and see how they were getting along. It was part of his job and he tried to shield Aaron from the hostile world. "I guess he was one reason I didn't realize I was crusading," Aaron said, "because he crowded out a lot of stuff and never let it get close to me."

Andrews wasn't supportive of Aaron because they were social friends; they were no Butch and Sundance. Logically, they should have been rivals trying to climb over each other to get to the Braves at the top of the chain. Andrews was doing what he thought was right.

⁘

Aaron came from Mobile, Alabama, where his father worked as a boilermaker's assistant at the shipyard. Henry learned the rules of life there, but never fully grasped why they should be so unfair. In his first professional season the Braves sent him to the Northern League in Eau Claire, Wisconsin, where there was one other black man in town and Aaron was the all–star shortstop. He had nice memories there, mostly of quiet times. Manager Bill Adair's report said he couldn't judge Aaron's IQ because he gave "nothing to go on" except what he could see. "The kid looks lazy, but he isn't," Adair wrote, piercing the stereotype.

"I never doubted my ability," Aaron wrote, "but when you hear all your life that you're inferior, it makes you wonder. . . ."

At Jacksonville he conducted himself with a sense of "knowing his place," absorbed from a childhood in racism, even after being exposed to Andrews's friendship. Andrews's first wife, Connie, and their two-year-old daughter, Joyce, would be waiting outside the Jacksonville ballpark as well as Barbara, Aaron's wife-to-be. Aaron would always greet them as "Miss Connie" and "Miss Joyce." Andrews told Aaron to call his wife Connie, but Aaron persisted: "Joe, you don't understand."

Andrews was a bonus baby from Durfee High School in Fall River, Massachusetts, a three-sport star in high school. He had worn uniform Number 44. Odd coincidence. He chose the University of Washington from dozens of college football scholarship offers and left as a freshmen in favor of a signing bonus from the Braves. He was highly regarded as a hitting prospect, but ultimately he chose drinking over baseball. Jacksonville manager Geraghty learned to rest Andrews on Sundays so he could recover from Saturday nights.

Aaron, Horace Garner, and Puerto Rican Felix Mantilla were the first black players in town. Aaron played second base, Mantilla shortstop. Garner played right field where the fans could reach him with the stones they threw. When Andrews's friendship became known to the fans they would say, among other things, "Andrews, you look blacker every time you come to town. You must be sleeping with Aaron's sister."

One night in Macon, Georgia, the pitcher for the home Peaches was Max West, who had been in the big leagues and was on the way down. Andrews was on second base when Aaron went to bat and heard West holler: "I got four for your head, nigger." The first pitch was over Aaron's head. The second was high and inside and Aaron tomahawked it so hard that the sound of the ball hitting the corrugated metal fence rang across the big field. "Must have been 600 feet," Andrews said.

Aaron had already won a number of games with his bat when a teammate from New Orleans was pitching for Jacksonville in the late innings and Aaron booted a ball that cost the game. Andrews recalled that the pitcher came into the clubhouse afterward and said something like, "You know, you can't trust a nigger. When pull comes to tug, they're going to go in the tank every time."

Nearly 50 years later, Andrews recalled banging a Louisville Slugger on the lockers and saying, "'Whoa! Whoa! We got enough aggravation outside. We don't need it in here. I'm just going to say this once and only once: If I ever hear that word used in here again, this bat's going to go across somebody's skull. I don't care much what happens to me. It doesn't happen in here again.' No one moved. No one said a thing. And it didn't happen again. It didn't."

Andrews played first base and heard whatever was shouted at Aaron. He marveled that Aaron never revealed his anger. Andrews recalled saying, "'Can you hear that, Henry? Do you hear him?' And Aaron said, 'What do you think, I'm deaf?'

"We'd get to the dugout and I'd say, 'They're on me and I haven't done anything. They're picking on me, I guess, because I'm sticking up for you, I guess. I'm looking blacker to them.'"

By the end of the season, Aaron won over many of the fans because the team was winning and they hadn't had a winning team to watch for a long time. Not only was he the best player in town, he was clearly the best in the league. Aaron led the South Atlantic League with a .362 batting average, runs, hits, and 125 RBI. They appreciated him on the ball field but not in the restaurants.

Aaron was judged ready in 1954 to move up to the Braves, then in Milwaukee. He hit his first home run off Vic Raschi, now a significant name in baseball trivia as the first home–run victim, in a career total of 755 home runs. He left Ruth's monumental mark of 714 well behind. Joe Andrews lingered another half season at Jacksonville, was dropped down a league and at 24 left baseball. He ran a successful car dealership in Fall River, Massachusetts, on the strength of his name in the community for a while but lost that and his health to cocaine and alcohol.

In the winter of 1973, when Aaron was on the brink of his record, he had a business engagement in Providence, Rhode Island. Andrews traveled to greet his old friend. Andrews phoned from the hotel lobby and Aaron invited him up. The FBI, responding to the death threats, frisked Andrews. Then Aaron opened the door and the two old teammates hugged. "Nice," Andrews said.

In 1998 Aaron appeared at a fund–raiser for Andrews's campaign for sheriff and accompanied him to speak to high school students.

Aaron was giving thanks for the support Andrews had given him so many years before. Andrews died in 2001 at 68.

Together they survived the trials in Jacksonville. In later years a columnist in the Jacksonville Journal gave credit to Aaron for starting the city on the road to racial understanding. Aaron wrote, "I'm not sure I've ever done anything more important."

⁂

Aaron looked back on his Milwaukee years as sweet times, but that was relative. In 1954, his rookie year, the Supreme Court voted, in *Brown v. Board of Education*, that "separate but equal" was illegal. The Braves were already together and equal when they traveled on the trains— unless the black players wanted to go to the dining car. Eddie Mathews or one of the other white veterans would bring food for Aaron back to his compartment, and later he would listen to Mathews or Del Crandall or Warren Spahn talk baseball.

One time when Martin Luther King Jr. was courageously leading civil rights marches, Spahn asked, "Henry, just what is it you people want?" Was it a question that anybody should have had to ask or answer, then or now? By then, Aaron had been warned not to drive at night during spring training in Bradenton, Florida. The local police would stop taxis and order black people to get out; they scrutinized black drivers. Typically, John Roseboro, a black man from Ohio playing in the Dodgers' farm system about that time, said images of 14-year-old Emmett Till being lynched in Mississippi constantly flashed in his mind. John Roseboro or Henry Aaron or any black person in the South had good reason to be wary.

"All we want," Aaron answered Spahn, "is the things you've had all along." Spahn appeared to accept that answer and the two got along well—great pitcher and great player.

Aaron did delight in putting one over on Jim Crow when he could. These moments were especially delicious in retrospect. Time does have its way of tempering pain into humor. He'd be barnstorming through the South in a black group with Willie Mays, Ernie Banks, Roy Campanella, and Sam Jones, playing a local team before driving to the next place, hoping to find a place to eat on the way. Too often they came upon doors that were shut to colored people.

"You remember Sam Jones," Aaron said with a conspiratorial laugh. "Big pitcher with light skin. As long as he kept his mouth shut, a lot of people thought he was white. We'd write down a list, Sam would get a cab to the finest white restaurant, pull a hat down low, walk right in the front door and give them the list. We ate good as long as he never opened his mouth."

He loved passing on the story. "Believe it or not, we laughed at a lot of things," he said.

Milwaukee was deliriously in love with Number 44, and with the Braves in general in 1957, and the feeling was mutual through the 1950s until they moved to Atlanta. Aaron hit the 11th–inning home run that clinched the National League pennant for the Braves, he was voted MVP, the Braves beat the Yankees in the World Series, and for a long time he regarded that as the sweetest season of his career.

It was so sweet that his youngest sister Alfredia eagerly decided to live with Henry and his wife so she could go to school in their white suburb. So parents of children in that school began picking up their kids after school so they wouldn't have to walk home with Alfredia. Aaron wrote in *I Had a Hammer*, that the principal told him, "There wouldn't be a problem if you hadn't brought her to this school." The educational logic was withering. Alfredia went home to Mobile.

By the time the Braves abandoned Milwaukee for the emerging metropolis of Atlanta in 1966, Aaron had hit .300 10 times in 12 seasons, led the league in average and home runs twice each and RBI three times—all of it with understated grace. The new Atlanta was the city where black men in suits and neckties carrying briefcases were most apparent. National League cities welcomed Aaron and admired him; Atlanta did not.

Atlanta called him "jagaboo" [sic] and "nigger," "nigger," "nigger." He began to speak out about conditions and shared his wisdom eagerly with younger black players. He was a mentor. He counseled young Dusty Baker not to miss too many games for being hurt. He advised against making a conspicuous show after home runs—something he never did. "We used to go to Hank for everything," Baker said.

Aaron would have Maynard Jackson and Andrew Young, forces in the civil rights movement, to his home and would invite young Baker to join them.

Baker was obviously a bright man and star in the making. Aaron reached out as well to Sandy Alomar, the shortstop hopeful from Puerto Rico who was trying to adjust to the harsh rules of the American South. "Hank was taking care of me," Alomar said. In Atlanta he invited Alomar to stay at his apartment and let him drive his car. When Alomar was uncomfortable going out in Atlanta, Aaron often would sit with him and talk. "He took so much care of me," Alomar said. "People don't recognize the kind of human he was, and how good a player he was. For a long time not even players recognized that."

Willie McCovey, a Hall of Fame player but never a teammate of Aaron, chose to wear Number 44 when he burst upon the scene as a star with the Giants in 1961. "For Hank, of course," McCovey said.

Hank never had a single season that challenged Ruth's 60 or Roger Maris's 61 home runs. What he did have was one 47, one 45, and three of his four league–leading totals were 44. Once he tied with McCovey at 44—another great bit of trivia.

He was so good that players referred to him as Bad Henry. He had astounding durability. By 1972, his 19th season, it was clear that unless he was seriously hurt, he was going to top Ruth's career total of home runs. It should have been a time of joyous anticipation and of celebration. Instead it was a time of sickening insults and "Dear nigger" letters. The fact that the Braves were a bad team emphasized Aaron's stardom.

There is some sense of equality in recognizing that people are normally uncomfortable with the new challenging the old. Ruth's 714 had stood since 1934 and he was Babe Ruth like Hercules was Hercules. He was of colossal proportions—of the called shot, the big belly, and hot dog binges. For generations a kid would take a big swing on the sandlot and another kid would demand, "Who do you think you are, Babe Ruth?" He did things that were so big they were called Ruthian.

Aaron just kept on at his personal pace, wonderful as it was, but he appeared so relaxed he was colorless. It was said with admiration that he could fall asleep between pitches while at bat and wake up to hit a line drive.

The reality, though, was that his color was black. And the mail poured in. Some of it was favorable. The total was so great the Braves had to give him a private secretary. The U.S. Post Office said that the only American to get more mail that year was Dinah Shore. And she didn't get the kind of mail Aaron did. Henry didn't answer the bad ones, but he didn't throw them away, either.

One from Tennessee said: "You can hit all dem home runs over dem short fences but yo can't take dat black off yo face."

One said: "Dear Nigger Scum, Niggers, Jews, Yankees, Hippies, Nigger Lovers are the scum of the earth. Niggers are animals, not humans. . . ."

Another said: "Dear Hank Aaron, Retire or die. . . Will I sneak a rifle into the upper deck or a .45 into the bleachers? I don't know yet. But you know you will die unless you retire."

Multiply these by 10,000, "not all from the South," Aaron said pointedly. He always thought pressure intensified his concentration. Sometimes he could make himself the butt of jokes. One time in Montreal the Braves had lost eight in a row and Aaron hit a drive that appeared certain to be a three–run homer that would win the game. The team in the dugout jumped up. The wind caught the ball and dropped it to the left fielder at the fence. "I'll bet any amount of money," Aaron said, "that damn Babe Ruth was blowing that ball back."

He didn't need this kind of pressure. When threats were more specific, they were passed to the Atlanta police. Aaron kept repeating that he didn't intend to replace Babe Ruth; that was impossible. He just wanted to be treated like a human being and be permitted to do his job. He paid his own tribute to Ruth. "I never said I was better than Babe Ruth," he said. "But what am I supposed to do, stop hitting?"

He thought it was appropriate that somebody was challenging the record of a man who'd been dead since 1948. "I think it's good for all

America," Aaron said. "The world keeps going on. Kids today can relate to me. I think it also gives black kids hope. It shows them that anything is possible today.

"Maybe they can't be a ballplayer like me but they can strive for excellence and be a good doctor or lawyer or anything. I believe that. I would have tried to be the best at whatever I did, even if it was being a dirt shoveler."

When Aaron was growing up, Babe Ruth was not a glowing image for him. "Ruth was in a different world," Aaron said. "Baseball when he played was something no black kid could relate to. We had nothing to wish for. You know, of all the pictures I've ever seen of Babe Ruth, I've never seen one with him and black kids. Have you? This is no knock on Ruth. It's just the way it was." (No, I don't recall having seen a picture of Ruth with black kids either.) In the pressure cooker, Aaron was more expressive, more insightful than ever.

He hit 34 home runs in 1972 to pass Willie Mays for second place, and 40 more in 1973. He needed one to tie Ruth and one more to break the record. When he flied out on his last at bat of the season, the largest crowd of the Atlanta season stood and applauded, demanding that he stand on the field for five minutes of appreciation he didn't expect. It wasn't how Atlanta had greeted him.

❖

He had to spend the winter reading mail and waiting. The Braves opened 1974 in Cincinnati and Aaron, needing two to set the record, wanted to accomplish it at home in Atlanta. Commissioner Bowie Kuhn justifiably said no, he had to play in Cincinnati. In spite of other interests, the concept should be to honor the game.

Opening Day 1975 in Cincinnati, Ralph Garr pointed out to Aaron, that it was the anniversary of the assassination of Martin Luther King Jr. Aaron asked Reds' management for a moment of silence before the game and was denied. Aaron noted that America should be more concerned with Dr. King's legacy and less with Babe Ruth's record.

On his first swing of the season, against Jack Billingham, whose name will live forever in trivia, Aaron was tied with the Babe. Self-consciously he ran out this home run a little faster than usual and was greeted at the plate by a hug from the Reds' great catcher Johnny Bench. It's one thing to be received by teammates; it's a deeper thing to be acclaimed by an opponent. What Bench portrayed was the respect and admiration the players in the league had for Aaron.

The next game was rained out and then manager Eddie Mathews, who didn't want to play Aaron on a wet and chilly field or break the record before the 11-game Atlanta home stand, submitted to Kuhn's pressure. Aaron's book gives too much credit and too much blame to the New York press for forcing the commissioner to make Aaron play. (The power of the press over things players don't like is not as great as they think.) Anyhow, Aaron played, was hitless, and the procession went home to Atlanta.

Aaron's father threw out the ceremonial first ball the first night home against the Dodgers. The Los Angeles pitcher was Al Downing, an intelligent left-hander who had grown up as one of the few black players with the 1960 Yankees, the team of Babe Ruth. Downing is one of the 13 Black Aces, as Mudcat Grant identifies black pitchers who have been 20-game winners.

Bowie Kuhn was conspicuously absent, speaking at the Wahoo Club booster luncheon in Cleveland. Apparently he judged that booster club date to be more important than the commissioner of baseball being on hand to honor the breaking of the biggest record in the game. Kuhn's blunder left deputy Monte Irvin to bear the resentful booing from 54,000, the largest crowd in Braves history. Aaron took Kuhn's absence personally, apparently as a racial slur. That was his inference. It is giving white people too much credit, however, to think that every time they blunder at the expense of a black that it's deliberate.

Aaron walked his first time up and the run he scored broke Willie Mays's National League record for runs scored—and put him behind only Ty Cobb, the bitterly racist Georgia Peach, and Ruth himself. Scoring runs is the great objective of the game, and Aaron performed that chore quite well.

In the fourth inning he hit one of those shots that earned his Hammerin' Hank nickname: The shortstop flexes his knees as if to leap for the line drive and the ball keeps rising until it clears the fence. Bill Buckner leaped against the left–field fence. The ball was gone. Number 715 was now in the glove of relief pitcher Tom House in the Braves' bull pen.

The crowd was on its feet roaring. Dodgers first baseman Steve Garvey shook Aaron's hand as he ran the bases in what seemed to him to be slow motion. Photos of the event show two young men who had jumped out of the grandstand, rounding the bases with Aaron. Ralph Garr was waiting to make sure Aaron touched home plate before the team mobbed him. House ran in with the baseball and made certain to give it only to Aaron. "Hammer, here it is," he said.

And in the brief ceremony at home plate, Aaron said, "Thank God it's over." Atlanta, Georgia, stood again and gave a black man an ovation.

The next time Aaron came up, Garr said, "Come on, break Hank Aaron's record."

Someday it will happen. Maybe Barry Bonds will break Hank Aaron's 755. Or maybe it will stand 40 years until someone yet unborn does it.

Comparisons will be there: Ruth hit home runs when nobody in his time did; Aaron hit his when everybody hit home runs. Ruth played in the daylight while Aaron played at night when only the top half of the ball was lighted. Ruth hit home runs in the growing dark of twilight because there were no lights to be turned on. Ruth didn't have to play coast–to–coast as Aaron did. Ruth had to ride and sleep on trains while Aaron got to fly. Ruth wrapped himself in wet sheets because his hotels didn't have air conditioning, which Aaron's did. Aaron had to hit against so many fresh relief pitchers while Ruth often had the benefit of tiring starting pitchers. Ruth was extending his own record with none of the pressures of battling tradition.

They were the same comparisons Maris heard in 1961. Ruth played in the major leagues while the talent of the whole population of coloreds, Negroes, blacks, and African Americans—whichever term was in vogue at the time—was closed out.

In his triumph, Aaron felt the tears run down his cheeks. This time congratulations ruled his mail. He was welcomed at the White House and his motorcade was cheered in Harlem. He had a forum to push for more opportunities in management for black people.

Just once in all the pressure he lost his composure. The *Atlanta Journal* had run a picture of Billye, Henry's second wife, with a caption Aaron interpreted to mean that she was manipulating him. He was so angry that he pushed a basket of clubhouse strawberries in the face of reporter Frank Hyland. Aaron understood that Hyland had nothing to do with the caption, but Hyland did work for the paper and that was enough. It was a rare lapse in dignity and judgment for Aaron. They later patched up their relationship and Aaron said he regretted the incident. (Athletes do have an adversarial relationship with the press, whose role most athletes do not understand.)

⁂

Aaron finished 1973 with 40 home runs, a remarkable feat at age 39. He played another season with Atlanta and two more in Milwaukee almost as his victory tour of the American League. By his last game he had played more games than anyone. On his last at bat, his infield single gave him one last RBI, more than anyone had ever had. He was on second base and, he wrote, he hoped he would not score the run that would break his tie with Ruth behind Cobb. He was pleased when he was replaced by a pinch runner.

"I sort of liked the idea of sharing something with the Babe," Aaron wrote.

Then came the hard part. It has been said that most of us die only once; an athlete dies twice. What does a man who left the side of mama and daddy as a teenager and played baseball for 25 years do with the rest of his life? There is no cheering when he sits down at a desk. Aaron felt unprepared for the position of a beer distributor that he sought.

Ted Turner, the maverick owner of the Braves, offered him a position as director of player development. It suited Aaron's skills and powers of observation developed over all those years. It was a real job. It also gave him a real forum from which to discuss the role of minorities in baseball; if Henry Aaron spoke, someone would listen.

Twice Turner offered the managing job. "I never once was interested in managing," Aaron said. He didn't want to be a general manager either. When former brother–in–law Bill Lucas, who was in effect the Braves' general manager, died, Aaron became the highest–ranking black in baseball. In 1989 Bill White became president of the National League. And Bob Watson with the Yankees and Ken Williams with the White Sox won World Series as general managers.

The job of farm director Aaron had was difficult enough. He had to release his own son, Lary, after two seasons in Class A with the Braves. In 1982 Aaron was elected to the Hall of Fame; only Cobb was elected with a higher percentage of votes. Anyone who did not vote for Aaron should have his sanity checked.

As senior vice president and assistant to the president of the Braves, he continues to speak out on issues of his choosing. Once he discouraged black college students from entering baseball because ultimately they would be shortchanged and because making a success in baseball is a long shot at best. Better, Aaron said, they should study to be doctors or lawyers or teachers. "Baseball needs me because it needs someone to stir the pot," he said.

Attitudes have evolved and opportunities have improved since 1951, although not enough. In 1989 Major League Baseball and MasterCard had a major promotion in which a public vote identified Aaron's breaking Babe Ruth's home run record as the greatest moment in baseball history. Of course, it was absurd to think that all of baseball history could be shaved to a single point by public vote. Aaron did what he did over a prolonged period—23 years of greatness. If he didn't hit his 715th on April 8, 1974, he would have hit it on April 9th or 10th or 25th.

Jackie Robinson's breaking the color barrier was a greater single moment, and his impact was over a period of years. If there was one brilliant flash of light, perhaps that was Bobby Thomson's home run in 1951, or Kirk Gibson's home run in 1988. Or maybe it was something much earlier.

But Aaron's selection was a sign of something else to him. "Slowly, attitudes are changing," he said. "Jackie passed the torch. Thirty or 40 years from now when my record is being broken, people will be saying, 'You're not as good as Hank Aaron.'

"Times must have changed. If not, I could not have won the award."

18

What Would Jackie Do

Dusty Baker Finds His Answers

(Born Riverside, California, June 15, 1949–)

DUSTY BAKER WAS A BRIGHT AND WORLDLY YOUNG MAN coming out of very hip northern California and out of the encouraging home of his parents. He was Johnnie Baker Jr. Johnnie Baker Sr. had been around the world in the segregated navy and both of Dusty's parents were strongly involved in the NAACP. *Ebony* and *Jet* magazines were around the house regularly, as was the *Pittsburgh Courier*, which had editorialized so hard for Jackie.

When Baker was playing right field in his first professional game with the Braves organization in 1967 at Little Rock, Arkansas, of all places, management let in a number of patients from the mental institution next to the ballpark. They were seated in a section of the grandstand in right field. "They sat by me in right field and I dropped the first fly ball hit to me," said Baker, now a successful big–league manager and a very sophisticated man. "They called me names I had never heard before. And I started crying and wanted to come home. It was painful. I shouldn't have been shocked but until you're really there, the first time of that magnitude in your face . . ." No man can understand fully until he has dropped a fly ball in his own skin.

"I wanted to go home," Baker said, "only my mama said it was too late, I had already signed. I was 18 years old, man."

While Baker was recounting history in his office, filling out his lineup card for the Chicago Cubs, Sonny Jackson, one of Baker's coaches

and a former shortstop, came into the room. "The thing," Baker said, "that kept me going a lot—Sonny will tell you the same thing—we would think: what would Jackie do?"

"You deal with it," Jackson said. That's what Jackie did. "I'd call my Dad and he'd tell me the same thing. Those words keep coming into your mind: what would Jackie do?"

No copper bracelet engraved with that philosophy was necessary as reminder. Jackie was the hero to the generation of Baker's parents. Robinson's impact was in their daily lives whether it was said or unsaid. Like Robinson dealing with significantly more stress than white baseball players, black people do have to cope with another level of pressure in their daily lives. As Baker put it, "I'm not a racist, but I live in the real world."

Baker went to Del Campo High School in Carmichael, outside Sacramento, California. "We were the only black family in the community," he said. "There were only two black kids in the high school—me and my brother. Only one black kid in junior high—my sister. It was a good thing I could play football, baseball, basketball, and run track, just as I was expected to do."

When the Bakers moved in, for-sale signs went up on houses across the street. A neighbor told his sister to get on her side of the street. "A lot of people really didn't want us there," Baker said.

The football coach called a meeting of his team and accused the white players—that is, all the players but the Baker brothers—"because he thought they were missing blocks on purpose trying to get us killed," Baker said.

Four decades later, Baker declined to make that accusation himself: No complaining; deal with it. "Well," he said, "the coach thought they were. It didn't matter what Baker thought, I was going to get my touchdowns, no matter what, anyway."

Baker laughed at what back then had been a kick in the stomach. "You laugh now," he said. "Well, I think we were able to deal with adversity. . . ."

Sonny Jackson completed the thought for Baker: "Ain't no choice. Otherwise we don't survive."

❖

All the minor–league teams of the Braves were in the South. That first full season at Greenwood, South Carolina, Baker experienced the standard indignity of having to accept meals on the bus. All the players lived with families, white players with white families and one pair of black players living behind Momma's, the soul food restaurant. To watch television, the black players had to go to a white player's house, as long as they were careful not to attract much attention.

In spring training in Moultrie, Georgia, spectators would call the few black players names and throw black cats on the field as a normal ritual. The black players did find some encouragement from teammates after a night–long bus trip. When they stopped for breakfast and the black players were told they had to eat in the kitchen, the white players chose to get back on the bus. If they couldn't all eat together, they weren't going to eat at all.

Baker's reflection at age 56 is that young people then were generally open to blacks and whites working and playing together, it was their elders who supported the old barriers. Of course, there was the time one of Baker's minor–league managers told his players, "All you guys from California, dress over there so you don't mess up the rest of the team." He was kidding about the California lifestyle and dress, but his directive had its element of kidding on the square. To that manager, baseball players from California needed separate handling, and who were they to argue? Baker laughs at that now.

By 1967, when Baker began in the minor leagues, black players were not uncommon. Black players had been stars on the highest levels for some time. Racist laws had been struck down in the courts. Attitudes that had been ingrained for a century, however, were slower to change. In many of the minor–league towns, the presence of black players was still unwelcome.

After a game in Charleston, West Virginia, around 1970, Baker and some black teammates were riding in a car on a dark rural road next to a river when they saw they were being pursued by white men in another car. Were the white men trying to drive them off the road, down the embankment into the river? Did the white men intend to block the road and give them a beating or worse? American history made Baker consider all those possibilities, none of them acceptable.

Baker and his teammates had no choice but to flee. "Being caught was not a good thing," Baker said. "We outran them in the car and one guy threw a softball at us, hit the window where I was sitting and didn't break it. We're going 80 miles an hour and our driver's door came open." The driver managed to keep control of the car and pull the door closed. Eventually, Baker's car emerged from the secluded road into relative safety of town and their pursuers drove off. It had been a frightening time. Backer sighed recounting his relief.

Another time in Palm Beach, Baker and some other minor–league teammates from the Braves system were playing pool. Some Spanish–speaking players, plus Baker and Mike McQueen, a white ballplayer, were all speaking Spanish. Baker had learned enough Spanish to get by while playing winter ball in the Caribbean. But once Baker spoke English in the pool hall, the proprietor asked where he was from. When Baker answered that he was from California, he was told to get out. Latin American blacks were acceptable; American blacks were not.

The proprietor said, "We didn't serve Maury Wills and we're not going to serve you." Baker impulsively tried to overturn the pool table, but it was bolted to the floor.

By then Baker had learned that Henry Aaron, a star with the Braves and 15 years older, had room under his wing to help young black players. Baker, "mad as hell," went directly to Aaron's room. Aaron explained that Wills was light–skinned and therefore might be perceived as a Latin player. He would be more acceptable than a dark–skinned American. If they didn't serve light–skinned Wills, Aaron said, they certainly weren't going to serve Baker.

"We used to go to Hank for everything," Baker said.

At Richmond, Virginia, in the AAA International League, the Braves' highest farm team, black players couldn't rent in the nicer areas of the city and they couldn't rent on the other side of Nickel Bridge where several white players lived. Baker was left to stay at a room in the Eckleston Motel, a hotbed establishment in a black neighborhood. "And that's where I got my introduction to a man called Bimbo, pimps, and prostitutes," Baker said. "It was a good lesson for me because you learn everybody's people. Those were my partners, so to speak, and they took care of me."

On an AAA International League road trip to Shreveport, Louisiana, a bastion of old–guard segregation, Baker went to a dinner with a white former minor–league teammate—Ted Bashore, now a doctor in Colorado—and his wife. Baker waited outside after dinner while Bashore paid the bill. When Bashore emerged, police were holding Baker in a spotlight, spread–eagled against the wall. "The cop said it was against a city ordinance for blacks and whites to be on the street together," Baker said. "Then Ted came out and saved me."

He and Bashore get together from time to time and always talk about the incident. "It was the first and last time I was ever spread against the wall," Baker said. "I didn't know what the cop was going to do." Actually, the cop could have done almost anything and Baker knew it. As Lou Brock said, it was the ever–present danger.

After each season Baker would go home to California and be drawn to the tumult at Berkeley and the continuous demonstrations intended to change society. Baker was drawn to the Black Panthers and Malcolm X. For a time Baker seriously considered changing his name to Dusty X. "My Dad wouldn't let me," Baker said. He was still the son of Johnnie Baker Sr.

Baker's father, a longtime navy man, was always called "Mr. Baker" with considerable respect by Dusty's friends. To him, the Panthers would have been the other side of the same coin of racism. "He wouldn't let me go to Berkeley to hang out with the Panthers," Dusty said. Mr. Baker also refused to let Dusty shine shoes or caddy on the golf course. His son was not going to be subservient to anyone.

While Baker was trying to find where he fit into the spectrum between Martin Luther King Jr. and Malcolm X, his baseball performance earned him a promotion as a regular with the Braves in 1972. In Atlanta, Aaron welcomed Baker's curiosity about life and the strength of Baker's black identification. Aaron had become active in the Georgia community of black civil rights leaders, communicating often with Dr. Martin Luther King Jr. Aaron frequently hosted meetings at his home and invited Baker to join the company of Maynard Jackson and Andrew Young and Herman Russell, black civil rights leaders Baker's mother had made him read about. Baker absorbed a sense of balance that has contributed to his success as a manager.

As a teammate, Baker witnessed Aaron's excruciating time while chasing down Babe Ruth's career home–run record. Baker and outfielder Ralph Garr were obliged to sit with Aaron on the airplane and make him laugh to relieve the relentless pressure. Sometimes when they thought Aaron was asleep they'd try to get up and move about the plane and Aaron would grab a wrist, tell them to sit back down, and laugh. Aaron's contagious laugh is legendary among teammates. So is the strength of his hands.

Baker and Garr read some of Aaron's hate mail and death threats and saw how he coped. Baker recalls that at the time he saw Aaron as a second father. As a manager, Baker gets some of that hate mail and shows it to white and black players. Some of that mail is directed at Baker as a black man and some of it demonstrates that any manager is blamed when things go wrong. "I think Hank prepared me for now," Baker said.

❖

Being a Californian used to few restrictions, Baker found Atlanta in the early 1970s a trial. It was even more stress being identified as "the next Hank Aaron." Opponents nicknamed Aaron "Bad Henry" because he was so good. Baker was a fine player—a good outfielder, a consistent hitter and a reliable teammate. He was named Most Valuable Player in the 1977 National League Championship series for the Dodgers, but he wasn't another Henry Aaron. "There wasn't a next Hank, there'll never be another," Baker said, "but you know we're always looking for the next something or next somebody."

Having to live up to "expectations" often makes a player bitter as it did famously for Darryl Strawberry, who railed at the mention of what was called his "potentials." Dusty Baker was able to accept doing his best no matter what others thought he should do. Mr. Baker taught his son Dusty to protect himself from anger. "It only eats you up," Dusty Baker said.

Baker was building a barrier made out of resentment to protect himself in the early 1970s from the white society that demeaned him when his childhood friend from Sacramento Dennis Kludt found Baker in Florida in the Braves' training camp. This white man, Baker says, reminded him that not all the white world was hostile. "Dennis didn't have parents; it was just him and his sister. He didn't have much food," Baker said, recalling their childhood together. "He came to my house to eat all the time. He's still my main friend." But later when Kludt was writing letters and phoning his friend Dusty, Baker refused to answer because he was stung by the treatment he was receiving in the minor leagues. "I was mad," Baker recalled.

Baker was mad at the way he was being treated as a black man, mad enough at the white world that he couldn't make the distinction between the tormentors and a treasured friend. "All of a sudden," Baker said, "I was driving down the street in West Palm Beach with the Braves and I saw somebody stopped at a light. It was Dennis and his wife, Yvonne. He told me since I didn't answer his letters he was going to drive to Florida from California. Damn, I felt bad. How many people would have done that, white or black?" Dennis Kludt, a white man, was upset that he was losing his link with Dusty Baker and drove 2,000 miles out of his way to renew their friendship.

He stayed with Baker for a week before driving to Maine to visit his wife's family. Baker called that renewal "a turning point in my life." In his mind, the doors Baker was closing off to the white community were reopened.

Baker's education in race relations advanced another step when he was traded to the Dodgers in 1976. There were still Dodgers whose roots were entwined with Jackie Robinson and with PeeWee Reese, the white Kentuckian who reached out to Robinson. Jim Gilliam, then a wise coach and a former teammate of Robinson's, told how Jackie gracefully but forcefully caused the Chase Hotel in St. Louis to accept black Dodgers in the dining room.

Henry Aaron used to talk about Robinson's legacy, and now Gilliam spoke of playing with Jackie. He told of how Robinson would be literally sick at what he had to take and how he disliked having to turn his back on it, but understood the cross he was carrying.

"The Devil—that's Gilliam's nickname—told me Jackie died of a broken heart and everybody said it was diabetes," Baker said. "Stress. But back then they didn't call it stress; that's a relatively new term."

Jackie, through college and sports stardom, was used to a predominantly white society that was intent on marginalizing him. Reese, shortstop and captain, was the strongest leader on the Brooklyn Dodgers, and conspicuous in his support of rookie Robinson when he was so alone. When Robinson was being abused ruthlessly in Cincinnati, there was Reese, with family and friends from across the river in Kentucky, to put his arm around Robinson in the face of the crowd.

In recent years some people in the black community have said that giving Reese credit is actually saying that this black man Robinson could not have succeeded without white Reese's patronization. Gilliam, who played second base beside Reese and gained from Reese's presence, thought otherwise. "Gilliam loved PeeWee," Baker said. "He talked about PeeWee all the time." The experience Gilliam passed along provided one more facet to manager Baker's people skills.

Today there are still times Baker feels responsibility to a whole race. He says he didn't feel that way as a player, because many black players had succeeded or failed before Baker. But he does feel the pressure of identification as a manager, being one of so few given authority over white men, being tested for wit and wisdom rather than for a strong back. When Aaron came to Chicago, Baker and Aaron would go to Jesse

Jackson's home and they'd discuss that issue of accountability to the race. "I'd hear it and feel it," Baker said.

The utopian ideal is to be identified as a manager, and not a black manager. Sometimes Baker feels he's getting closer to this ideal, but when things don't work out his mail reminds him that some fans still see his blackness before they evaluate his ability. Then he remembers that the contents of his mailbag aren't as vile as Aaron's. That must be progress.

The breadth of Baker's awareness—the things he sees and feels—is uncommon among managers or former players whose sensibilities were bounded by the white lines of the playing field. He doesn't see the public resentment of Aaron challenging Babe Ruth's record as solely racial but also as an aspect human nature. "Most of us don't want to see the heroes of the past passed," he said.

Certainly it's in Baker's face that so many worthy black candidates to manage have been refused the opportunity. The specifics he sees are not so obvious. Gilliam, who died in 1978, was one of those passed over repeatedly although his baseball wisdom was apparent. While Baker was a Dodgers player and Gilliam a coach, they discussed that, and Baker came away recognizing critical factors that aren't racist.

"I thought he was going to be a great, great manager; I thought he was the brains of the operation," Baker said. "He told me, 'Dusty, I'm not as educated as I'd like to be.' I didn't know what he meant at that time, but he was so right."

Perhaps if Gilliam was educated in an environment other than what was available to a black man in Tennessee in the 1930s, he might have had the verbal skills necessary to manage. Baker acknowledges that no matter how much baseball a man knows, a manager must be able to communicate with newspapers, radio, and television, and must have the ability to reach a generation of players who need explanations who quickly turn off to a manager they can't understand or don't trust.

Baker's communication skills are assets beyond measure. "Players see through B.S. now more than ever," he said.

During those years with the Braves, Baker often discussed the experience Orlando Cepeda had with the successful racial mix of the

St. Louis Cardinals. In essentially a southern city, the Cardinals won championships and won the populace. "To this day, I think about that team, as far as how I like my team to be," Baker said.

⁂

Baker feels he got a better understanding of the role of manager from his time in the Marine Corps. He served six months of active duty, a weekend a month and two weeks every summer from 1969 to 1975. He spent time talking with men who fought in World War II, in Korea, and Vietnam, and learned how deeply they relied on the men in the next foxhole without regard to their nationality, race, or religion.

The definition of teamwork the Marine Corps offers is taken from the dedication of the Marine Corps cemetery on Iwo Jima, one of the bloodiest battlefields of World War II by Rabbi Roland Gittelsohn Chaplain of the Fifth Marine Division:

> "Here lie men who loved America . . . Here there are no quotas of how many from each group are admitted or allowed. . . . Whosoever of us . . . who thinks himself superior to those who happen to be in the minority makes this ceremony and the bloody sacrifice it commemorates an empty, hollow mockery. . . ."

Baseball is not war; a base runner slides into the second baseman to break up a double play and everybody gets up afterward. But a great team is defined by players sacrificing selfish interest for the good of the team. "I learned a lot about teamwork and stuff," Baker said of his service in the Marine Corps. "You save his ass and he's going to save yours—even if you don't like him and he doesn't like you. That's teamwork."

With his baseball career extended by his years as a successful manager, he has grown through generations of change and added substance to his life. He has taken input from all directions. Of course, there was his father, and the warm guidance of Henry Aaron as a teammate, exposure to the Black Panthers in tempestuous Berkeley, the childhood friend whose loyalty reminded him that not all white people were hostile, the influence of the Marine Corps, and the eulogy at Iwo Jima by a Marine Corps rabbi that has become a kind of monument in the corps. These things stimulated Baker's growth before he ever had to deal with managing Barry Bonds.

Dusty Baker's hope is to be identified just as "manager." Someday maybe that day will come.

19

Coping with the Ever-Present Danger

Lou Brock Outsmarted the Threats

(Born El Dorado, Arkansas, June 18, 1939-)

THE FIRST SEASON WAS CULTURE SHOCK for Lou Brock. In starting out in St. Cloud, Minnesota, he had gone from an all–black Louisiana community, where he had lived all his life, to an all–white community, where they had lived all their lives. If there was one black family in the area, Lou Brock never saw it.

"I knew there was a different culture," he said looking back with an adult's sophistication and wisdom. "Could I make an adjustment to the new culture without losing my identity? I can't lose my identity because I'm black. How can I adapt? They wouldn't change, I knew that."

To his surprise, he was welcomed. It was 1961 and he was playing on a farm team for the Chicago Cubs. He had trouble eating and sleeping because he was so consumed by his opportunity. "I've got to make it here," he told himself, "I just can't go back to Louisiana and Arkansas." He was the son of sharecroppers. He had been there and knew what was there.

He felt he needed to control his curious mind, to keep himself from reaching too far into this new world and having it blur his baseball focus. He had abundant baseball talent. If he let any side issue deter him, he wasn't going to reach his goal. He was going to be a big–league baseball player and he was never going back to that sharecropper's farm.

He led the Northern League in batting average, hits, and runs. It was his only season in the minors.

He had left what he calls the rule of the jungle of the South and its ever-present danger. "Don't break the rules or they can hang you from a tree without ever facing the law," he said, drawing a picture north-ern whites—even those of a certain age—can't visualize and southern whites find more comfortable to deny. "It's the cloud over your head, dictating what you can do, what to say, and when to say it," Brock said. "You grow up thinking white people are not your friends. You are a second-class citizen and they can wipe you out any moment they want to. So, if I'm going to survive, I'm never going to show up where there's a risk of them socializing."

He wasn't going to run the risk of socializing with white people. If he did, maybe there would be some accidental event and he'd be blamed, or maybe he'd just be rejected and insulted. If he did let down his guard, he said, "I'm running the risk. How often do you want to run that risk? And you're being told you're not good enough."

❖

Lou Brock was born in 1939 in El Dorado, Arkansas. He kids that the community called itself the land of opportunity and "the first oppor-tunity I have, I got the hell out of there." Nice line, except the next stop was Collinstown, Louisiana. He was the child of sharecroppers; he never knew his father. He knew too well that whether it was a good year or a bad year in the cotton field, his mother wound up owing the plantation owner $300. In spite of the poverty of his background he knew that education was a way out.

He won an academic scholarship to all-black Southern University in Baton Rouge as a math major. He was going to play baseball, but he was determined to get an education. Nobody was going to cheat him with numbers. In his sophomore year at Southern he hit .565, Southern became the first black school to win the NAIA baseball championship, and Brock was selected for the 1959 Pan-American Games. Not only was he black, he was so green that when the stewardess brought his meal in the first–class flight to the games, he thought he had to pay for the meal and it looked too expensive for the $3 in his pocket. He told the stewardess he never ate on airplanes.

Skip ahead to June of 1964, his third big–league season, and the trade that sent him from the Cubs to the St. Louis Cardinals. By then he had demonstrated he belonged in the big leagues and could survive in the white community, but the Cardinals were above and beyond what he had experienced with the Cubs. The Cardinals were close to what social scientists envisioned for Utopia. They had a white manager in Johnny Keane and white stars in Stan Musial, Tim McCarver, and Ken Boyer, and black stars in Bill White, Bob Gibson, and Curt Flood. Neither side of the divide resented the other. They were a good team on the verge of being a great team.

"They were tough on each other and just as tough—more so—on the opposition," Brock observed. "They had respect for each other. They never impugned that you could do more than you were doing or that you were holding back. They knew what to expect from each player and got what they expected. That allowed each player to become a confirmed member of the team, and yet be outstanding in his own right.

"That became the groupthink: can I be outstanding in my own right if I have great talent or less talent? The answer was yes. You have synergy, which means you're going to play at a consistent level, higher than if somebody walked in and tried to motivate you."

In an essentially southern city, players may have had their independent views on racial issues but they didn't apply them to teammates. "I don't think they looked at it as black and white," Brock said. "The uniform was the identity. The style of play became the motivation. Winning became the ultimate goal."

In rural Collinstown life was separated into two distinct worlds with no teams to bring them together. "And now you walk into that St. Louis clubhouse—remember the word 'clubhouse.' Then whatever your upbringing, your character, your family, your personality, your behavior, you are governed by a different set of rules—always relating to the team. Jim Crow was not in there, although he may have been in existence. Black power wasn't in there. White supremacy wasn't in there."

Such chemistry could not exist just anyplace. On "the Cubbies," as Brock calls them, a man was always trying to prove himself. "I never thought I had to prove anything to the Cardinals. Whatever I had to prove, they told me to prove it to the opposition," he said.

The Cardinals held their self–image as the Yankees had theirs: You act like a Yankee and you act like a Cardinal. "What is expected of me as a big–league ballplayer, aside from being a black player, aside from growing up in the South, aside from having a locker next to a white player, aside from not going into a restaurant he's able to go to, I come into this arena recognized for having performed at a certain level," Brock said. "Now I need a stage to play this out on."

The newcomer must learn that everybody plays by those same rules of the game. Brock tends to intellectualize the unstated rules. At St. Cloud, for the first time in his life he dressed next to a white player in the clubhouse. Whether or not they were comfortable, they had to make it work.

With the Cardinals he had to learn that relations with white play-ers weren't threatening. "It was the relationship after the game," Brock said. With the Cubs in spring training in Mesa, Arizona, players were required to eat together at the hotel. The Cardinals were free to come and go as they pleased. "But where did most players wind up?" Brock discovered. "You could go after a game and see five or six players together; invariably two or three of those guys would be black."

This was happening to Lou Brock who showed up for a tryout with the Cubs with baseball shoes so battered that first baseman Ed Bouchee, a white man, gave him a pair of his. They were too small, but Brock wore them because they were better than what he had. He had $10 in his pocket and washed floors at the YMCA in order to wait for the tryout.

He was still so green that when the Cubs elevated him at the end of 1961, he ran down a drive by the great Musial and clung to the ball in his glove. Richie Ashburn, the sage in center field, shouted, "Kid, sooner or later you got to throw it back." Legend says that the next spring Warren Spahn of the Braves hit Brock with a pitch and he ran to first thinking the bruise was a souvenir of the great Spahn. "Fall down, kid. Fall down," Spahn yelled. "Goddamn it, fall down so it will look like I'm throwing hard."

He was pursuing baseball as if it were a mathematical equation. He had speed, which was for him like the "given" in geometry. He ran so fast that when he played baseball at Southern that friends woke him at midnight and demanded he race the conference sprint champion, Harry Keyes. They had the lights on the football field turned on and Brock left the sprinter in the dust.

So he asked Maury Wills, the reigning base stealer, about telltale details of pitchers. At the start of 1964 he brought a video camera onto the field. Dodger pitcher Don Drysdale asked what in the world Brock was doing with the camera. "Just taking home movies," Brock replied with mock innocence. "I don't want to be in your goddamn home movies," Drysdale said. The next time Brock went to the plate, Drysdale threw at him.

Bob Gibson, the Cardinals pitcher destined for the Hall of Fame, often was called upon to retaliate against embarrassed pitchers who threw at Brock. Brock learned his craft as a base stealer so well that he wound up taking the career record of stolen bases away from Ty Cobb. Brock studied each pitcher for the giveaway that told him when to steal. He broke Maury Wills's five–year string of leading the league in steals and Brock led eight of the next nine seasons. His 118 bases stolen in 1974 stood as the major–league record until 1982 when Rickey Henderson stole 130 bases. However, it would be a deception to think Brock got into the Hall of Fame as a thief. He blossomed with the Cardinals, hitting .300 eight times. He is one of three players ever to hit a ball into the distant center–field bleachers at the Polo Grounds in New York. More revealing, in his first four seasons with the Cardinals they won three pennants and two World Series.

And once in Shea Stadium in New York, he pointed to the Band–Aid on his arm and said, "It says on the box, 'flesh colored.' Does this look flesh colored to you?"

Of course not. Brock was what he was: curious, insightful, and black, no matter how much more exposed he became to the world outside the Louisiana cotton field. At Southern, when freedom riders were boarding buses and young people were sitting in deliberately to be refused at lunch counters, the coaches ruled that any athlete who got caught demonstrating would lose his scholarship. "And I was one of them," Brock said. "I never did march."

His performance playing baseball served as his march, and his team won. America was watching and saw Jackie Robinson and Pee-Wee Reese shaking hands; they saw hugs in the clubhouse. The year after Robinson desegregated the major leagues, 1948, the army desegregated. "Why?" Brock said. "Because baseball had said it was okay. Baseball had shown it was okay. Now people could imagine. That's the beauty part of baseball: The daily box score.

"Nobody had to tell the world; people could pick up the paper and see it. Prior to that, a man, no matter what his work was, still was judged on his color. At this instant, in the civil rights movement, they were saying, do not judge me based upon my color; you must judge me based upon my work. And, I think, this is the first time that the work of a man really began to become public knowledge."

A black athlete being equal to a white athlete and working toward a common goal presented a conflict to the rules of Brock's childhood. Then it was understood that white people were not your friends. One of the kids Brock played with was white Billy Puckett. "We grew up together," Brock said. "He ate at my house; I went to his house; I ate with him. We didn't have any organized league; we played. The moment we put on the organized thing, we were governed by rules.

"That ever-present danger was over his head as well as mine, for knowing each other. We were at the point where you can reproduce. That is the ability to change the world without a weapon. That's when all the hostility takes place."

At Southern University Brock objected to the coaches' rules that said he mustn't break the rules. He was a subtle as he could be. To Brock in Baton Rouge that meant he better not be seen or caught breaking them. "You break the rule," Brock said. "You sit in a café, sit at the counter knowing they wouldn't serve you. I was riding on buses with people telling me to get up and go ride in the back. I was told, 'The bus is not going to pull off until you move.' I remember holding my grounds, sitting in the seat.

"If somebody shows up, what do you do? You do what you gotta do at the time you got to do it. I never experienced dogs and fire hoses. But the danger was ever present. Which means you just as well may have experienced it, except the physical aspect of it."

He stayed out of trouble but his baseball talent and the school's success made him highly visible. Scouts were working in their devious ways. National League scouts were telling black players there was better mixing of black and white in their league. American League scouts were telling white prospects in the South that they wouldn't have to deal with as many blacks in their league.

"But television was showing kids relationships between black and white teammates and friends," Brock said. "Maybe they have parents who say that is not how they do things. But, believe it or not, the relationship with the friend will always override the relationship of a kid to a parent.

"I had a white man tell me hate groups had come to him when he was 14 years old. 'But they came too late,' he said 'because I already knew about Bob Gibson and Lou Brock when I was eight years old. By the time they got to me, it was too late.' Because sports said it was OK to have that relationship. What they see, through the media, and by performance in the public arena permeates throughout society."

Through the 1960s and 1970s, Brock saw the concept of separate water fountains fading and the "ruling authority" becoming free to change its rules. Many people resented that they had to give up a fundamental rule of life they'd been taught for two or three hundred years. Black players said they were going to stretch that rule. Even if players never spoke out, their presence spoke out. Rickey and Robinson broke the rule in 1947. "Manifestation didn't need for them to speak, it needed them to perform," Brock said.

The early black players who passed through the slimmest of gaps were on the firing line. They knew the danger of their time and place.

They had their own trapdoor for safety in the line of fire. Brock points to a scene in the film *Ray*, the story of Ray Charles's life. In it Ray Charles's mother plants in her son's mind that what other people said did not matter as long as he didn't get too close to the ever–present danger. "When it gets that close, you will find a way to survive it," Brock said. "Don't ever forget that it exists."

20

The Only Black in the Room

Bob Watson Wears a Necktie

(Born Los Angeles, California, April 10, 1946-)

PEOPLE WHO HAVE KNOWN BOB WATSON from his time as a player call him Bull because he's so strong. Just ask the smartass bigots in Houston who thought they should run him off the road because no nigger like him should be driving such a nice car. That is, if you can find those guys.

In the office of the commissioner of baseball, Watson is known for no bull as the director of on–field operations, commonly known as the lord of discipline. He has a handsome corner office with big windows that look onto Park Avenue in New York. That's the highest position a black man has ever held in the chain of command.

Watson paid his dues for a lot of years. In 1975 he scored the millionth run in baseball history, which was happenstance; his shoe that touched home plate is in Cooperstown. He had a long and successful career as a player and when he coached the Oakland A's in 1988, he was the highest paid coach in the major leagues. He took a cut in pay to be the assistant general manager of the Houston Astros.

No black man had ever been that high in anybody's front office. It appeared that it might be a long time before there was another such minority opportunity and it was a job Watson had identified for himself for some time. Somebody had to go through the door first. Somebody had to effect change.

When the Astros elevated him to the general manager's position in 1993, they gave Watson the keys to the Astrodome. The Astrodome was the first of the domed stadiums, the place the Astros—then called the Houston Colt .45s—boasted as the Eighth Wonder of the World. They sent him out to do business with executives who had been making deals for years. He went to the general managers' meetings and was the only black person in the room.

And, as he recalls, he was seen as a black sheep to be fleeced. There wasn't even another black executive coming through the pipeline.

"People on the other side looked at you," he recalled. "They didn't know how you conducted business and how you went about making trades. There were things said that I know wouldn't have been said if I were someone else. Like, would you make this XYZ trade that was totally ridiculous? They were thinking normally they wouldn't even propose a deal like that, but here's a young black guy who didn't take the general manager's 101 course. We'll ask him and he might be dumb enough to do it. Out of respect, you think they would give you the benefit of the doubt, but that was not the case all of the time."

Sometimes Watson would back away from their implausible proposition and have an assistant or a limited partner in the Astros take on the conversation in order to get something constructive done.

Watson was speaking of this at his corporate office, having stepped in when Frank Robinson was assigned to manage the struggling Montreal team on its way to Washington. That was after Watson had been general manager of the New York Yankees and won the World Series in 1996 and 1997. That was no bull. He held the keys to the House That Ruth Built and then he grasped the championship trophy in Yankee Stadium. His stewardship restored the Yankees to their throne after an 18-year absence. In doing that he held his wide body in front of George Steinbrenner's arrows intended for the manager, Joe Torre, and players. And Watson took the arrows for the little people in the office who called him Uncle Bob.

Of course Watson knew what he was getting into by going to work as general manager for That Man. He had played for Steinbrenner's Yankees from 1980 through 1982, played in pinstripes in the 1981 World

Series. How could he not know? "How could you know?" Carol Watson, Bob's wife, said in an interview after her husband had moved out of That Man's clutches. "This is analogous to reading a book about having a baby." Bob had the strength to withstand Steinbrenner's abuse and he had the strength to say no more and walk away in February 1998.

Carol Watson had seen the toll her husband paid. Tenuous as any job is for Steinbrenner, the Watsons kept their home in Houston and Carol would visit New York and Bob's hotel suite when the Yankees were home. "I'd get up in the morning and walk to St. Patrick's Cathedral," she said, "and light a candle, and get on my knees and pray for an hour and I'm not Catholic. I'd go out the back door of St. Patrick's and sit in the garden at St. Bart's and just meditate. Because at the end of the day the game would be over, I'd come back to the hotel and there would be George blowing Bob up."

It wasn't that Steinbrenner was being racist; he did give a black man the opportunity to be general manager of the most successful franchise in sports. That man was an equal–opportunity abuser.

※

Watson was thoroughly tested before he ever got to the big leagues. He was part of the generation of baseball players who went through the minor leagues in the South in the late 1960s when the new civil rights laws said the community could no longer treat black people as its Jim Crow mentality had. And the community kept right on treating black people just the way Jim Crow had.

Bob and Carol grew up in Los Angeles where certain rules were understood. "Hats," she said. "Ladies couldn't try on hats in downtown stores. They didn't want our hair touching anything. But we had our own community and integrated schools. We didn't face any real prejudice until we left home and found out that white people didn't like black people. I really didn't know that."

Colleges in the South were recruiting athletes for the first time and plunging them into hostile communities. Baseball had been doing that since 1947 and hadn't learned much from it. The Houston ball club told Watson nothing about the segregation he'd face, and they certainly didn't tell his mother or the grandparents who raised him. "All they told me was: you're going to get an opportunity to play," Watson said. "I think it's the obligation of clubs to tell families what their young men are getting ready to face."

The most devastating moment in the Western Carolinas League for Watson was not having to live in the home with a 70–year–old black man or having to accept cold meals on the bus, but a local business pro-motion. Get a game–winning hit or hit a home run and get a Salisbury steak dinner, it promised. "Well, I'm the leading hitter on the team and I go to cash in my steak dinners," Watson said, "and they said, 'No, you can't eat here.' I said, 'Give me my steak dinner and I'll take it home.' They just said no. And I was devastated. I couldn't understand."

He was on the major–league roster the next spring but when he was reassigned, there was a lapse of a week between the time the major–league team moved out and the Class A Cocoa Beach team assembled. The organization had to find a place for the two black players to stay. The best the Houston organization could find for two black men in Cocoa Beach was beds at a black funeral parlor. They slept for four nights in the viewing room before a hospitable family agreed to put them up. That was when Watson called home and considered training as a chef or as a technical illustrator instead of trying to be a baseball player.

"Your life had no value where I was," Watson reflected. "Your exis-tence was just a matter of fact. A bunch of guys said the hell with it, I'm going home. Charlie Murray was one of them. Others said, this is my dream; I'm going to stick it out. I was one of them."

When Watson was eight or nine, he remembers his parents and grandparents raving about Jackie Robinson playing for the Brooklyn Dodgers. "He was so much the idol," Watson said. "We didn't have a bracelet, but when we got into situations in the minor leagues, we'd ask, 'How would Jackie handle this?' That became a battle cry."

He was catching and was the leading hitter when the Astros drafted a new catcher and tried Watson in left field. They were playing in Green-ville, South Carolina—brick wall in the outfield, no padding, and no warning track. Larry Bingham from Alabama was in center field and Edmundo Moxey, from the Bahamas, was in right. The ball was hit deep to left center.

"I'm running full speed and I get to the wall and the center fielder is coming and he doesn't say 'watch out' or anything," Watson said, "And—bam—I hit the wall, break my left wrist and break the tip of my shoulder and I'm lying there in pain. The right fielder is coming over to help me, and him and the center fielder get into it. Moxie said to Bingham, 'How come you didn't let him know he was close to the wall?' Bingham made a smart remark, and the next thing you know they're fighting there in the outfield.

"The ball is on the ground and the guy is running around the bases for an inside–the–park home run. Bingham said to Moxey, 'It seemed it was just another black guy and it doesn't matter. He used up all the room anyway.'" To Bingham, Watson was "just another black guy."

In Salisbury, North Carolina, of the Class A Western Carolinas League, Watson and two black teammates had a day off. They didn't allow baseball on Sunday in Salisbury in 1965, and the teammates went into town to the movies. They came out and it looked as if there was a parade coming their way. "Folks with torches and banners and they had sheets," Watson said. "I had never seen these people before—not even on the news."

Moxie was a little older and, even if he was from the Bahamas, he knew. "He said, 'Hey, *mon*, let's run.'" Watson said. "We concluded it was a Klan rally or demonstration and I wasn't about to stand there and debate them. I'm the slowest of the three guys but I kept up with them and they ran like hell. We beat it back across the tracks, cut through a little forest to get to the house where we were staying. That was 1965 in Salisbury, North Carolina."

By 1975 America was supposed to be more advanced. Watson was playing in Houston, a major American city, not backwoods North Carolina. Segregation prevents understanding among different people; integration is supposed to educate people about coexistence and the concept of working together. Watson was an established big leaguer. It was late in the season and Watson was among the league leaders in hitting. He was driving home from the airport at 2:30 or so in the morning, sitting high up in his Blazer. Two white guys in the car to his left were squeezing his lane, waving their fists and bottles.

"We pull up to a stoplight and the one guy hops out of the car, and I'm not taking this and I jump out of mine," Watson said. "The guy says, 'Why are you driving this big car, you black so–and–so?' I said, 'Why is it a problem with you what kind of vehicle I drive?'

"He says, 'Black folks are not supposed to have this, and we're going to run you off the road.' I said, 'Oh, really.' The guy came toward me and I hit him a left on the jaw, hit him so hard blood shot out of his ears and eyes. The other one takes off and runs. I reach in and take their keys and drive home in my Blazer."

Watson's swollen hand had what is known as a fighter's break. He missed the last three weeks of the season and ended up hitting .324, fifth in the batting race. "There's no doubt in my mind I would win the batting title," he said. "I let a racial incident get the best of me and it cost me. I was lucky the guys didn't have a gun and there was only two of them. I gave their keys to the police the next day in case a guy came in with a broken jaw. But how much restraint, how much can one person take is really the question."

There are lists upon lists of incidents of bigotry. There are always individuals who are drunk or are drunk with delusions of superiority. This was in 1975, not 1875. Bob Watson was a bright and insightful black man who was subjected to more than he could bear. He was not an isolated case; he was an illustration of life that was unreasonable and terribly common. He disagrees with Bob Gibson's assertion that they're all the same stories. "Little tiles make up the big picture," Watson said.

Bob and Carol Watson were uncommon people but that didn't exempt them from commonplace prejudice. When they were with the Astros, Carol invited the team's wives and girlfriends to her home for a pool party. Word came back from one Arizona–raised wife that she wouldn't go to the home of a black woman. "I don't know what happened to that husband and wife but I know where we are," Carol said.

She and Bob were not intimidated to move into new areas of life. They loved their time with the Red Sox in 1979, the last team in the American League to accept a black player. They loved the camaraderie among the players, the tradition of the team in Boston and the mystique of the Green Monster of Fenway Park. She gave dinners and "the girls got together and were friends," she said. Players and wives "were open the way I supposed a team was supposed to be."

The common people of Boston, that cradle of democracy, hardly mixed. The Watsons lived in Wellesley and met other black people only in church.

When Bob played with the Yankees in 1980, he and Carol wound up in Teaneck, New Jersey, in a predominantly Jewish neighborhood as the first black family on the block. He and Carol had read that Teaneck— the community that 20 years earlier had obstructed Elston and Arlene Howard—by then was identified by one publication as among the three top communities in the country in dealing with racial diversity. There were black children on the next block and Japanese and Spanish–speaking families nearby. The Watsons had done their homework.

The black community, however, was resentful. "Disappointing," Carol said. "They said, 'Oh, you live over there?' We just picked a house we could afford and put our children in predominantly Jewish schools. Black people thought, 'Don't be different.' I've received that from black and whites; any time you rise above, 'Do you think you're better?'"

They were different. Carol has a bachelor's and a master's degree and is a PhD candidate as a visual artist whose work with textiles is infused with elements of spirituality. She's a fiber artist and collage artist. She loves museums and exploring the world. Bob's ambition is not limited to the playing field. In the midseason strike of 1981, while he was playing with the Yankees, he worked in the institutional investment office of Cyrus J. Lawrence, carried his own briefcase to work and saw the world. When the strike was over and he went back to playing baseball, he was an adult in a league of perpetual adolescents. "I had no idea," he said, "what it meant to be up at 6 a.m. every morning, shave and shower, and ride the train an hour to get to the tube to Wall Street, elbow to elbow with those people who do it every morning. It opened my eyes to what's out there."

He could talk baseball with business investors for 15 minutes, and then they wanted to know what he could do for them.

When he interviewed for a coaching job in Oakland and general manager Sandy Alderson asked what his career goal was, Watson replied, "To sit in your chair."

Being the assistant general manager in Houston and then general manager were giant steps forward for Bob Watson and, by extension, for blacks in baseball. Going to the Yankees as general manager was a step into the fire. One of Watson's reasons for taking the job was that the Yankees office is such a showcase for a black man on the job. Jackie Robinson and Larry Doby were visible on the field; Watson defied the stereotype by doing what he could in a shirt and tie at a desk.

He told of standing with Carol, tears streaming down their faces, when the last out of the Yankees' 1996 World Series victory was caught. It was, he said, "letting the world know an African American can put together a championship team."

When he accepted the championship trophy on the makeshift podium in the champagne–soaked clubhouse, he said, "Fifty years ago Jackie Robinson was opening up this door. . . . He would be proud, and all the things he went through for this day when I could stand here and receive this trophy."

When the Yankees had their big celebration at Tavern on the Green in New York's Central Park, Omar Minaya, then a minor–league executive from the Dominican Republic in the Mets organization, congratulated the crosstown rival. "Mr. Watson," he said. "I want to thank you for holding open a space for me to possibly get in."

Watson held the space open for Minaya to rise to general manager with Montreal and on to the Mets, and for Kenny Williams to win as general manager of the White Sox, and there are female executives with the Dodgers and the A's. "When Bob and I went to his first general manager winter meeting," Carol said, "there were a few black secretaries and nothing."

After years of playing, coaching, aspiring, interviewing, and waiting, Willie Randolph got his chance to manage the Mets. "I was real happy for him because he had all those window–dressing interviews," Watson said. "He was sincere but they weren't.

"I feel happy for him as a black person and for him getting it here in his hometown, because he has family and friends and all of those expectations. He's a New Yorker. More than anything, I am happy for him to be a major–league manager in the capital city of the world and have a chance to put his mark on baseball history."

Watson put himself on the line when he left the comfort and relative security of coaching for the Oakland A's. He could have been somebody's coach for a long time. But he felt he could fill a general manager's chair and was willing to take his chance, first for Bob Watson, and then for any black man who might have baseball ambitions beyond the limits of the playing field. He proved his capability with Houston and then with the ultimate challenge of the Yankees: A black man could put a team on the field and win.

21

Epilogue

We Integrated Baseball and America Followed

"A life is not important except in the impact it has on other lives."
—*Inscription on Jackie Robinson's tombstone*

BEFORE JACKIE ROBINSON, America was the home of democracy, except for most blacks and other minorities. Before Robinson no blacks were permitted in major–league baseball or any of the significant sports in America, except as gladiators in boxing. Blacks couldn't buy homes in the South or in many neighborhoods in the North, and many colleges had strict quotas. And that was just the beginning.

The United States Army and Navy segregated personnel and limited black servicemen to menial positions. A black person in a position of authority over whites was virtually unknown. Nat King Cole, a huge star and wealthy man, could sing and play piano in showrooms of great hotels, but he couldn't sleep in those hotels.

In the South, life for black people was so severely limited that water fountains and restrooms were rigidly separated between black and white. Schools were called separate but equal, which meant they were separate and a world apart. A black and a white were not permitted to marry in many states. Some states didn't permit black and white athletes to compete on the same playing field. And Montgomery, Alabama, would not permit them to play checkers against each other in a public place.

A black man could be dragged from his bed or from a jail and hanged from a tree for suspicion of anything. And the law supported or accepted all of that and more.

Was it imaginable at that time that someday two black men would be general managers of World Series champions, that black athletes could be unlimited in baseball and be the majorities in football and basketball? Was it possible that America could have had a black man and a black woman as secretary of state? How could it happen that Mississippi, which had hidden—even encouraged—the murder of three civil rights workers, would 41 years later try to convict the instigator?

When did these changes begin?

The changes began to take hold of America on the opening day of the 1947 baseball season when Jackie Robinson played his first game for the Brooklyn Dodgers. "Simply by his presence on the field, Robinson persuaded more white people to be fair about black people than have all those endless government or university meetings," said Princeton sociologist Marvin Bressler. By his presence, Robinson told people who had never given the matter a thought that a whole race of people had been excluded from life. By his success Robinson opened the minds of people who thought Josh Gibson and Satchel Paige and their contemporaries were not as good as they seemed because they were merely competing against black players.

And then what? One black man or two—with the addition of Larry Doby later in 1947—could crack the surface. It was the often unidentified and largely unsung players who pushed through that crack in the surface and held it open for the tide of change that followed.

"There is a big difference in breaking a barrier and making it real," said Mario Cuomo, former governor of New York and himself a former minor leaguer who played in the segregated South. "We adopted the Constitution in 1789 and it took until 1954 to let blacks into the schools. And when the Supreme Court changed the law, it didn't change for real for years and years." The lasting impact came with the flood of black talent into baseball, carried on the great new wave of television into homes and bars in the South, the North, the Midwest, and the West.

The depth of change came with the strength and the tears of young men whose names are largely dim in the light of history.

Jackie Robinson was a grown man in 1947, an educated man and a mature athlete, experienced in the outrageous ways of segregation when he integrated baseball. If he had been white when he played football at UCLA it's likely that he would have won the Heisman Trophy as the nation's best college football player. And he had been a lieutenant in the segregated army and fought discrimination there.

The pressure of simply being the first of his race to be permitted to play major–league baseball was excruciating. But Robinson was 28 years old and he had the help of his educated and supportive wife, Rachel. He was a valued teammate among professionals at the highest level, men who would reap a reward if this black man helped the team win. All but a few of the Brooklyn Dodgers accepted that. The ownership of the team was behind him.

Robinson did what he did on the grand stage of the major leagues in the New York spotlight. The media in New York, which at the time meant newspapers, was not actively opposed to his presence.

At the same time as he was breaking through, much of America was trying to close the door behind him. At the time there were 16 major–league baseball teams playing in 10 cities in the Northeast—none farther west than St. Louis and none farther south than Washington, D.C. Television was in its infancy. The historic Dodgers–Giants playoff of 1951 was the first series of games telecast coast–to–coast. Radio gave images to be seen only in the mind. Essentially, to see major–league baseball players a fan had to go to a major–league game in those 10 cities. With the coming of television, people could see even on the early black–and–white screens that some of the great players were white and some of them were black.

Minor–league baseball was spread all across an America that was governed by Jim Crow and by people who wanted their communities to stay segregated and unequal. After World War II there were 366 minor–league teams playing in 52 leagues from Maine to California and Cuba to Alberta, Canada. In 1950 North Carolina alone had 45 teams. Leagues were categorized from the lowest, Class D, to the highest, AAA. (With later major–league expansion and minor–league shrinkage the spread became simply A, AA, and AAA.)

At any given time there were 10,000 players in the minor leagues, and all of them were white until Robinson's performance ignited the great change. In some of those leagues, the spectators and the people of the community had never seen a black person before those young baseball players.

Those who came after Robinson were 17, 18, and 19 years old, unprepared and uninformed about what they faced. In Columbia, South Carolina; Jacksonville, Florida; and Reading, Pennsylvania, they were left to withstand the vile pressures on their own. If teammates hated them, so what! Players were competing as much or more against teammates as against other teams in their leagues because the reward was to get moved up eventually to the big leagues.

If the community hated the new black players, there was little support of any kind, including from the major–league teams to which those players belonged. Local management was rarely more cordial than the community that supported them, and the owners were far away.

Hall of Famer Willie McCovey began as a 17–year–old professional in 1955 with the Sandersville Giants of the Class D Georgia State League. He led the league with 113 RBI over 107 games. "I never stole a purse," McCovey said, mocking the perception of many southern women that any black person was a potential thief.

He had a sympathetic white player–manager at Sandersville named Pete Pavlick from New Jersey. "He had a beautiful young wife and in Sandersville you could walk home from the ballpark," McCovey recalls. "I lived on the other side of the tracks with the rest of the colored guys and she'd see me walking home. She'd pick me up and drive me home. And she didn't know how much trouble she could have got me in by doing that. I was scared to death but it didn't faze her at all." McCovey could have been set upon when he got out of the car and beaten or worse. Such things happened. McCovey doesn't know whether some citizen complained or not, but the owner of the team made her stop.

Mingling with white players was the fact of the minor leagues. "You knew the guys who was with you and who was against you," McCovey said. "I mean, you didn't have a lot of guys that come up and say things to you in your face. You're supposed to be on an even keel with them. And you have people on the outside, rebelling against that."

At Sandersville there were a few sympathetic northerners and some others on the team who stood beside McCovey. He said there were enough guys on that team "to ease the pain, guys that didn't look the other way," McCovey said. "They were right there with you."

When he was in the Georgia State League or Carolina League— McCovey isn't certain which—the manager from the opposing team in his home city went up in the stands because he wouldn't accept the razzing some fans were giving McCovey and his black teammates. "You needed some support like that," McCovey said.

In the Texas League, black players were not permitted on the field in Shreveport, Louisiana, so McCovey stayed behind. By then he had learned to accept what he had to accept. At Sandersville, McCovey had a black teammate from New York City, Ralph Crosby. "He just quit and went home," McCovey said. "He couldn't take it."

⁘

Baseball is the most imprecise of all the games to scout and predict. Players whose talent matures early often fail at a higher level of competition. Some have talent that is revealed at a higher level of competition as they mature as players. They are 17 or 18 years old and baseball's parent organizations have to fill out teams in the minors. Players are cheap. If some of them walk away, chances are they weren't going to be of great value anyhow. "I don't know how good Ralph Crosby would have been," McCovey said. "I don't think he would have become a star, but you never know."

Jackie integrated the major leagues. Those people who bore the burden in the minor leagues, and ultimately survived more terrible bigotry in the minor leagues, integrated baseball.

Joe Louis was respected as a boxing champion in the 1930s and 1940s even if he was a black man, but all the while America searched for a great white hope to dethrone him. For the first time with Robinson—except for the fleeting triumph of Jesse Owens in the 1936 Berlin Olympics—white Americans were willing to root for a black man. On the 50th anniversary celebration of Robinson's debut, President Bill Clinton, historian in addition to politician, said that "a 28–year–old rookie changed the face of baseball and the face of America forever."

The Robinson effect was so profound, his influence and his talent so obvious once he had a chance that, in retrospect, he hardly appears to have been an experiment.

"When something happens that turns out to be so successful, it's seen as inevitable," says Jules Tygiel, a San Francisco State professor and author of *Baseball's Great Experiment*. "Nothing surrounding Jackie was inevitable. This was an experiment. And experiments can fail."

Surely it was inevitable that another black man, perhaps in another sport, would have risen. America was opening its eyes. But when would it have happened? How much longer would it have taken? And what would the public reaction have been?

Those same questions had to be answered by the contemporaries of Ed Charles, Frank Robinson, Curt Flood, Mudcat Grant, and the others who carried Jackie's torch. How would the fans take to him? How would his teammates? Would he bear up under the pressure? Would he lose his temper in a way that would sink the whole project? Someone had to be first. Someone had to be able to withstand awful demands.

This Robinson was a man of fiery convictions; he was no lamb. Branch Rickey, the president of the Brooklyn Dodgers, had made it abundantly clear to Robinson that he had to confine himself to the narrowest standards of behavior in the face of terrible opposition. Years later, Robinson recalled Rickey's lecture in *Look* magazine: "He told me that one wrong move on my part would not only finish the chances for all Negroes in baseball, but it would set the cause of the Negro in America back 20 years. I was on guard night and day."

The major leaguers who followed had to deal with the same challenge. Young minor leaguers had to cope while they had little or no benefit of protection.

It's no coincidence that President Harry Truman ordered the army integrated the year after Robinson integrated baseball. The trail had been broken in snow–white America.

Had Rickey embarked on his experiment out of a desire to do good? Or was he a baseball executive who didn't care what color the player was as long as it was somebody who would make his team better and make money for his team? The latter was Rickey's ideal.

Robinson understood that his personal and professional qualifications enabled him to reach people and accomplish things beyond baseball. The scope of his role is obscured by time and the fact that young people today start from such a higher base. They wouldn't begin to accept the restrictions that black athletes—black people in general—saw as major advances. They have no idea what Robinson and Banks and Aaron had to endure. When Robinson was integrating the major leagues, the threat of lynching in minor–league towns was real.

Ed Charles and Ernie Banks were players people could see. There was no hiding the box score every day from April to October. This was before Dr. Martin Luther King Jr. emerged as the driver of the civil rights movement. King once told pitcher Don Newcombe, who along with Roy Campanella followed Robinson from the Negro Leagues to the Dodgers, "You'll never know what you and Jackie and Roy did to make it possible for me to do my job."

❖

I was surprised and dismayed when some of the black players who endured those years refused to be interviewed about what they had overcome. They have reached a certain age. Was it too painful to recall, similar to combat veterans and Holocaust survivors who refuse to look back? Or did they deny an obligation to help young people to understand progress and how the struggles of others made it happen? "Some of the young players don't have a clue," said Henry Aaron.

If his story helped "just one person" to understand history and enabled him to cope with life, Bob Watson said, it was worth telling his story.

At first baseball had its unwritten quota system. In 1967, Philadelphia manager Harry Walker, once a confirmed segregationist, started eight black men and a white pitcher whose turn it was. In 1971 Pittsburgh manager Danny Murtaugh fielded a team with nine black players in the lineup and there was no rebellion.

Black managers and black general managers are still rare enough to be identified by their race. So are black executives outside of baseball. That's still America. Some people who espouse a politically correct position are racist behind closed doors. Some of those people are decision makers of industry. But they can look out the window and see their white children playing with black children.

The pendulum of the 21st century has not swung so much as it has twisted. Read the papers and listen to the news and you don't hear the voice of today's Jackie Robinson using his influence to push for real–life advances. To the contrary, when Michael Jordan was asked why he hadn't campaigned for a democrat to unseat Jesse Helms in the North Carolina Senate, Jordan explained, "Republicans buy sneakers too."

Turn on the television and see how many black athletes dominate the small screen. In the background hear the late Arthur Ashe warning several years ago that blacks "were spending too much time on the playing field and not in the libraries."

Instead of advancing from the gains won by blacks in education a decade ago, there has been a regression. Frank "Bishop" McDuffie, president and former basketball coach of Laurinburg Institute in North Carolina, which produced musician Dizzy Gillespie and black pioneer Atlantic Coast Conference basketball player Charlie Scott, said, "It will change when as many parents go to PTA meetings as to basketball games."

Parents and students have been seduced by the very public and highly unlikely riches of athletes and entertainers, while the reachable professions of accountants, teachers, doctors, and lawyers are dismissed. Studies have shown that nearly half of high school seniors in football and basketball believe they will be professional athletes. At the same time, nearly one in three is functionally illiterate upon emerging from high school. When the NCAA wrote its original "700 Rule," which required a minimum 700 SAT score for freshman eligibility, the intent was to tell high school athletes they'd better pay some attention to schoolwork if they expected to be college athletes. With athletes like Kobe Bryant bypassing college and going directly to the pros, high school minimum standards became irrelevant to them. Just play.

And what happens when the playing stops?

Henry Aaron, who often talks to young people emphasizing education rather than home runs, tells of the experience with his son, who was in the Braves' farm system while Aaron was making decisions in the front office. "I brought him in the office and told him he had to do something else," Henry said. "He wanted to play baseball. Just because I was a baseball player, he thought that he was going to play. And I saw him going no higher than A ball. So I told him, 'You've got two choices. Either I can keep you here in A ball or you can go back to college, get your degree, come back out, and have a family.' So he thought for a while, and I said, 'While you're thinking, here are your release papers.' It was hard, but I had to make the decision for him. He wasn't able to make that decision because he wanted to play baseball, and I just saw him floundering around in the minor leagues for the rest of his life."

At first young Aaron resented what his father did. "He went through some traumatic times," Henry said. But he went back to school and became a schoolteacher. "He came up to me and hugged me and kissed me," Henry said, "and told me, 'Thanks for making that decision, because I couldn't have made it.'"

Baseball has suffered from another twist of the pendulum in that there are now fewer blacks playing baseball than 30 years ago when there still were lingering barriers. For the 2006 Hall of Fame induction, which spotlighted the honoring of 17 pioneers of the Negro Leagues, conspicuously absent was Reggie Jackson, who has often and loudly spoken of baseball's debt to the Negro Leagues. Increasingly, athletic ability is taking black athletes to basketball and football. "In baseball almost everybody goes first to the minor leagues and nobody in the neighborhood knows where they are," said Ken Singleton, college man, big–league outfielder, and current Yankees broadcaster. "If they play college basketball or football, even Division III, everybody at home knows they're playing." If those routes don't lead to instant riches, they do lead to instant cred in the neighborhood.

Lou Brock, the intellectualizing Hall of Fame baseball player, sees another rationalization for the focus on sports in the face of overwhelming odds against the great reward. "I would take that chance," Brock said. "The lottery is by chance. Sports says if I work hard and sacrifice I can make it. So I mold my thinking. Unlike even music, sports still stays within the bounds of fair play. I got referees telling me when I step out of bounds. You don't have that in music; you don't have that in business. Kids think they will be cheated."

A perceptive young black minor leaguer in the spring training camp of the Mets looked at it from the understanding that bad slumps and bad seasons are more a fact of life in baseball than in any other of our games. "Baseball is a humbling game," he said. On the contrary, he said, the black high school basketball and football stars, coddled from their earliest years, especially in the inner city, don't like to be humbled. They've been stars all their conscious lives. They don't want to take the chance of going to the minor leagues and coming home with nothing.

As President Clinton said in that anniversary celebration, "Jackie Robinson scored the go–ahead run that day; we've all been trying to catch up ever since."

Bibliography

Aaron, Hank, and Lonnie Wheeler. *I Had a Hammer*. New York: Harper-Collins, 1991.

Adelson, Bruce. *Brushing Back Jim Crow*. Charlottesville: University Press of Virginia, 1999.

Angell, Roger. *Game Time*. New York: Harcourt, Inc., 2003.

———. *Late Innings*. New York: Simon & Schuster, 1982.

Ashford, Adrienne Cherie. *Strrr–ike!!* Bloomington, IN. AuthorHouse, 2004.

Deford, Frank, and Verne E. Smith. "Crossing the Bar." *Newsweek*, April 14, 1997.

Dorinson, Joseph, and Joram Warmund, eds. *Jackie Robinson/Race, Sports and the American Dream*. Armonk, NY: M.E. Sharpe Inc., 1998.

Epstein, Jack. "Baseball's Conscience Finally Gets His Due: Communist Ties Obscured Walnut Creek Retiree's Success Fighting Racism in the Sport." *San Francisco Chronicle*, July 10, 2005, p. A–1.

Flood, Curt, and Richard Carter. *The Way It Is*. Naples, FL: Trident Press, 1971.

Gibson, Bob, and Lonnie Wheeler. *Stranger to the Game*. New York: Viking Penguin, 1994.

Gibson, Bob, and Phil Pepe. *From Ghetto to Glory*. Upper Saddle River, NJ: Prentice Hall, Inc., 1968.

Golen, Jimmy. "Providing a Shield from the Storm: Andrews Helped Aaron in Racist South." *Journal Sentinel*, May 13, 2001.

Halberstam, David. "But Could We Be Friends," *Parade Magazine*, July 24, 1994, pp. 4–6.

Halberstam, David. *October 1964*. New York: Villard Books, 1994.

Jacobson, Steve. *The Best Team Money Could Buy*. New York: Atheneum, 1978.

Littwin, Mike. "An American Hero." *Baltimore Sun*, April 15, 1997.

Moffi, Larry, and Jonathan Kronstadt. *Crossing the Line*. Jefferson, NC: McFarland & Company, 1994.

Robinson, Frank, and Berry Stainback. *Extra Innings*. New York: McGraw–Hill, 1988.

Silber, Irwin. *Press Box Red*. Philadelphia Temple University Press, 2003.

Silverman, Matthew, Michael Gershman, and David Pietrusza. *Baseball: The Biographical Encyclopedia*. Total/Sports Illustrated, 2000.

Sports Illustrated. "A Lot of Things Seem to Be Better." Roundtable discussion, August 5, 1991.

Wills, Maury, and Mike Celizic. *On the Run*. New York: Carroll and Graff, 1992.

Index